■ A F T E R   T H E   L A W

A book series edited by John Brigham and Christine B. Harrington

INSIDE THE STATE

A. Robert DeHart
Learning Center

Presented by
Friends of the
Chicanos for
Multicultural Awareness
in Education

De Anza College Library
Cupertino, California

■ *AFTER THE LAW*
A book series edited by John Brigham and Christine B. Harrington

Also published in the series:

Gigs: Jazz and the Cabaret Laws in New York City
by Paul Chevigny

A Theory of Liberty: The Constitution and Minorities
by H. N. Hirsch

INSIDE THE STATE

THE BRACERO PROGRAM, IMMIGRATION, AND THE I.N.S.

KITTY CALAVITA

ROUTLEDGE NEW YORK LONDON

Published in 1992 by

Routledge
An imprint of Routledge, Chapman and Hall, Inc.
29 West 35th Street
New York, NY 10001

Published in Great Britain by

Routledge
11 New Fetter Lane
London EC4P 4EE

This material is based upon work supported by the National Science Foundation under Grant #SES-8618999. Any opinions, findings, and conclusions or recommendations expressed in this publication are those of the author and do not necessarily reflect the views of the National Science Foundation.

Printed in the United States of America on acid free paper

Library of Congress Cataloging in Publication Data

Calavita, Kitty.
    Inside the state : the bracero program, immigration and
the INS / by Kitty Calavita.
        p. cm.—(After the law)
    Includes bibliographical references (p.   ) and index.
    ISBN 0-415-90537-0;   ISBN 0-415-90538-9
    1. United States. Immigration and Naturalization Service.
    2. United States—Emigration and immigration—Government policy.
    3. Aliens, Illegal—Government policy—United States. 4. Alien
    labor, Mexican—Government policy—United States. 5. Migrant
    agricultural laborers—Southwestern States.   I. Title. II. Series.
    JV6493.C35 1992
    353.0081'7—dc20   92-12340
                                                                   CIP

British Library cataloguing in publication data also available

For Nico, Joe, and Marco

CONTENTS

Acknowledgments   ix

Chapter 1.   Introduction   1

Chapter 2.   The Formative Years   18

Chapter 3.   Formalization and Informal Control:
              The Bracero Program Comes of Age   42

Chapter 4.   Let's Make a Deal   73

Chapter 5.   "Wrangling" with the Department
              of Labor   113

Chapter 6.   Loss of Control   141

Chapter 7.   Conclusion   167

              Notes   184

Appendix A.   Illegal Aliens Apprehended by the INS,
              1940–1976   217

Appendix B.   Mexican Foreign Workers Admitted
              Under the Bracero Program, 1942–1964   218

Appendix C.   Mexicans Admitted on Permanent
              Visas, 1940–1971   218

              Bibliography   219

              Index   235

ACKNOWLEDGMENTS

I had the help and support of a number of colleagues, friends, archivists, and government officials, in the preparation of this book. The staffs at the National Archives and the Freedom of Information and Privacy Act Office of the Immigration and Naturalization Service (INS) gave generously of their time to help me locate the archival material upon which much of this book is based. Many past and present INS officials were equally generous in allowing me to interview them at length. In one case, a former immigration agent took the time to write detailed letters responding to my many queries. Without the good will and hard work of these people, this book would not have been possible.

I would also like to thank Wayne Cornelius and the staff at the Center for U.S.-Mexican Studies at the University of California, San Diego, where I was awarded a research fellowship during the early stages of this project. Their continued interest in my research has been an important source of satisfaction and moral support.

Bill Chambliss, as usual, has been a good friend and colleague, not only contributing an important intellectual grounding for the book, but helping me put in perspective the inevitable "dry spells" of archival research. His encouragement and friendship have meant a lot to me. The insightful and constructive criticism of Marjorie Zatz, John Brigham, and Christine Harrington on various drafts of the book eased the always difficult process of revisions. I also thank Cecelia Cancellaro, Michael Esposito, and the staff at Routledge, Chapman and Hall, who did an excellent job with copy editing and the many other details of preparing the book for publication.

The Program in Social Ecology at the University of California, Irvine has provided me with the ideal work environment in which to finish writing the book. I especially appreciate the expertise of Judy Omiya and Diane Christianson who helped me with the administrative and word processing tasks involved in manuscript preparation. Their patience and efficiency are without equal.

Finally, this research was funded by a grant from the Law and Social Science Division of the National Science Foundation. I want to thank Felice Levine and the panelists of the National Science Foundation for their interest in the project.

CHAPTER I

INTRODUCTION

On September 29, 1942, five hundred farm workers from Mexico arrived in Stockton, California. Transported by the United States government and delivered to California growers, these Mexican workers were the first installment of a wartime emergency program designed to fill the declared labor shortage in agriculture. Over the next twenty-two years, in what turned out to be the largest foreign worker program in U.S. history, five million "braceros" were contracted to growers and ranchers in twenty-four states. The term "bracero" comes from the Spanish word for arm, "brazo," and can be translated loosely in this context as "farmhand." Its literal meaning, "arm-man," hints at the function these braceros were to play in the agricultural economy, supplying a pair of arms and imposing few obligations on the host society as human beings. The Bracero Program was operated jointly by the State Department, the Department of Labor, and the Immigration and Naturalization Service (INS) in the Department of Justice. The INS was critical, for in its capacity as official gatekeeper, it controlled entries, departures, and bracero desertions, giving the agency substantial power, not only over the braceros themselves, but ultimately over the entire program.

This is the story of how immigration officials used that power, why they used it the way they did, and what forces impinged on them in the process. It is a story about informal lawmaking and the ability of one federal agency not just to interpret and implement the policy agenda handed down by Congress, but in fact to set the agenda. As the story unfolds, we will see the immigration agency, beset by contradictory pressures embedded in the broader political economy, alternately stretch Congressional statutes, "walk around" those that seem insurmountable, and invent its own to fill inconvenient voids.

The Bracero Program was born and raised on administrative powers, not just the power of the INS but of all government agencies that participated in bracero operations. What came to be called the Bracero Program was in fact a series of programs initiated by administrative fiat, subsequently endorsed by Congress, and kept alive by executive agreement whenever foreign relations or domestic politics threatened their demise. The foreign contract labor system, designed by a small group of federal administrators in the spring of 1942, was launched with very little public notice. The Immigration Service and the Departments of State, Labor, and Agriculture, together with the War Manpower Commission, in early 1942 formed a Special Committee on Importation of Mexican Labor, drew up plans for the first installment of Mexican contract labor, signed a bilateral agreement with Mexico, and arranged for the importation of workers, all in the absence of congressional legislation or public debate. Not that Congress opposed the idea; within a few months, Congress gave its nod of approval, officially endorsing the wartime emergency program that outlived World War II by more than two years and provided growers, at government expense and under government contract, with an uninterrupted supply of cheap, essentially captive, Mexican workers.

By 1947, with the war long over, and with it the labor shortage that had provided the rationale for the bracero importation, Congress allowed the statutory basis for the program to expire. But administrative action took up where legislation left off. The government contract system was temporarily replaced by direct employer recruitment of braceros, supervised and assisted by the Immigration Service and the rest of the bracero administrative apparatus, but unencumbered by much of the red tape of the legislative program. To accommodate employers who complained that recruiting braceros from Mexico was expensive and time-consuming, the INS devised an even simpler arrangement: on-the-spot legalization of illegal Mexican farm workers. Indeed, the official policy during this period gave *priority* to illegal immigrants found in the United States. By 1950, the number of Mexicans "legalized" and "paroled" to growers as braceros was five times higher than the number actually recruited from Mexico.

In 1951, President Truman's Commission on Migratory Labor reported that employer abuses and lax enforcement produced deplorable working and living conditions for braceros; that the INS had effectively abdicated its border control responsibility which, together with legalization policies, had given rise to unprecedented levels of illegal immigration; and that the steadily increasing number of braceros and illegal aliens had depressed wages and undermined collective bargaining efforts by domestic farm workers. As damning as the Commission's conclusions were, its recommendations to restrict the contract labor system were ignored.

Instead, the Bracero Program was expanded and entrenched, the outbreak of war once again providing the justification for a congressionally sanctioned program. As the Korean War escalated and growers' allies in Congress warned of new labor shortages, the formal program was revised. PL 78, which served as the statutory basis for the Bracero Program until its termination in 1964, passed in June 1951 with very little discussion and virtually no opposition. The government was back in the business of recruiting, contracting, and delivering workers to agriculture. But if the system was thus formalized, it was by no means rendered inflexible. Rather, the Immigration Service used its considerable administrative ingenuity over the next thirteen years to mold and shape the program to maximize its utility to bracero employers. By the time the increasingly controversial labor system wound down in 1964, it had supplied millions of Mexican workers to Southwest growers and ranchers, and in the process inevitably had a substantial negative impact on farm wages, working conditions, and labor relations. As one observer summed up the benefits of the program to bracero employers: "For the growers the program was a dream: a seemingly endless army of cheap, unorganized workers brought to their doorstep by the government."[1]

This study of the Bracero Program as it provides growers with an "endless army" of cheap labor not only highlights the informal policymaking process and the role of administrative discretion, but also contributes to the theoretical debate over the nature and functions of the state. In some respects, the role of the INS in shaping the Bracero Program to suit the needs of growers seems to fit well the structural model of state action proposed by Althusser,[2] Poulantzas,[3] and others. Indeed, a number of immigration scholars have offered implicit structural explanations for the evolution and demise of this contract labor system. Bach,[4] for example, argues that the state, in an effort to maximize profits on one hand and contain legitimation problems on the other, constructed bracero policies to undermine the power of domestic farm labor by increasing the size of the agricultural work force, while periodically placating the political demands of opponents of the program with poorly enforced and generally ineffective safeguards. Others have pointed to direct personal, political, and economic links among bracero employers and the legislators and public administrators who set bracero policy, in a depiction more reminiscent of the Marxist instrumentalist model of state action.[5]

However, neither the Althusserian structuralist rendition nor the more straightforward instrumentalist account of the state's role in designing and implementing the Bracero Program are entirely supported by the historical record. A close look at the immigration agency that shared responsibility for running the Bracero Program reveals a far more complex scenario, and greater inconsistencies and ambiguity of state action, than either of these perspectives can account for. In the first place, as we will see, INS policies were not simply a response to the demands of the capitalist class—in this case growers—but were first and foremost the product of the bureaucracy's own institutional needs. Perhaps most important, this study finds a "state" that is rift with internal divisions, as the policy agenda of the Immigration Service collides head-on with the policy goals of other state agencies, most notably the Department of Labor. The following section sketches a theoretical model of immigration policymaking that may help us make sense of the shifting patterns of INS policymaking. It also describes the agency's precarious alliance with growers, and the pronounced divisions within the state that periodically escalated into bitter administrative crossfire.

THE CONTRADICTIONS OF IMMIGRATION POLICYMAKING: A THEORETICAL FRAMEWORK

Since Alexander Hamilton warned Congress in 1791 that European immigration to the United States must be encouraged in order to increase the size of the work force and mitigate the "dearness of labor,"[6] U.S. policymakers have recognized the importance of immigrants as a labor supply. Throughout most of the 19th century, an open-door policy prevailed, with much of the early legislation designed to *encourage* immigration. The first federal immigration law, appropriately titled "An Act to Encourage Immigration," was passed in 1864 in response to industrialists' complaints of reductions in the labor supply during the Civil War, decreases in immigration, and rising wages. This law established the first Bureau of Immigration—located in the Treasury Department—whose primary function was to encourage emigration from Europe and to arrange for the transportation and distribution of immigrant workers upon arrival in the U.S.

Employers applauded the ever-increasing influx of immigrants. Andrew Carnegie referred to immigration as "a golden stream which flows into the country each year" and valued each adult immigrant at $1500, "for in former days an efficient slave sold for that sum."[7] The *New York Journal of Commerce* declared appreciatively, "Men, like cows, are expensive to raise and a gift of either should be gladly received. And a man can be put to more valuable use than a cow."[8]

4

Minor restrictions by the turn of the century barred a few "undesirables" but were carefully worded and implemented so as not to interfere with the golden stream. As the 19th century came to a close, nearly a million immigrants entered the United States every year, most of whom took up industrial employment in the urban centers of the East and Midwest.

If Carnegie and other capitalists of the period appreciated the new immigrants, domestic workers were less enthusiastic. Not surprisingly, the influx of hundreds of thousands of desperate, mostly unskilled, immigrant workers each year had the effect of depressing wages and undermining the power of the fledgling labor movement.[9] The contradiction between capital and labor on this issue was fundamental and irresolvable. It was precisely because the immigrants provided abundant cheap labor that employers welcomed the new immigration and workers demanded its restriction.

As the American labor movement organized nationally and increased its ranks in the late 19th century, this contradiction presented a thorny dilemma for immigration lawmakers. The Anti-Alien Contract Labor Law of 1885, which barred the importation of foreign labor on contract, was the legislative response to this dilemma. Proclaiming that the law would "prevent pauper-wage prices for labor" and bring "relief to the labor of this country," Congress enacted a measure that responded politically to the demands of organized labor but did not interrupt the immigrant stream.[10] By the time the law was passed, only a few highly skilled immigrants were being imported on prearranged contracts. While earlier in the century employers had often contracted workers with special skills directly from Europe, by 1885 the vast majority of European immigrants were unskilled and the private labor exchanges of New York and other port cities had replaced the direct contract system. Thus, although Congress promised rhetorically to save American labor from the pauper labor of Europe, the potential of the Anti-Alien Contract Labor Law to curtail the immigration of this unskilled labor was virtually nil.

As the size of the immigrant influx continued to increase, a contradiction of a somewhat different nature became apparent. If immigrants supplied a work force, that work force was made up of human beings, and because it was a cheap labor supply that they provided (and for which they were so appreciated by employers), these human beings were frequently destitute. The same policies that increased the size of the cheap labor supply and depressed wages, simultaneously increased the fiscal burden associated with a burgeoning poor population. By the end of the 19th century, much of the immigration debate in Congress reflected this contradiction: on one hand a surplus labor supply was useful to the rapid development of the emerging capitalist democracy, while on the other hand the poverty it brought required unprecedented expenditures on poorhouses, asylums, hospitals, and jails.[11]

These contradictions are not confined to the United States in the 19th century; they permeate the policy debate whenever immigration is used as a way to expand the unskilled work force. Referring to the "guest worker" system in Europe in the 1960s and 1970s, Swiss playwright Max Frisch once said: "We called for workers, and there came human beings."[12] The European guest worker program not only ignited the labor movement in protest over competition with Third World workers, but also imposed a series of unanticipated social and fiscal costs. Compounding these tensions, guest workers—whose primary virtue had been their presumably temporary status and the flexibility to which this was thought to contribute—increasingly chose to remain and become permanent members of the European host societies.[13]

In the United States, Congress attempted to resolve immigration dilemmas by placing restrictive quotas on Eastern Hemisphere immigration in the early 1920s, while exempting from those quotas migration from Mexico and other Western Hemisphere countries. The Chair of the House Committee on Immigration and Naturalization, in debates preceding the quota legislation, questioned the director of the U.S. Employment Service on the experience with Mexican labor during World War I. He was particularly interested in the flexibility of the Mexican labor source, asking, "You reserve the right to deport them when you get too many?" Another representative interjected, "How did the thing work out? Were you able to deport them when the need had passed?" Another persisted, "Are you having any trouble in getting them out of the country since bringing them in?"[14]

What this brief overview suggests is that immigration policymakers historically have faced a number of contradictions to which modifications in immigration law are one response. Immigrant workers are a "golden stream" to be used as cheap labor to expand the economy and maximize profits; but at the same time, they trigger a political backlash against the resulting wage reductions and exact a fiscal toll in the form of social welfare costs, broadly construed. Some of the most important U.S. immigration policies have attempted to resolve the conflicts stemming from such contradictions. The Anti-Alien Contract Labor law of 1885 is one example, and the public charge provisions barring anyone with a "predisposition" to poverty—first enacted in 1882 and still on the books—is another.[15]

Within this context, Mexico has long been considered an ideal backdoor source of cheap labor. In the 1880s, Mexicans provided a critical supply of cheap labor for rapidly expanding agricultural production in the Southwest and constituted a large portion of the railroad workers on the Southern Pacific and Santa Fe Railroads which transported the agricultural produce.[16] In recognition of their important role in the economy, the immigration restrictions of the early 20th century included specific exceptions for Mexicans. For example, when a literacy test for entering immigrants was passed in 1917, Southwest growers convinced policymakers to exempt Mexicans.

These were not merely "good neighbor" policies. Rather, the advantage of immigration from Mexico was the flexibility derived from Mexico's proximity to the United States and the related ability to expand and contract the supply of Mexican workers with the labor need, thus easing the tensions associated with the more permanent European immigration. If immigration from Europe had been hailed earlier because "men like cows are expensive to raise," Mexican immigration was doubly beneficial. Not only were the majority of Mexican immigrants adult males unaccompanied by dependents, but their stay in the United States was contingent on a continued demand for their labor. The temporary nature of Mexican immigration and the marginal status of the migrants were periodically reinforced by formal and informal policies. For example, during the 1920s, in order to ensure the departure of Mexican immigrant workers, the Department of Labor instructed employers to withhold 20% of their pay to be deposited with immigration officials and returned to them on their way back to Mexico.[17] The debates surrounding the Quota Laws of the 1920s attest to the congressional intention to use Mexican immigrants as a malleable supply of labor.[18] The massive repatriation of Mexicans during the depression of the 1930s—many of whom were in the U.S. legally and some of whom were U.S. citizens—left little doubt of policymakers' willingness to act on these intentions.

Half a century later, with undocumented immigrants supplying a substantial portion of the work force in Southwestern agriculture, the garment industry, janitorial services, construction clean-up, hotels and restaurants, and other seasonal and minimum-wage jobs, the Immigration Reform and Control Act of 1986 (IRCA) once again wrestled with the dilemmas surrounding immigration policy. While IRCA contained amnesty provisions that legalized close to three million undocumented immigrants, an employer sanctions measure, which for the first time made it illegal to knowingly employ an undocumented worker, was the indisputable political centerpiece of the law. Responding to widespread public pressure to "regain control of the border" yet concerned not to "harass" employers, Congress crafted employer sanctions that were largely symbolic. Republican Senator Alan Simpson, the principal Congressional sponsor of IRCA and an adamant advocate of border control, explained to his colleagues in the Senate that, despite the appeal of employer sanctions, "It must be the type of program which does not place an onerous burden upon the employer. . . ."[19] As passed, employer sanctions sent the message that something had been done to restrict illegal immigration, but contained substantial loopholes through which most employers could escape detection and prosecution.

The reform package attracted bipartisan support. However, a few members of Congress observed that IRCA, presented as a restrictive measure, would in fact have the opposite effect. Citing the abundant loopholes in employer sanctions and the generosity of the bill's farm labor provisions, Democratic Representative Roybal of California said, on the day of the final vote in the House: "They [members of Congress] thought . . . that they voted for immigration reform with sanctions, but they did not. What they voted for is a farm labor bill, a bill that is designed to provide cheap labor for the farmers and growers of this country."[20] Fellow Democrat Henry Gonzalez, Representative from Texas, complained, "Let there be no mistake about it. This bill . . . guarantees that those who want to exploit cheap, foreign labor . . . can continue to do so with impunity."[21] Republican Senator McClure of Rhode Island said simply that the bill was "a failure, a sham, and a fraud."[22] After an initial decline in border apprehensions following the law—probably in part the consequence of the broad legalization program—by 1991 apprehensions were at their highest level in five years and climbing steadily.[23]

This interpretation of U.S. immigration policymaking and the contradictions driving it draws from the dialectical-structural model of law and the state.[24] This dialectical model posits that the political economy of a capitalist democracy contains within it specific contradictions, and that law often represents the state's attempt to grapple with or reconcile the conflicts derived from those contradictions. To the extent that the contradictions are entrenched in the political-economic structure, the attempted resolutions are not only doomed to failure but give rise to further conflict. From this perspective, the Bracero Program is one piece of an on-going dialectic in which the structural contradictions surrounding immigration precipitate conflicts and dilemmas for policymakers, to which Mexican immigration historically has been both a temporary resolution and a trigger for future dilemmas. But, if this dialectical-structural model of state action helps explain the rough outlines of the Bracero Program, the account is at best incomplete, at worst misleading. The data uncovered in this study reveal a "state" that is fragmented across institutional lines, at least in the short term and close up; that faces contradictions not just from without but from within as well; and that sets policies less according to some grand plan to rescue the political economy than in response to immediate institutional needs. Furthermore, the data, much like Dorothy's Toto in *The Wizard of Oz,* pull back the curtain of structural analysis to reveal real-life human beings sitting at the controls.

The picture that emerges from my research is of structural contradictions penetrating the institutions and bureaucracies of the state in different ways, posing different dilemmas, and eliciting different responses depending on the location of those institutions in the state apparatus. Thus, political actors in the highly visible arena of Congress dodge contradictions associated with immigration by delegating authority to the less visible and less politically vulnerable administrative enclaves of the state. As we will see, Congressional actors, faced with the no-win politics of the Bracero Program, shunted policymaking power for the controversial labor system to the INS and other administrative agencies.

The way the immigration agency used that power was shaped, in large part, by its own bureaucratic interests, within the context of the contradictions confronting it as the federal agency responsible for immigration control. While it is true that INS policies usually advanced the interests of growers, close attention to the archival record reveals that this was neither because the agency was coopted by agricultural interests, as instrumentalists would have it, nor because of a direct "objective relation" between the state and capital, as structuralists would maintain.[25] Rather, the Immigration Service pursued growers' interest in a generous bracero system at least in part in order to realize its own. The contradictions outlined above presented the agency with a bureaucratic dilemma related to its unenviable mandate to control illegal immigration despite the powerful economic forces driving that migration. Securing growers' cooperation in using braceros rather than illegal workers—cooperation that was contingent on the INS providing growers with "a seemingly endless army of cheap, unorganized workers"—was the immigration agency's response to this institutional dilemma.

Not only are the contradictions of the larger society reflected differently in the various institutions of the state, but, as we will see, they resurface as inter-agency conflict. Immigration officials struggled to solve their bureaucratic dilemma by fashioning policies that maximized the supply of braceros to agriculture and enhanced bracero vulnerability; but by the late 1950s, their controversial policies were contested by the Department of Labor, the federal agency whose hapless task was to reconcile class interests and defuse conflict. As the Labor Department was pressed by organized labor to impose restrictions on the contract system, INS officials worked behind the scenes to minimize Labor Department control of the Bracero Program and to expand the much smaller H-2 program over which the Immigration Service had greater jurisdiction.[26] Ultimately the two agencies were forced to present a "united front," to compromise, and to coordinate their policies, but they did so reluctantly and only after sometimes prolonged and hostile negotiation.

This focus on one federal agency as it interacts with other institutions of the state in formulating program-specific policies contributes to an empirically informed understanding of state action that avoids the ungrounded abstractions of much structuralist theory without succumbing to the equally abstract empiricism common to many micro-level analyses.[27] I have taken seriously Skocpol's warning that "[w]e do not need a new or refurbished grand theory of 'The State,' "[28] a goal that anyway is doomed to failure. Instead, "we . . . need to probe the internal complexities of state structures, without going to the extreme of treating states simply as disconnected collections of competing agencies."[29] This look inside the state takes a step in that direction, by documenting decision-making in one agency while locating that agency in its broader institutional and structural context.

DATA SOURCES, "FREEDOM OF INFORMATION," AND THE ARCHAEOLOGY OF ARCHIVAL RESEARCH

The data for this book come from a variety of sources, some relatively easy to access and others posing almost insurmountable difficulties. Fortunately for historical research of this sort, the U.S. government produces reams of official information, providing one important source of data. I used congressional hearings and reports, as well as the *Congressional Record*, to document various aspects of congressional policymaking affecting the Bracero Program. These congressional materials not only provide a formal chronology of events and a synopsis of policy outcomes, but allow us some limited access behind the scenes where it is possible to watch the meandering course of policy, to glimpse disagreements among state actors, and to be privy to sometimes remarkably candid statements of intent. Other government publications, including General Accounting Office reports, Congressional Research Service studies, official reports of the INS and other federal agencies, supply a wealth of additional information about the Bracero Program and the congressional and administrative roles in its formulation and operation.

While these documents have the distinct advantage of relatively easy accessibility—they are prepared in large part for public consumption—there is both good news and bad news here. For such official records are by definition *political* documents, precisely because they are published with the public eye in mind. Thus, while the *Congressional Record* may be a source of periodic insights into congressional motives, its contents are not to be taken at face value. Not only are political actors inevitably "on stage" in the congressional arena, but they have the option of retracting or revising their remarks before publication in the *Record*. With this limitation in mind, I have used these documents conservatively, depending on them primarily for informational purposes or as supplements to other types of data.

A second major source of data is provided by in-depth interviews with former INS employees and other government officials involved in bracero operations, some of whom were central players in bracero policymaking, while others were lower-level district managers or field-level employees. The interviews were unstructured, providing the opportunity for free-flowing dialogue, and generally lasted at least two hours, with some key interviews lasting much longer and extending over the course of several days. In no case was my request for an interview denied, and in most cases the respondents, all of whom were assured confidentiality, spoke freely and at length. In addition to these personal interviews, extensive correspondence was carried on for several months with a former top official who was with the INS for the duration of the Bracero Program. Finally, oral histories conducted as part of the Eisenhower Administration Project of the Columbia University Oral History Research Office provide a unique opportunity to hear the stories of the most senior participants in bracero policymaking, most notably Attorney General Herbert Brownell and INS Commissioner Joseph Swing. These interviews, correspondence, and oral histories collectively yield insights into the informal policymaking process and the *modus operandi* of the INS that could be provided only by those actually inside that process.

While these official and personal accounts are critical to the project, the most substantial source of data—both in terms of volume and theoretical importance—is the paper trail left by administrative decision-makers in the form of unpublished reports and communication internal to the INS, and between INS officials, other branches of government, and interested outsiders. These unpublished documents provide the single most important source of data; perhaps not coincidentally, they were by far the most difficult to obtain. Unlike most other government agencies, the Immigration Service has relinquished virtually no internal documents since World War II to the National Archives in Washington, D.C., which serves as the official repository of the government's written historical record.[30] This single fact complicates immeasurably the researcher's task, as she must both track down the relevant INS data within the agency and persuade the bureaucracy that the data are suitable for academic consumption. But the fact that so few INS documents are housed at the National Archives is of more than direct pragmatic import. More fundamentally, it is symptomatic of the strong preference for secrecy on the part of the immigration bureaucracy.

The INS's narrow interpretation of its obligations under the Freedom of Information Act (FOIA)[31] exemplifies this penchant for nondisclosure. This act, passed in 1966 as an amendment to the Administrative Procedure Act, was designed to enhance the public's access to information about the workings of government, and to provide for a mechanism with which to sue for disclosure if necessary. Jack Wasserman, well-known immigration lawyer, optimistically reported to his colleagues in 1976 that FOIA "will bring sunshine and openness not only to you and your clients but, maybe, also to our bureaucratic agencies."[32] While FOIA has been used effectively by immigration lawyers to secure information critical to their clients' lawsuits, it has by no means brought "sunshine and openness."

In the 1980s, the American Library Association sounded the alarm that the Reagan Administration was unilaterally narrowing the interpretation of FOIA so as to deny access to information that had previously been available under the law.[33] The restrictive interpretation of FOIA by the INS stands out even against this context of retrenchments. A 1970 *Iowa Law Review* Note, entitled "The Secret Law of the Immigration and Naturalization Service," documents the immigration bureaucracy's hostility to FOIA from the beginning.[34] Despite the fact that full disclosure is required unless the documents in question fall into one of the nine exceptions specified by the act, there has been since the act's inception a "pervasive attitude of nondisclosure prevalent in that agency [INS]," an attitude that is apparently based on an "agency-oriented" memo from the Attorney General in 1967.[35] Among the many illustrations of this "climate of nondisclosure," the law review author describes a personal interaction with an INS official in which he asked the official about the meaning of 8CFR, Section 103.9(d), the section of the *Code of Federal Regulations* that details the requirements of FOIA. The official's indignant response was, "Where did you get that? 8CFR is confidential, isn't it?"[36]

This concern to control access to information is not limited to the bureaucracy's public encounters. The Select Commission on Immigration and Refugee Policy, a prestigious panel made up of members of Congress and other high-profile participants in the immigration policy debate, was formed by President Carter in the late 1970s to make recommendations to Congress on immigration reform. An INS employee temporarily detailed to the Commission resigned from the INS in protest over the constraints placed on her efforts to provide the Commission with pertinent information. In her letter of resignation, she told INS Commissioner Crosland:

> These restraints clearly constitute an attempt to influence and control the legal research activities of the Select Commission through me, an INS detailee. . . . [T]he detailees to the Commission from other agencies are not operating as agents or representatives of their departments; nor are any of them subject to the type of control you are imposing on me. . . . I refuse to be a party to the proposed charade.[37]

Compounding the impact of bureaucratic secrecy, archival research of this sort is not unlike archaeology; having specified the general area of interest, a certain amount of digging is required. And, as in archaeology, it is usually not possible to know in advance precisely what remnants to look for. After persistent negotiation with the information gatekeepers at the INS in Washington, numerous dead-ends, and personal pleas for mercy, I obtained a limited digging license from the FOIA office. In the process of this struggle to gain access to the INS paper trail with which to tell the bracero story, it soon became clear that the struggle itself was part of the story, or at least a kind of methodological subplot. The following attention to that saga will demystify the misleadingly tidy concept of "methodology" as it applies to this kind of historical research, and at the same time introduce the bureaucracy which is the main protagonist in this story.

Since I was interested in the internal workings of the INS and the motivations and dynamics driving its bracero policies, and since few internal documents had been transferred from the INS to the National Archives, I was dependent on the cooperation of the immigration bureaucracy for much of my data. Painfully aware of the INS reputation for secrecy, I was not to be disappointed. My first encounter with the administrators who were to determine whether I saw any INS archival materials—and if so, what, how much, and under what procedure—hinted at the scale of the task ahead. Most of the historical materials, I was told, are stored in a government document warehouse in Suitland, Maryland, in the suburbs of Washington, DC. These records are filed in large cardboard boxes and catalogued according to a variety of overlapping and unwieldy systems, the most complete of which is a 300-page "Subject Index"—a lofty label for this slippery, vague, and only sometimes alphabetized listing.

After extensive negotiation, during which I attempted unsuccessfully to secure permission to browse in the stacks of the Suitland facility in order to bypass the time-consuming and inefficient FOIA process (and because the nature of the research precluded advance knowledge of what documents existed), I was informed that I would have to request individual documents through FOIA on the basis of the cumbersome subject index. Relieved at least that there *was* an "index" in this otherwise depressing scenario, I asked for a copy. One of my unflappable hosts told me, "I believe you have to file a FOIA request for that." Perhaps sensing the utter dejection that took hold of me when, with this notice, I ascertained the density of the bureaucratic fortress around the data I needed, and moved by simple compassion, one official risked the censure of his colleagues by reaching into his briefcase and handing me his copy of the coveted subject index. This first step in the data collection process set the pattern for what was to follow. For, in the course of my research, I was repeatedly confronted with mostly well-intentioned individuals operating within the confines of an extraordinarily cautious, self-defensive, and understaffed bureaucracy.

With my copy of the subject index now in hand, I identified large clumps of subjects of potential interest for my research. My next task was to approach the Freedom of Information Office at the INS—a division separate from the archival administrators already dealt with—to request the relevant data. Long-distance telephone contact up and down the FOIA hierarchy led to the same unyielding impasse: I could request documents one by one, and wait. If government functions are funded according to some priority system, then providing outsiders access to INS documents through FOIA is a very low priority indeed. I was informed that the backlog at the INS FOIA office was two years and steadily increasing, meaning that the staff operates entirely on the basis of crisis management. I was discreetly encouraged by the FOIA staff to *sue* them, since lawsuits are virtually the only way to activate the creaking and overburdened "freedom of information" machinery.

But lawsuits take substantial investments of time and resources, both of which were in short supply. Besides, I needed a data access procedure that would allow me "to get into the stacks," to sample the range of documents available. After lengthy telephone negotiations and several trips to Washington to plead my case, a compromise was finally reached. I could request entire boxes of documents, which would be shipped from the Suitland warehouse to the Central Office in Washington, where a FOIA officer would skim the contents for classified material and "sanitize" (the bureaucracy's evocative word for blacking out sensitive sections) them.[38] The FOIA staff were as accommodating as possible under the circumstances, setting me up in their overcrowded office for a week at a time over the course of two and a half years, as I pored over the boxes of data as they became available. I was even included in office birthday celebrations and retirement parties. But I never got over the feeling that the staff collectively cringed when I submitted requests for more documents, and were enormously relieved when I announced my departure, for the INS is ill-equipped to share its historical record.

The effects of understaffing are compounded, as I soon found out, by a level of file disorganization that is matched only in some people's attics. Working from the subject index and a variety of other partial and haphazard listings, I accessed approximately 100 large cardboard boxes containing thousands of file folders. These boxes are labeled by general subject, such as "Southwest Border Activity," and/or by time period. But nowhere are there any files marked by specific policy, or even generically "Bracero Program." In addition, the labels do not always accurately reflect the contents of the boxes, which I found on some occasions contained a wide assortment of extraneous documents, while including no trace of the subjects promised on the label.

Despite these considerable obstacles, the hours of tedium sifting through these files ultimately paid off, as rich veins of data documenting the internal policymaking process periodically surfaced. After one particularly productive day, during which extensive documentation of informal bracero policies was uncovered, the request of a FOIA officer reminded me how far I had come in my search for the bracero record, and the depths of the bureaucratic disorganization that had posed the single greatest obstacle to that search: "Oh, that's interesting," she said. "People have wondered where that material was. Maybe you can keep a list for us of what you find!"

While the bulk of the data for this study is the product of this labor-intensive excavation of INS archives, additional data were provided by the extensive Department of Labor files at the National Archives in

Washington. Contrasting markedly with the difficulties of accessing historical materials from the INS, these Labor Department files are readily available, well-organized, and carefully catalogued. They are critical not only for the reconfirmation of data obtained through other sources, but as documentation of the disagreements and sometimes open hostility between the Labor Department and the INS as they attempted to coordinate bracero policy.

These internal records from the INS and the Department of Labor are invaluable sources of primary data, relatively uncontaminated by self-censorship and official posturing. The potential drawback of such data and the "archaeological" collection process itself, is that the accessed material is inevitably incomplete and at best provides only a partial glimpse into the day-to-day workings of administrative policymaking. There are no doubt records not uncovered, perhaps even entire issues left unexplored. But the volume, quality, and diversity of the data obtained, and the fact that as data collection proceeded, a consistent pattern emerged and was repeatedly confirmed, give me considerable confidence in the analysis presented here.

This book is organized according to both chronology and analytical logic. As the Bracero Program comes of age, so does the analysis, with the evolution of policies adding cumulatively to our understanding of the complexities of agency action. Chapters Two and Three lay the descriptive groundwork for the more detailed analysis in the rest of the book. Relying primarily on secondary materials, these chapters trace the formative years of the Bracero Program, during which a comparatively small number of braceros were imported, and describe the operating procedures that characterized the program for its duration. Chapter Two examines the initiation of the contract labor system during World War II, and its post-war extension, as well as the accompanying increase in illegal immigration that was triggered by bracero policies. Chapter Three describes the entrenchment of the program in the early 1950s, the dramatic reduction of illegal immigration following "Operation Wetback," and the advantages of the subsequent expansion of the Bracero Program for agricultural interests. The chapter closes with a look at the INS "walking around the statute," or circumventing formal program guidelines and ostensible congressional intent, in order to maximize the utility of the contract labor system to growers—a theme that recurs throughout these first chapters and provides an important analytical thread that weaves through the rest of the book. Chapter Four investigates more closely the internal archival record, and it is here that the real substance of the argument emerges most clearly. Memos, unpublished reports, notes of telephone calls, and other fragments of the informal paper trail allow us to watch the effects of the structural contradictions outlined in the earlier chapters, as they impinge on immigration decision-makers in concrete ways, thus connecting the structural, the institutional, and even, as we will see, micro-level political feuding. Examining the confrontation between the INS and the Department of Labor as the contradictions of bracero policymaking generate inter-agency conflict, Chapter Five adds the final ingredient to the model of the state proposed here—a model that depicts the state as neither monolithic, nor, ultimately, uncoordinated. Chapter Six describes the demise of the Bracero Program, the last desperate efforts by the Immigration Service to salvage the foreign labor system, and ultimately the defeat (and retreat) of the immigration bureaucracy as an effective state agency. The book closes with a discussion of the strengths and weaknesses of prevailing theories of the state, and argues that if we are to advance beyond the current impasse in state theory, we must bring human agency back into state theorizing.

CHAPTER 2

THE FORMATIVE
YEARS

Major changes in law are typically preceded by voluminous commission reports, lengthy public hearings, and Congressional negotiation. In contrast, the Bracero Program was born virtually overnight and with remarkably little fanfare. When Congress quietly authorized the program in 1943, the labor importation system had already been operating for seven months. Its inconspicuous beginnings belie its significance and impact. This program, that delivered millions of Mexican farm workers to employers in the United States, is unique in U.S. immigration history. For over two decades, the U.S. government recruited, distributed, and controlled a massive foreign labor force for agriculture. It was an experiment that, as we will see, was mired in controversy while it lasted, and had enduring ramifications for both domestic farm labor and subsequent immigration patterns.

This chapter begins with an overview of the early years of the Bracero Program, providing a chronology of its development and a description of its basic operating procedures. Two interrelated themes recur throughout this overview. First, INS policies favored growers. Second, a high degree of administrative discretion permeated the program and was instrumental in tailoring it to growers' needs. But, if the Bracero Program fulfilled for growers their every dream of a plentiful and cheap labor supply, the use of foreign agricultural labor presented the INS with a series of stubborn dilemmas. The chapter closes with an examination of the most fundamental of these dilemmas, related to the rapid increase in illegal migration in the early years of the contract labor system—an increase that was in many ways a product of prevailing bracero policies.

THE WARTIME EMERGENCY PROGRAM, 1942–1947

Early in 1940, vegetable and cotton growers in California, Texas, and Arizona sounded the alarm of impending labor shortages. Reminiscent of their pleas for access to Mexican farm workers in the post-World War I period, farm employers in a number of Southwestern states in 1941 formally requested permission from the Immigration Service to import Mexicans to cultivate and harvest crops. All such requests were denied.[1] The following year, with the attack on Pearl Harbor and the entry of the United States into World War II, the official attitude towards Mexican contract labor changed abruptly. In April of 1942, the INS formed a committee bringing together top officials from the Departments of Justice (the INS parent agency), Labor, State, and Agriculture, and the War Manpower Commission, to study the possibility of launching a labor importation program. By May, this Special Committee on Importation of Mexican Labor had formulated a temporary worker program ostensibly designed to offset wartime labor shortages. Informal negotiations with Mexico had been ongoing, and on April 4, 1942, the two countries signed the bilateral agreement upon which the wartime Bracero Program was based.

According to President Truman's Commission on Migratory Labor,[2] "The negotiation of the Mexican International Agreement is a collective bargaining situation in which the Mexican Government is the representative of the workers and the Department of State is the representative of our farm employers." The compromise that was hammered out in 1942, and that served as a blueprint for subsequent agreements, established that braceros were not to be paid less than domestic workers doing similar work—and in no case were to be paid less than 30 cents an hour—and specified that piece rates be calculated to allow the average bracero to earn at least the minimum hourly wage.[3] At the insistence of Mexican negotiators, a subsistence wage of $3 per day was to be paid to braceros who were unemployed for more than 25% of the contract period; for those who were unemployed for less than 25% of the period, Mexican officials insisted on the payment of whatever unemployment benefits U.S. farm workers received (negotiators for the United States apparently kept to themselves the fact that domestic farm workers enjoyed no unemployment benefits). In addition, braceros were to be permitted to elect representatives to discuss complaints with their employers, as long as these discussions did not involve attempts to upgrade the terms of the contract, which were non-negotiable. Finally, Texas employers were excluded from eligibility for braceros, as Mexican negotiators cited a history of discrimination and abuse of Mexican workers in that state.

The bracero contract was initiated by requests from agricultural employers in the United States for a given number of Mexican workers for a specified period of time. After the U.S. Employment Service (USES)[4] had certified that a "shortage of labor" at "prevailing wages" existed, an order for braceros was placed with officials in Mexico City. Mexican officials selected bracero candidates from regions around the country, who were then transferred to recruitment centers in the interior of Mexico. Representatives from both countries made selections from this pool and processed the workers for distribution to their agricultural employers in the United States. Transportation and subsistence from the Mexican recruitment centers to places of employment were paid by the U.S. government, to be partially reimbursed by the employer. The actual work contract during this early period was technically between the Farm Security Administration (FSA), located in the Department of Agriculture, and the individual braceros who were then subcontracted to employers. The Cooperative Employment Agreement, which constituted the contract between the FSA and the employer, bound employers to the terms of the international agreement with Mexico; stipulated that employers make a $5 contribution to the transportation of each of their braceros; and required employers to pay a "performance bond," to be forfeited should they violate the terms of the contract.[5] In return, the government delivered a guaranteed source of labor. The vast majority of braceros in this period came from the least developed, poorest, and most remote areas of Mexico. As Gamboa explains, "This meant that in spite of the fact that the contract was explained to them before they affixed their signatures, most of the men did not have a rudimentary understanding of the terms and conditions. The whole idea that a young person from a tiny community in Michoacan could comprehend the meaning . . . was farfetched. In reality, the workers understood little beyond the fact that they were going to work in the United States."[6]

From 1942 to 1947, the Department of Agriculture had primary authority for coordinating the Bracero Program, but its operation involved a complex network of interagency responsibilities. The agreements with Mexico were negotiated largely by the Department of State; the United States Employment Service was responsible for certifying labor shortages and estimating prevailing wages; the Farm Security Administration—and later the War Food Administration—did the actual recruitment and contracting; and the INS authorized and oversaw the admission and return of the workers.

The wartime Bracero Program provided over 219,500 Mexican workers to farm employers in twenty-four states (see Appendix B). Although this constituted only 2.7% of the wage labor force in agriculture, braceros were an integral component of agricultural production in some states and for some crops. During 1945, for example, California growers employed 63% of the total bracero work force, and in the off-season months from January to April, 90% of the braceros went to California. The bracero work force was concentrated in cotton, sugar beets, fruits, and vegetables, and in some areas comprised the bulk of the unskilled labor for these crops.[7]

One contemporary researcher observed that the wartime bracero program was a grower's "dream of heaven."[8] Growers were the obvious beneficiaries of this infusion of hundreds of thousands of additional farm workers. But the advantages of the system went far beyond what numbers alone might suggest. Remember that Mexicans had been considered an ideal labor source in the early 1900s due to the vicinity of Mexico and the ability to expand and contract the supply at a moment's notice. The bracero system institutionalized that flexibility and injected an important element of control over both the timing of the entrance and the certainty of the departure. The President's Commission on Migratory Labor explained these advantages of the system: "[Growers] want a labor supply which, on one hand, is ready and willing to meet the short-term work requirements and which, on the other hand, will not impose social and economic problems on them or on their community when the work is finished. . . . The demand for migratory workers is thus essentially twofold: To be ready to go to work when needed; to be gone when not needed."[9] A grower from Colorado told the President's Commission, ". . . any nation is very fortunate if [it] can, from sources near at hand, obtain the services on beck and call of labor, adult male labor, on condition that when the job is completed the laborer will return to his home."[10]

The *New York Journal of Commerce* in 1892 had compared immigrants to farm animals, arguing that "a gift of either should be gladly received."[11] From this perspective, the bracero was the perfect "gift." Not only did he arrive as "adult male labor," but unlike European immigrants of the 19th century, he could be sent home upon completion of the contract. Furthermore, by definition, the bracero was a *contract* laborer, a status that placed him outside the free labor market.

As war industries siphoned off the number of domestic workers available for the civilian labor market, the Bracero Program filled the gap with workers who were tied *by law* to agriculture. Likening the bracero to a prisoner of war, one observer noted the unique advantage to the grower of a work force that was "indentured to agriculture and prevented by law from listening to the siren call of the shipyards."[12]

Beyond these benefits that were inherent in the labor importation scheme, growers quickly succeeded in molding both the mechanics and the content of the program to their liking. The first concrete indication of the power that growers were to have in the evolution of the Bracero Program came with the transfer of responsibility for the program from the FSA to the War Food Administration, a decidedly "friendlier agency."[13] Growers had always been wary of the FSA, which they saw as a "social reform" agency.[14] When the FSA began extending certain provisions of the Bracero Program—such as wage and work guarantees—to domestic farm workers, accusations that it was engaging in "socialist experiments" reached a new pitch.[15] In addition to these ongoing complaints about the FSA's purported "socialist" tendencies, growers protested that the agency "stalled around" in providing bracero labor.[16] In March 1943, in response to continued pressure from growers, the program was removed from the jurisdiction of the FSA.[17]

One month later, on April 29, 1943, Congress enacted Public Law 45, officially endorsing the Bracero Program.[18] The law established the parameters of the wartime program that endured until 1948, and in acceding to most of the demands made by the American Farm Bureau, moved it even closer to a grower's "dream of heaven." The law, for example, prohibited the FSA practice of using federal money to recruit and transport domestic workers to areas with labor shortages before importing braceros, and stated explicitly that domestic migrants were not to be covered by the protections required by international agreement for braceros.[19]

While PL 45 required growers to offer employment to domestic workers at "prevailing wages" before being certified to employ braceros, in practice the provision was rendered virtually meaningless by decentralizing the responsibility for determining prevailing wages in the State Extension Services. The Extension Services were everywhere allied with local Farm Bureaus.[20] So close was this alliance in California that it was reported that the County Extension Agent ". . . functions as an employee of organized farm groups . . . and is therefore of doubtful impartiality."[21] The typical procedure for setting wages was for growers to meet at the beginning of each season, determine the wages they were willing to pay, and then inform the appropriate state officials.[22] The "prevailing wage" thus came to mean "the wage that prevails" within the context of a non-competitive labor market.

Perhaps most remarkably, PL 45 authorized the Immigration Commissioner to admit Mexican contract workers on his own terms, in what Kirstein calls a "dramatic reversal of the bilateralism" of the bracero agreements.[23] From the beginning, the Bracero Program had been a creature of administrative discretion. Not only had it been mounted entirely through the efforts of administrative agencies, but the importation of foreign contract labor was dependent on the Attorney General—and through him, the INS Commissioner—admitting the inadmissible. The Anti-Alien Contract Labor Law of 1885 had prohibited the importation of contract labor, a provision that was incorporated into the Immigration and Nationality Act of 1917. But the Ninth Proviso to Section 3 of the 1917 law gave the Attorney General the authority to "issue rules and prescribe conditions . . . to control and regulate the admission and return of otherwise inadmissible aliens."[24] PL 45 reconfirmed this administrative discretion to admit the inadmissible, authorizing the Immigration Commissioner to waive the prohibition against contract labor "for such time and under such conditions" as he shall prescribe.[25]

This provision offered a temporary reprieve to growers who resented having to go through the Mexican government for their workers. As initially interpreted by the Immigration Service, the provision allowed employers to recruit Mexican workers at the border, with their braceros being admitted directly by the INS, bypassing the Mexican recruitment process altogether.[26] Besides permitting growers to select their own workers and cutting down on the time consumed in government processing and transportation, border recruitment had the effect of opening up the program to Texas employers who were specifically excluded by the international agreement. During the month of May, 1943, the INS admitted over 2000 braceros who were contracted at the border to employers in El Paso County, Texas, with 1500 entering in one day.[27]

Although direct recruitment by Texas employers was stopped only weeks after it began,[28] the episode provides an important indication of the impact that administrative discretion was to have on the operation of the Bracero Program, and the role of grower interests in shaping the use of that discretion. Furthermore, it highlights the differing concerns of the various institutions of the state and the conflicting pressures under which the INS operated. While the State Department urged immigration officials to terminate border recruitment in the interests of international relations, influential members of Congress from border states applauded the policy. One senior immigration official sent a confidential memo to his counterpart in the State Department explaining that if they stopped admitting braceros directly at the border, "a good many members of Congress would be on Immigration's neck."[29] Finally, the INS interpretation of PL 45, although short-lived, was an important harbinger of things to come, for border recruitment continued to be a major priority of the agency in its efforts to maximize the utility of the program to agricultural employers.

In addition to administrative arrangements that bypassed certain requirements of the bilateral agreements, employers often simply ignored contract provisions they found inconvenient. Wages did not consistently meet the 30 cents per hour minimum, hours actually worked were not always correctly recorded, payments were delayed, and housing and food frequently failed to meet the minimum standards required by the contract.[30] Such flagrant violations prompted a curious kind of double-speak from political scientist Richard Craig, who in his analysis of the period seemed intent on giving employers every benefit of the doubt. "In such areas as housing, wages, food, standards of transportation, and unemployment and subsistence payments," he said, "farmers did not necessarily violate the provisions of the agreement; they either ignored them or fulfilled them in a manner more to their liking."[31]

On October 24, 1945, the Secretary of Agriculture, members of Congress from bracero using states, and growers' representatives appeared before the House Committee on Appropriations, urging an extension of the labor importation program, even though the war was by now over.[32] Arguing that domestic workers were unwilling to do the "stoop" labor of agriculture, and that therefore braceros continued to be vital to the agricultural economy, they managed to keep the "wartime" Bracero Program alive long after hostilities had ended.[33]

While the farm labor program continued through 1947, very few braceros were actually imported that year. Instead, the INS devised a *de facto* legalization program, whereby they legalized on the spot illegal Mexican immigrants found employed in agriculture and contracted them to their employers as braceros. During the summer of 1947, when only 31,331 braceros were imported or recontracted, the Service legalized 55,000 undocumented workers in Texas alone, once again effectively circumventing the exclusion of Texas from the formal program. This legalization of undocumented Mexican farm workers by the INS continued for the next several years to be an integral part of the Bracero Program—sometimes sanctioned by international agreement, at other times used as an administrative bypass of the conditions imposed by those agreements.

DIRECT GROWER PARTICIPATION, 1947–1951

Two years after the end of World War II, Congress officially declared an end to the wartime labor program. Public Law 40, passed on April 28, 1947, provided that the Bracero Program "may be continued up to and including December 31, 1947, and thereafter *shall be liquidated within thirty days.*"[34] Agricultural employers, alarmed at the impending deadline, and warning of continued labor shortages, swamped the INS with petitions to extend the stay of their braceros and to allow for additional admissions. Despite the unambiguous termination of the program by Congress two months earlier, on February 21, 1948, the State Department arranged a new accord with Mexico, and labor importations were resumed.

Perhaps it should not be surprising that the executive agencies that had conceived, formulated, and implemented the labor importation system, were aggressive in perpetuating their program. What is more surprising, or at least potentially puzzling, is that Congress let them do it. Peter Kirstein offers an explanation for these events that emphasizes a balance of power favoring the executive branch, noting tautologically, "The fact that the executive branch was able to continue the bracero program despite Public Law 40 indicated that the locus of power in managing the bracero program lay with the executive branch."[35]

But subsequent events undermine this interpretation, implying as it does that Congress and the administrative agencies were at loggerheads, and that Congress was powerless to impose its will in this area. The evidence suggests instead that the two branches worked in tandem to perpetuate administratively what Congress was for the moment unwilling to legislate. When Congress passed Public Law 40, it was seen primarily as a six-month *extension* of the Bracero Program. Appropriations for the wartime program had been scheduled by Public Law 521 to expire on July 1, 1947; however, proponents of the extension maintained that there were still critical shortages of "stoop labor."[36] A small minority of Senators sympathetic to the interests of labor opposed PL 40, arguing that the six-month extension constituted an unnecessary federal "subsidy" to agriculture and would displace domestic workers and depress their wages, but they were quickly discredited.[37] When Senator James Kem (R-Missouri) suggested that the stoop labor argument was no longer valid and cited earlier testimony from Elizabeth Sasuly, Washington State representative of the Food, Tobacco, Agricultural, and Allied Workers' Union of the CIO, that growers were using the Bracero Program "to create a surplus pool of labor so as to depress wages," he was met with ridicule.[38] Senator Millikin (R-Colorado), a primary spokesperson for the extension, retorted that "the lady [the union representative] was 'talking through her hat,' " punctuating his disdain with, "[i]f she was 'talking through her hat', I am sure it must have been a very attractive hat," whereupon the all-male Senate gallery filled with laughter. The labor representative's credibility—and that of Senator Kem who had cited her testimony—was thus effectively undermined, and the opposition silenced.[39] So focused was the Senate debate on the provision of the law that *extended* the program for six months, that one Senator was moved to point out, "I wonder if the Senate is not somewhat confused about this particular piece of legislation. As at present constituted, the importation of foreign labor into this country is subject to complete termination within a very few months."[40]

Two months after the enactment of the extension, new legislation was introduced that would have given the Department of Agriculture and the INS the authority to admit foreign contract labor administratively—even in the absence of a congressionally sanctioned program—upon the determination of labor shortages.[41] Congress adjourned before the bill was acted on. Instead, in December 1947, just a few days before the end of the six-month extension, the House Committee on Agriculture held hearings on the issue of labor importation. The Chair of the Committee described its purpose: ". . . the hearing is purely informal, just for the purpose of having those who are directly concerned with this problem as users of labor to present their views to the committee and to the Government officials who are most directly concerned with it, having in mind the thought that by talking the matter over we might be able to solve some of the problems that admittedly do exist in connection with foreign labor."[42]

The meeting served to bring together growers and federal administrators, and to sanction a *de facto* extension of the contract labor system through administrative action. The hearing opened with the declaration "that the interest of this committee is primarily that of doing what it can to make available an ample labor supply for the producers of crops which require the foreign labor, the stoop type of labor."[43] The Commissioner of the INS, Watson Miller, assured the committee that he too recognized the continued need for Mexican labor. Speaking first of the wartime program, Commissioner Miller explained his agency's plans to continue to admit Mexican contract laborers: "It was pointed out to us that the emergency was not over . . . and that it was not likely to be over for several years. We had as many as a hundred experienced growers . . . with whom we consulted. Some of them expressed the thought that they could not see the end as yet."[44]

Having established that bracero importations would continue administratively beyond the expiration date of the law, most of the hearing focused on the details of the plan, with the agriculture committee primarily interested in its acceptability to growers. One concern had to do with the departure of braceros who were already in the United States, as Public Law 40 required that they leave by January 30, 1948. The Immigration Commissioner and the Committee Chair agreed that it would be undesirable "to rush these people [braceros] back at an undue rate."[45] In fact, the Chair told the head of the INS, "It was our hope that the matter could be delayed as long as possible in order that the work of these people could be continued to the latest possible date."[46] Far from fighting the administrative plan that was an apparent violation of the intent of PL 40—which had ostensibly *terminated* the Bracero Program—Congress helped hammer out its practical details. Not every member of the House Committee on Agriculture was pleased with this expansion of administrative power. A few, in the distinct minority, agreed with Representative Granger of Utah when he complained, "It seems to me this is just another way to break down the immigration laws of the United States, when discretionary power is given to anybody under even the pretext that we want to raise food. It seems to me it is the wrong thing to do."[47] Seven months after the congressional deadline for the Bracero Program had lapsed, Congress passed Public Law 893 with little discussion and no public hearings. The law officially transferred responsibility to the USES, which it authorized to "direct, supervise, coordinate, and provide transportation" for the program. One year later, this law too expired, once again leaving the program to operate completely outside of any formal Congressional endorsement or oversight.[48]

The labor program that was worked out by administrative agreement and international negotiation with Mexico differed in a number of important ways from its wartime predecessor. Most significantly, the government-to-government contracts that Mexico had insisted on during the war were replaced by direct grower-bracero work agreements. Now that growers and their representatives contracted directly with braceros at recruitment centers, and were responsible for the cost of transportation to places of employment, the longstanding demand that recruitment centers be set up at the border intensified. This had always been one of the most hotly disputed and enduring issues for negotiation, and one on which Mexican officials rarely were willing to compromise. Policymakers in Mexico were convinced that border recruitment contributed to illegal immigration, as workers who congregated at the border and were not selected as braceros, often immigrated illegally. Such a mass exodus from the northern border was not only embarrassing for what it said about the Mexican economy, but it also depleted that rich agricultural region of seasonal farm labor. When Mexican negotiators proved intransigent on the issue, the extra expense and effort of having to recruit at reception centers in the Mexican interior convinced many growers that hiring illegal workers was far simpler and less expensive than contracting braceros, a response that contributed to a substantial increase in illegal migration.

Acting on the belief that it would decrease the number of illegal immigrants in the United States and thus reduce employer abuses of vulnerable undocumented workers, Mexican negotiators agreed to a provision in the 1949 bilateral accord that illegal immigrants already in the United States be given preference for bracero status over newly imported braceros. While the provision originally allowed for the legalization of only those illegal workers already in the U.S. at the time the agreement was signed, the deadline for legalization was continually extended to cover the most recent arrivals.[49]

The President's Commission on Migratory Labor protested that this legalization of undocumented workers by the INS constituted a blatant "erosion of immigration law."[50] The Commission noted, "The ninth proviso [of the 1917 Immigration and Nationality Act] allows the temporary admission and return of otherwise inadmissible aliens. . . . In the contracting of wetbacks, we see the abandonment of the concept that the ninth proviso authority is limited to *admission*. A wetback is not admitted; he is already here, unlawfully. We have thus reached a point where we place a premium upon violation of the immigration law."[51]

Although legalization—the official slang for which was "drying out the wetbacks"—clearly made "recruitment" easier for growers, Mexico's hopes that it would reduce the number of illegal immigrants in the U.S. proved to be misplaced. Instead, it *increased* illegal immigration as word spread that the way to get a bracero contract was to cross the border illegally. Between 1947 and 1949, approximately 74,600 braceros were contracted from Mexico, while 142,200 undocumented workers were legalized and contracted directly to growers.[52] In 1950, fewer than 20,000 braceros were imported, and over 96,000 illegal aliens were paroled to local farmers.[53]

Not only did INS legalization practices effectively circumvent the recruitment requirements of the bilateral agreement, but direct grower-bracero contracts had the effect of minimizing the already lax enforcement of contract provisions. Mexican negotiators insisted on government-to-government contracts in the earlier stages of the program because they anticipated—correctly, as it turned out—that enforcement would be perfunctory if the U.S. government was not held directly accountable. The President's Commission on Migratory Labor described the deterioration of enforcement in the post-war period: "Following the war . . . we virtually abandoned effective scrutiny and enforcement of the Individual Work Contracts to which private employers and individual Mexican aliens were the parties."[54] A secret U.S. Embassy report in 1950 concluded that "employers had committed mass violations with regard to recruiting, wages, general hiring conditions and utilization of non-contract [illegal] labor," and that federal agencies were "not enforcing certain wage requirements and assumed a partial attitude in favor of agribusiness."[55] The comments of a grower from New Mexico to the President's Commission reveal the cavalier attitude of employers toward the work contract and the ease with which contracts were violated: "I know that we can't live up to the contract 100 percent. It is just a piece of paper. If we get along with the men and are able to satisfy them and they don't go to the Mexican consul and kick, we get by."[56] While the USES was still responsible for certifying a shortage of labor before braceros could be contracted, and the INS and the Department of Labor officially shared responsibility for contract enforcement, in practice a hands-off policy prevailed.

While this was a "laissez-faire era"[57] with regard to enforcement, U.S. officials did not simply watch from the sidelines. Not only were federal officials responsible for negotiating acceptable agreements with Mexico, but periodically they actively *abrogated* those agreements, both to satisfy growers and as a show of force in their relations with the Mexican negotiators. The most notable example of such unilateral action occurred on October 16 and 17, 1948, on the border between El Paso, Texas, and Ciudad Juarez. A combination of factors—including the continued refusal of Mexico to allow Texas employers to contract braceros, the lack of a formal border recruitment system, and the virtual employer boycott on recruiting braceros from the interior of Mexico—had resulted in the piling up of thousands of hopeful braceros in border towns, particularly at Ciudad Juarez. On October 1, the Mexican government, in a bid to offset an impending crisis, issued the order that U.S. growers could recruit 2000 workers from the overrun border town. Before the contracting could begin, thousands of desperate workers stormed the border. After an initial attempt to stop the influx, the INS simply opened the border for the weekend, paroling the workers to growers through the Texas Employment Service.[58] Mexican officials were understandably outraged by this "El Paso Incident" as it came to be called, and temporarily voided the entire international labor agreement. It took eight months for a new agreement to be negotiated, but the supply of braceros continued uninterrupted. Operating outside of any congressional endorsement, and now disconnected from its bilateral foundation, the Bracero Program was implemented unilaterally by the INS, the Department of Labor, and other administrative agencies, until the international program could be restored.

Although the opening of the border was triggered by the rush of Mexican workers into Texas, the USES and the INS had been contemplating such a move for several months. According to documents unearthed by Kirstein in the files of the Truman Library, a meeting had been convened between representatives of the Department of Labor, the INS, and the State Department in the summer of 1948 to discuss the merits of an administratively arranged open border.[59] Kirstein concludes from the records of this meeting, "The Labor Department supported such activity [an open border] and the Immigration and Naturalization Service concurred, provided that the influx was manageable and easily apportioned among the farmers and ranchers."[60] The INS District Director in El Paso later told the *New York Times* that he opened the border to Mexican workers because "they need the work, our farmers need them and the crops were going to waste."[61] The few thousand Mexicans who entered during the El Paso Incident was a small number compared to the estimated 100,000 illegal immigrants in Texas already; but the incident serves as a dramatic example of the blatant and unilateral abrogation of the bracero accords on the part of federal agencies, and the role of grower interests in that abrogation.

By the end of the first decade of the Bracero Program, labor importation had significantly advanced grower interests in the balance of power with their workers, both bracero and domestic. As the program insulated agriculture in the Southwest from the principle of supply and demand in the labor market, farm wages were stabilized, and in some cases reduced. The President's Commission on Migratory Labor correlated farm wages and concentrations of braceros, and concluded that the influx of foreign workers had been central in depressing wages.[62] In light of these wage reductions, the Commission was suspicious of growers' cries of labor shortages, remarking pointedly, "A labor shortage with falling wages is difficult to understand." The Commission reasoned that "if there is a shortage, the price of labor should rise. Yet the opposite of this actually has occurred."[63]

Additional data gathered by the Commission confirm the validity of their suspicions. According to their report, the number of workers required to do the nation's farm work actually went *down* between 1940 and 1950. Mechanization of agriculture dramatically increased productivity, and a number of traditionally stoop labor tasks were done almost entirely by machine by 1950.[64] Mechanization not only reduced the per-unit demand for workers, but had the effect of shortening the harvest season, making it increasingly difficult to eke out a living as a farm worker. As a result, agricultural production expanded, while the total number of farm workers dropped.[65] With domestic farm workers unemployed, mechanization steadily advancing, wages depressed, and agricultural production at an all-time high, it was apparent that the advantage to growers of the labor importation system was not just that it provided them with labor, but that it provided that labor at wages and under conditions of their choosing.[66]

As the system that was conceived as a wartime emergency measure approached its second decade of operation, there was no question that it generously served the interests of southwestern agriculture, and that it did so in no small measure through the administrative discretion and inventiveness of the Immigration Service and other responsible agencies. But, while the program provided growers with a guaranteed labor supply with few strings attached, the increase in illegal immigration that accompanied the bracero movement introduced a series of dilemmas for the immigration bureaucracy that shaped important components of INS policy for the duration of the program.

ILLEGAL IMMIGRATION: CONFLICTING PRESSURES ON THE INS

The Bracero Program in this period was complemented by an informal, implicitly sanctioned system of illegal farm labor. During the first years of the program, the number of illegal immigrants in farm employment far exceeded the number of legal braceros. From 1942 through 1952, when a total of 818,545 braceros were imported from

Mexico, the INS apprehended over two million undocumented workers, the vast majority of whom were Mexican (see Appendix A). Illegal migration increased dramatically over the course of the decade. In 1943, approximately 12,000 illegal immigrants were apprehended; by 1945, the number had jumped to almost 70,000. By the end of this period, the gap between apprehensions and legal braceros was widening rapidly. In 1949, when there were 107,000 braceros, the INS apprehended slightly over twice that many undocumented workers. Two years later, the ratio was 3 to 1.[67]

There are several problems with using INS apprehension statistics for estimating the number of illegal aliens in agricultural employment. In the first place, it is impossible to tell exactly what proportion of the apprehended aliens were farm workers, since the immigration bureaucracy did not record occupational data until 1953. However, researchers of the period note that "[o]ccupationally, the majority of [undocumented] workers were engaged in hand or stoop labor in agriculture," and given the concentration of Border Patrol activity in the rural border regions, it is safe to assume that most of those who were apprehended were farm workers.[68] The second difficulty, of course, is that not all illegal aliens are apprehended, and some may be apprehended more than once in a given year. Finally, apprehension statistics necessarily vary with enforcement policies and resources.[69] Taking these potential biases into consideration and given the lax enforcement policies of this period, to be discussed below, it is likely that these border apprehension statistics underestimated the number of illegal alien farm workers.

The increase in illegal immigration was in part the side effect of bracero policies. The "drying out" of illegal workers found in the United States and the preference given to illegal aliens for bracero employment provided little incentive for aspiring braceros to remain in Mexico until they were legally contracted. The Bracero Program triggered illegal immigration in other ways as well. For example, Hadley, calling this period "the wetback decade," argues that the program precipitated the influx, as returning braceros spread word of employment opportunities in the United States.[70] Since there were more bracero candidates than there were official slots for them, and because it was quicker and cheaper[71] to bypass the contract system, many Mexican workers took matters into their own hands, crossing the border illegally.

Substantial evidence suggests, however, that the increase in illegal immigration was not simply a byproduct of the Bracero Program, but was encouraged by INS enforcement policies. The Border Patrol was notoriously reluctant to apprehend and deport illegal farm workers during the harvest season or at other times of peak labor demand. During the war, the INS District Director in Los Angeles explained to the Department of Labor that it was their policy not to check farms and ranches for illegal aliens while harvest work was being done.[72] In 1949, the Idaho State Employment Service reported, "The United States Immigration and Naturalization Service recognizes the need for farm workers in Idaho and . . . withholds its search and deportation until such times as there is not a shortage of farm workers."[73] Similarly, the Chief of the Border Patrol in Tucson, Arizona, told the President's Commission that the District Director in El Paso issued orders each harvest season to stop apprehending illegal Mexican farm workers.[74] In South Texas, some farm employers were reportedly immune to border patrol enforcement.[75]

This reluctance to detain illegal farm workers was not confined to the idiosyncrasies of regional enforcement. Instead, it seems to have been the official policy through much of the 1940s and early 1950s. A senior immigration agent told a State Department official in 1944, according to a memorandum of their telephone conversation, that "the Immigration Service was concentrating on those who were not engaged in the preparation and harvesting of perishable crops."[76] In 1949, the Immigration Commissioner explained to Congress that "the Border Patrol would not go on the farms in search of 'wetbacks,' but would confine their activities to the highways and places of social gatherings."[77] Willard Kelly, Chief of the Border Patrol, testified before the President's Commission in 1950 that orders went out regularly from the central office to "cooperate" with farmers in Texas: "Service Officers were instructed to defer the apprehensions of Mexicans employed on Texas farms where to remove them could likely result in loss of the crops."[78] The following year, Kelly told the House Committee on Agriculture, "We do feel that we have the authority to permit to remain in the United States aliens who are here as agricultural laborers, whether they are here legally or illegally."[79] Summing up the non-interventionism of his predecessors, newly appointed Immigration Commissioner Joseph Swing told a House subcommittee that prior to 1954 the Border Patrol did not have "any real fervor to get anything done."[80] Political considerations compounded the economic imperatives. It was well-known within the agency, for example, that the chief of the Border Patrol in the early 1950s directed his agents to stay away from Governor Shriver's Texas ranch—reportedly one of the biggest employers of illegal immigrants in Texas—while a highly publicized visit from President Eisenhower was underway.[81]

The failure of the immigration agency to curtail undocumented migration has often been attributed to a lack of sufficient resources.[82] It is true that the INS budget has rarely kept pace with inflation, and that in the period between 1942 and 1951, while apprehensions of illegal aliens rose over 400 percent, Border Patrol personnel was *reduced* by more than one-third.[83] However, the Immigration Service was confronted by more complex pressures than simply an inadequate budget. In fact, the lack of resources was at least as much a reflection of these underlying pressures as it was their cause.

Addressing the issue of the "wholesale violation of the [immigration] law" in South Texas, an article in *Newsweek* claimed that the INS was driven by economics: "They [INS] know that the wetback is the very backbone of the prosperity of the . . . lower Rio Grande Valley. . . . Without him, bank vaults in the Valley towns might not be bulging— as they are now—with farmers' cash."[84] This mass media interpretation was periodically validated by statements of immigration officials who underscored the importance of illegal aliens to agriculture—particularly in Texas where braceros were not available—and their reluctance to damage the agricultural economy with rigorous enforcement. Consistent with this economic interpretation, Immigration Commissioner Watson Miller told the House Committee on Agriculture in 1947 that it was the "duty" of the agency "to protect valuable and necessary crops."[85]

Should immigration officials occasionally forget this obligation, growers did not hesitate to protest. When border apprehensions increased during the summer of 1943, farmers quickly complained. The head of the Chamber of Commerce in McAllen, Texas, wrote to the War Food Administration in June 1943 on behalf of area growers: ". . . the labor shortage can be easily solved in the Texas Valley merely by the Border Patrol . . . relaxing their vigilance on the deportation of so-called wetbacks. . . . Now which is more important, punctilious execution of immigration regulations . . . or the saving of food crops?"[86] Members of a South Texas farm association, writing to Senator Connally in 1944, expressed their irritation at having their cooperative "arrangement" with the INS violated:

> For a number of years citizens of Mexico entered the United States both legally and illegally, engaging in agricultural work. . . . While from time to time they have been picked up by the Border Patrol, there has been a tendency on the part of the Border Patrol to concentrate their efforts on deporting only those who were bad citizens. . . . This arrangement, although it did not have the stamp of legislative approval, has worked

out very nicely for our farmers down here. . . . [But] during the past few weeks the Border Patrol has picked up and deported hundreds of wetbacks.[87]

In February 1950, when the Border Patrol increased their monthly apprehensions by 30%, Texas farmers again launched a counterattack.[88] Growers in the Rio Grande Valley called the Border Patrol a "Gestapo outfit."[89] The *New York Times* underlined the sense of betrayal felt by growers: "The border patrol, long known for its anomalously amicable relations with . . . the farmers whose fields it periodically raids . . . was accused of almost as heinous a roster of outrages as was laid to the Nazi government."[90] Local newspapers protested that the farmers were "justifiably resentful" at having their labor supply interfered with.[91] Representative Lloyd Bentsen (D-Texas), who himself came from a wealthy family of Rio Grande Valley growers, addressed the floor of Congress following the raids and insisted on a full-fledged investigation of INS tactics.[92] The Border Patrol campaign was short-lived, and by June 1950, it was estimated that as many as 50,000 illegal aliens were crowded into the Lower Rio Grande Valley, causing one State Department official to wonder how they would all find employment.[93]

Congressional representatives of grower interests were influential in a number of ways in limiting the effectiveness of the Border Patrol, sometimes through blatant pressure such as that exerted by Representative Bentsen after the 1950 raids, but more often through implicit, indirect means. Two types of indirect pressure were most important in reducing the ability and the motivation of the Immigration Service to curtail illegal immigration. First, the agency was regularly reminded that Congress found the rigid interpretation and enforcement of immigration laws undesirable if it meant the reduction of the farm labor supply. When Border Patrol chief Willard Kelly told the House Committee on Agriculture in 1951 that the agency had the authority to allow illegal aliens to remain in the United States, Representative Poage, Vice Chair of the Committee from Texas, made it clear not only that the Committee would tolerate such an apparent distortion of the law, but that it was counting on it. Kelly had admitted that it was a "strained construction" that permitted the immigration bureaucracy to allow illegal labor to remain in the U.S.; Representative Poage continued to press Kelly, demanding confirmation that in spite of its ambiguous legality, the INS would continue to exercise this authority to tolerate illegal labor: "So long as you are running the show, we can anticipate that that will be the interpretation, is that the idea?" And later, ". . .

I think so far as the power is concerned, it leaves it completely in your hands. . . . You have given us the assurance that I think takes care of the situation, so long as you are in charge of it."[94]

Second, not only did the limited budget of the INS hamstring the agency in this period, but the budgetary process and the debates surrounding it highlighted the reasons behind this underfunding. Senator Patrick McCarran (D-Nevada), known generally for his immigration restrictionism, supported *reductions* in appropriations for the Border Patrol in 1953, leaving little doubt about his motives:

> . . . [o]n this side of the border there is a desire for these wetbacks. . . . Last year when we had the appropriations bill up, the item that might have prevented them coming over . . . was stricken from the bill. . . . We might just as well face this thing realistically. The agricultural people, the farmers along the . . . border in California, in Arizona, in Texas . . . want this help. They want this farm labor. They just cannot get along without it.[95]

In the House, representatives from Texas, with its huge concentration of illegal workers, spearheaded reductions in appropriations. In spite of INS figures that revealed that the number of undocumented workers far exceeded the number of legal braceros, Representative O.C. Fisher (D-Texas) argued successfully against supplemental funding for the agency in 1952 declaring, "I do not find ample justification for that kind of expenditure."[96]

Hadley noted the "social paradox" that while Congress stringently limited the number of refugees to be admitted after World War II and jealously guarded the front door of legal immigration, it was "splendidly indifferent" about the mounting number of illegal aliens who entered the back door, cutting funds to the Border Patrol just as the illegal traffic increased.[97] When apprehensions of undocumented aliens tripled from 1943 to 1944, Congress responded by eliminating over 100 positions from the Border Patrol. By 1954, this frontline enforcement arm of the immigration agency had been cut by one-third. So blatant was the discrepancy between Congressional restrictionism regarding legal immigration and the tolerance of the illegal flow that a *Washington Post* cartoonist poked fun at the hypocrisy by depicting a member of Congress proclaiming righteously, "I don't want any *legal* immigration around here."[98]

Those few members of Congress who spoke for budget increases were skeptical of their colleagues' motives. In 1952, Senator Hubert Humphrey, frustrated over the congressional reluctance to fund the

Border Patrol, told a State Department representative during hearings on Migratory Labor:

> I am going to be honest and frank with you . . . because of the economic interests that are involved in the wetback problem, no real, sincere effort has been made to solve it. . . . As long as it is possible to hire the wetbacks at 10 cents an hour, they will be coming across the border until kingdom come. . . . Somebody is making a filthy dollar out of it.[99]

Later during the same hearings, Senator Humphrey relayed his frustration to Immigration Commissioner Argyle Mackey and Border Patrol chief Willard Kelly, saying that he would "never be convinced that a majority around here are sincere about wanting to do anything about the wetback problem."[100] Kelly responded, "It would almost seem that the reason for the failure of the United States to properly protect its borders is to make way for the illegal entry of cheap alien labor. . . ."[101] He was in a good position to draw such conclusions. As head of the Border Patrol, Kelly had primary responsibility for implementing enforcement policies, and it was he who generally appeared before Congress to explain or defend those policies, promising the House Agriculture Committee in 1951, for example, that he would continue to permit illegal agricultural workers to remain in the U.S.

The Congressional pressure on the immigration bureaucracy to go slow on enforcement was thus twofold. Not only was the agency appropriated insufficient funds, but the budget debates sent an unequivocal message to the Immigration Service, underscoring the Congressional unwillingness to interfere with a plentiful farm labor supply. Summarizing the pressures on the agency not to enforce the law, and the only partial validity of budgetary explanations of Border Patrol inadequacies, the INS District Director in El Paso testified to the President's Commission on Migratory Labor in 1951, "All we need is a go-ahead signal and we can enforce the law 90 to 95 percent."[102]

So lax was enforcement and so pervasive was the perception that illegal aliens were a necessary and integral component of the farm labor supply, that increased Border Patrol enforcement was often a *Mexican* demand in negotiating bracero agreements, and was seen by U.S. negotiators as a concession. Indicative of the relative importance that Mexico, as compared to the United States, attached to the reduction of illegal immigration, one State Department official told Congress in 1947 that "the 'wetbacks' as we call them . . . were giving considerable worry to the Mexican Government."[103] Senator Allen Ellender (D-Louisiana) reminded the Senate Committee on Agriculture in 1953 that the "wetback problem" was primarily a Mexican problem. Mexico's concern about illegal immigration was occasionally used as a bargaining stick, as when Senator Bourke Hickenlooper (R-Iowa), perturbed by Mexico's assertiveness on bracero wages and working conditions in the spring of 1953, suggested militantly, "I wonder what kind of consternation would go on in Mexico if our people got tough themselves on the negotiations down there and said that we would not be suckers anymore." Later the Senator was more specific on how the U.S. might "get tough." "I am wondering if a device could not be worked out to say 'Come on boys, there is work here, come in under your own power and go back under your own power.' We could work it out without the law."[104]

Periodically, Mexican pressure had an effect. In the winter of 1950, the INS launched a special enforcement campaign along the Texas border, and was accused by newspapers in the Lower Rio Grande Valley of "siding with Mexico."[105] In 1951, when Mexico stalled bracero negotiations until the U.S. showed an effort to halt the flow of illegal workers, the INS undertook an all-out enforcement effort in the Lower Rio Grande Valley and instituted an airlift to deport the apprehended workers to the interior of Mexico.[106] But such campaigns generally constituted little more than highly visible episodes of enforcement in an otherwise hands-off era. Plentiful, cheap, unencumbered by the red tape of the government program, and for the most part tolerated by the Immigration Service, undocumented workers provided growers with an inviting alternative to the Bracero Program.

The increases in illegal immigration in this period, and the laissez-faire approach of the Immigration Service that contributed to it, were clearly tied to the utility of illegal aliens from Mexico for the agricultural economy of the Southwest. At the same time, however, the influx presented the immigration bureaucracy with a knotty problem. As we have seen, a number of recurring contradictions have surrounded immigration policymaking since the 19th century. While immigrants have historically provided employers with an abundant and cheap labor supply, this very fact has provoked anti-immigrant backlashes and demands for restrictions by domestic labor. A second contradiction stems from the fiscal burden of subsidizing immigrants' poverty wages in the form of social and welfare costs.

In the 1940s and early 1950s, these contradictions were intensified as an increasing proportion of the immigrant population entered illegally. Illegal migrants from Mexico provided southwestern agriculture with a seemingly ideal labor supply, as their illegal status made them highly vulnerable and difficult to organize. Not surprisingly, wages in regions with high concentrations of undocumented farm workers were well below the average for agricultural employment.[107] Many of the same protests that had traditionally been registered against unrestricted *legal* immigration—that massive numbers of immigrants depressed wages and exacted a burden on local communities—were now applied to the illegal supply.[108] And the illegal nature of the flow enhanced the political legitimacy of those complaints.

In addition, a new contradiction appeared as policymakers were caught between the economic utility of illegal immigrants and the hypocrisy of an immigration policy that systematically violated its own terms. The *New York Times* summarized the bind of immigration policymakers, noting that "[m]embers of Congress [were] whipsawed between the constant farm pressure for alien labor and the obvious need to do something about the 'wetback' traffic."[109] A State Department official, addressing a congressional subcommittee on the issue of illegal migration, laid out the myriad and entangled controversies and lamented, "It is just like fighting a windmill."[110]

A vast literature on the rise of the administrative state suggests that Congress has delegated increasing authority to federal bureaucracies in the 20th century.[111] It is frequently noted that this delegation is not randomly distributed, but is concentrated in controversial or problematic policy areas that present Congress with no-win political dilemmas.[112] Following this logic, it makes sense that administrative discretion in the areas of illegal immigration and foreign worker programs would be significant. Buffeted by electoral pressures and the irresolvable quality of immigration conflicts, Congress attempted to resolve its dilemmas by shunting them to the federal bureaucracy. Thus, the discretion exercised by the INS not only was tolerated by Congress, but in important instances—such as the administrative extension of the Bracero Program in early 1948 after Congress had terminated it— was actively encouraged.

If the immigration policy arena was permeated with contradictions, nowhere were they more pronounced than in the Immigration Service itself. In the first place, the wide discretion accorded the agency meant that it necessarily played a pivotal role in fighting the windmill of illegal immigration. More important, the contradictions and conflicts associated with illegal immigration were heightened in the agency whose official mission is enforcement of the immigration laws and control of the border. Faced with the economic utility of illegal aliens on one hand, and its bureaucratic mandate to halt the flow on the other, the INS found itself in a catch-22 that almost perfectly mirrored the underlying structural contradictions. This interpretation is compatible with, but not identical to, Rourke's observation that some federal agencies are placed in a bind by the fact that their primary clients, or "constituencies," are interest groups whose goals are antithetical to the formal function of the agency.[113] While Rourke's discussion is based on pluralist assumptions of interest group politics, the present analysis places the bureaucratic bind in the context of broader structural contradictions. Instead of focusing primarily on the conflicts between various interest groups, this approach views such interest group conflicts as symptoms, or reflections, of underlying contradictions in the political economy.

This structural approach allows for a fuller understanding of both the congressional delegation of these issues in the first place and the origins and precise nature of the dilemma faced by the agency in addressing them. So, for example, the structural contradictions of illegal immigration, and the politically sensitive, but economically useful, scheme of importing hundreds of thousands of foreign laborers, are key ingredients in understanding Congress's reticence to assert itself in this area and its proclivity for passing the buck to the administrative arena. Furthermore, while Rourke's focus on "constituencies" is useful—as far as it goes—in understanding the administrative response, his essentially pluralist framework is unable to account for the anomaly at the very heart of his analysis, that is, that some federal agencies have clients whose interests clash with the official goals of those agencies. The broader dialectical perspective taken here suggests that it is no accident the INS is stuck catering to an interest group with goals apparently opposed to its own official mandate. Rather, as the agency responsible for controlling the border and limiting illegal immigration, the Immigration Service is in a sense the bureaucratic embodiment of the contradiction between the economic utility of immigrant labor and the political, social, and fiscal costs associated with that labor supply.

The symptoms of the bureaucracy's catch-22 were widespread and unmistakable. The severely limited budget of the Border Patrol was the fiscal symptom of the dilemma, but there were other indicators as well. Perhaps most obvious were its highly erratic and selective enforcement procedures. Pressed to do something about the "wetback problem" for which it was officially responsible, but precluded from eliminating a major source of agricultural labor, the INS was limited to "restricting illegal immigration to the level of active public alarm."[114]

Finally, there is evidence that the agency struggled with the discrepancies between *de jure* and *de facto* law that reflected its bureaucratic quagmire. One example is particularly striking, as it highlights both the centrality of INS discretion and the dilemmas posed for the agency in the exercise of that discretion. When the International Agreements with Mexico stipulated that illegal workers already in the United States be given preference for bracero status over newly imported workers, the INS was initially skeptical. The President's Commission on Migratory Labor explained the source of its concern and the subsequent solution:

> To be prevented from deporting a deportable alien is, in effect, to be prevented from enforcing the law. A technique more insidious than ingenious was devised and put in effect. . . . In this improvisation, the Immigration and Naturalization Service would be allowed to "deport" the wetback by having him brought to the border at which point the wetback would be given an identification slip. Momentarily he would step across the boundary line. Having thus been subjected to the magic of token deportation, the illegal alien was now merely alien and was eligible to step back across the boundary to be legally contracted.[115]

The ritual of having illegal aliens step across the border to be brought back as legal braceros was referred to by the INS as "a walk around the statute," suggesting that the agency was fully aware of its role in circumventing the inconveniences of the law.[116] Confronted by the economic pragmatism of contracting illegal immigrants as braceros and the formal mandate of the INS to apprehend and *deport* illegal immigrants, the bureaucracy's "ingenious" response attests to the truth of the adage that necessity is the mother of invention.

Just as the INS used its administrative power to shape the Bracero Program to suit growers, its less than enthusiastic approach to the roundup of undocumented workers was tied to the long-standing role of Mexican immigrants in the agricultural economy. These formal and informal arrangements dovetailed well with growers' needs, but the rising influx of illegal aliens presented the immigration bureaucracy with increasingly vexing problems of its own. These problems, and the contradictions from which they derived, were central ingredients in the formulation of INS policies for the remainder of the Bracero Program.

CHAPTER 3

FORMALIZATION
AND INFORMAL
CONTROL: THE
BRACERO PROGRAM
COMES OF AGE

Direct employer recruitment, the contracting of illegal immigrants, and lax enforcement by the INS and other federal agencies further consolidated growers' power over their workers—bracero as well as domestic. In fact, the 1948–1951 Bracero Program was "tailor-made to the demands of growers."[1] Convenient as the system was for employers, it was far from perfect. For one thing, the haphazard nature of the decentralized recruitment process was wreaking havoc. Periodic oversupplies of aspiring braceros in border towns led to rioting and health and safety concerns—a situation that was compounded by the unpredictability of on-again/off-again open border policies and the paroling of illegal aliens directly to employers. Noting the volatility and instability of the poorly regulated system, the American Consul in the border town of Reynosa, Mexico, warned that the Bracero Program was "in a state of what almost might be termed chaos."[2]

The direct recruitment system not only created confusion at the border, but it ultimately contributed to unpredictability of the contract itself. With no effective enforcement of bracero wages and working conditions, and no meaningful possibility for collective bargaining, desertion was one of the few recourses open to dissatisfied braceros.[3] Braceros complained to Mexican Consuls in the United States of insufficient and substandard food and housing, inadequate wages, deplorable working conditions, and insufficient work during the contract period. Growers sometimes kept braceros unemployed for several hours a day or for weeks at a time due to weather conditions, a late harvest, or over-contracting. In some cases, braceros were charged for room and board during these slack periods, which they had to pay off out of their future wages, creating a system that some have likened to debt bondage.[4] Under the circumstances, it should not be surprising that employers began to register complaints of increasing bracero "skips," or desertions.[5] The President's Commission on Migratory Labor estimated that the desertion rate in some areas approached 50%.[6] Since growers were required to post a $25 bond for each bracero they contracted, to be repaid when the bracero completed his contract, desertions exacted a direct financial toll along with the more indirect cost of high labor turnover.

If "skips" were costly to growers, the diplomatic fallout of the appalling conditions that underlay this discontent threatened to undermine the contract system altogether. Mexican policymakers had never approved of the direct contract arrangement and had for years lobbied for a return to a government-sponsored program, which they were convinced yielded them more leverage in limiting employer abuses.[7] With the entry of the United States into the Korean War in 1950, and growers' rising calls for more farm labor to meet wartime needs,[8] Mexican negotiators upped the ante. When U.S. officials met with their Mexican counterparts in Mexico City in the winter of 1951, they were given an ultimatum. Unless a bill was introduced in Congress to reestablish government sponsorship of the bracero system, Mexico would terminate the bilateral agreement.[9] As braceros "skipped" their contracts and border tensions mounted, even the staunchest supporters of the labor program had already begun to fear that it was deteriorating into "chaos." Now it seemed the whole system was on the verge of collapse. At the conclusion of the Mexico City conference—which was attended by Senator Allen Ellender (D-Louisiana) and Representative W.R. Poage (D-Texas), Chairs of the respective Congressional Committees on Agriculture—the U.S. agreed to reestablish the government-to-government program.

EXPANSION AND INSTITUTIONALIZATION

Within days of their return to Washington, Congressman Poage and Senator Ellender introduced legislation that would formalize and stabilize the bracero system. Hearings on the bill began in March, and by June, Congress had passed the measure that became PL 78, adding Title V to the Agriculture Act of 1949.[10] PL 78 for the first time explicitly authorized the importation of contract labor for agriculture, officially voiding the prohibition against foreign contract labor that had been on the books since 1885. In response to Mexican pressures and the unpredictability inherent in the direct contract system, the U.S. government itself was to be the official contractor of Mexican labor, and hence technically the guarantor of the terms of the contracts. The law placed some restrictions on the administrative transformation of illegal workers into braceros, stipulating that only workers contracted from Mexico, Mexicans legally in the U.S., braceros in the U.S. whose contracts had expired, and Mexicans who had been in the U.S. illegally for at least five years, would be eligible for bracero status. It further required that before braceros could be imported, the Secretary of Labor must certify (1) that a labor shortage in agriculture existed; (2) that the importation would have no "adverse effect" on local farm workers; and (3) that the employer requesting braceros had made an effort to recruit domestic labor at comparable wages. In addition, braceros were to be paid the "prevailing wage" of the area, and employers of illegal aliens were to be ineligible to receive braceros.

Noticeably absent from the legislation were the recommendations of the President's Commission on Migratory Labor, whose final report was submitted as the hearings on PL 78 were taking place. Specifically, the statute provided no guidelines for the determination of what constituted a "labor shortage" or how "prevailing wages" were to be set. Nor did it include any fines or criminal penalties against employers of illegal immigrants, a provision that the President's Commission had insisted was critical not only to the reduction of illegal migration, but to the elimination of substandard wages and working conditions.

The American Federation of Labor (AFL), its fledgling National Farm Labor Union, and the Congress of Industrial Organizations (CIO) were vehemently opposed to this institutionalization of the program that had originally been designed to fill temporary labor needs during World War II. Noting that the requirement for Department of Labor certification of a labor shortage and the provision that the importation of braceros must not adversely affect domestic labor were included in previous bracero regulations, labor representatives protested bitterly that in the absence of more specific protections the new program would recreate the abuses of the past.[11] However, only a few liberal Democrats spoke against the bill, and agribusiness staunchly supported it. The large growers of the powerful American Farm Bureau not only lobbied for the law, but took the opportunity to make a pitch for "opening doors so that farmers and their organizations can do the job for themselves."[12] Just as the outbreak of World War II had justified Congressional legislation officially validating the Bracero Program a decade earlier, Senator Ellender warned that the emergency labor need precipitated by the Korean War left no time for further deliberation or foot-dragging.[13] In the end, PL 78 passed with little opposition and in near-record time.

The law was extended four times through 1959, each time with relative ease and very little debate. Not that the Bracero Program was uncontroversial. Rather, the program's congressional sponsors were clever in introducing the legislation as an amendment to the Agriculture Act. This ensured that it was routed through the Agriculture Committees, whose Chairs (Senator Ellender and Representative Poage) were known to be aggressive allies of agribusiness, and where the program was likely to receive a favorable response. Critics of the program point out that this committee assignment was in violation of the Congressional Reorganization Act of 1946 which specified that all bills having to do with "the regulation of foreign contract labor" must be referred to the House Committee on Education and Labor and the Senate Committee on Labor and Public Welfare.[14] These critics not only maintain that pro-bracero forces managed to bias the congressional proceedings by locating them in the "friendly" Agriculture Committees, where Senator Eugene McCarthy was the sole opponent of the program; they go one step further and suggest that the State Department had influenced the proceedings from the beginning by inviting only the Chairs of the Agriculture Committees to the Mexico City negotiations, setting the stage for their domination of the issue in Congress.[15] State Department officials later apologized for the exclusive invitations and promised that in the future any such invitations would be forwarded to the Vice President and Speaker of the House to be distributed appropriately.[16] As it turned out, after the critical 1951 conference, no members of Congress received invitations to Mexico City negotiations. Periodic attempts were made to transfer jurisdiction over the Bracero Program to the Labor Committees in Congress, but they were met with strong opposition from the powerful Agriculture Committees and their farm block constituents.[17]

Fifteen minutes after PL 78 was signed by President Truman, U.S. negotiators met with Mexican officials to arrange a new bilateral agreement.[18] With only minor changes, the Migrant Labor Agreement of 1951, together with PL 78, set the official parameters for the Bracero Program until its termination in 1964. The agreement stipulated that the U.S. government, not individual employers, was the guarantor of bracero contracts. It provided for recruitment centers in the interior of Mexico as before, but supplemented them with border "reception centers" where braceros were distributed to their U.S. employers. Contracting illegal workers already in the U.S. was not permitted under the bilateral agreement, at the insistence of Mexican negotiators who were by now convinced that such legalization encouraged illegal immigration. Braceros were to be paid the prevailing wage for given crops in specific regions or a piece rate equivalent of that wage. As in the past, if braceros were unemployed for more than 25% of the contracted period (which varied from a minimum of 6 weeks to a maximum of 18 months), the grower was to provide them with a subsistence wage. Housing and meals for a nominal price were to be provided. Finally, no state was to be blacklisted or barred from importing bracero labor. This last provision was in clear reference to Texas which, in all previous agreements, had been excluded from bracero eligibility.

In response to the demands of Mexican negotiators, braceros were not to be used to break strikes, or to replace striking workers. Furthermore, they were to have the right to elect candidates of their choice to represent them in disputes with their employers. This by no means meant that braceros were free to negotiate wages and working conditions, as another article of the agreement specified that "all negotiations . . . shall be carried out exclusively between the two governments," leaving workers with only the right to dispute the way the contract was carried out.[19] Neither did the provision imply the right to unionize, as the joint interpretation of the accord was careful to make clear: "This article does not have any reference to union memberships or collective bargaining activities."[20] Instead, "Mexican workers may . . . designate representatives *from among their own numbers* for the purpose of discussing with the employer any question arising under the Individual Work [contract] but not for the purpose of changing its terms or conditions."[21]

PL 78 and subsequent international agreements reestablished the role of the state as farm labor contractor par excellence. As Runsten put it, "The Bracero Program . . . represented the entry of the state into the regulation and management of cheap labor for agriculture."[22] PL 78 formalized that commitment, and in so doing injected increased predictability and control into the contract labor system that had begun a decade earlier as a wartime emergency measure.

OPERATION WETBACK AND THE EXPANSION OF CONTROL

With the Bracero Program now secured by PL 78, attention shifted to the increasingly vexing problem of illegal immigration. Stability of the Bracero Program was enhanced by the government's official role as labor contractor, yet it was becoming clear that uncontrolled illegal immigration—as advantageous as it might be to agriculture in the short run—threatened to undermine that stability in the long run.

The President's Commission on Migratory Labor sounded an alarm over the rise in illegal immigration, warning ominously, "The magnitude of the wetback traffic has reached entirely new levels in the past 7 years. ... In its newly achieved proportions, it is virtually an invasion."[23] It concluded, "The wetback traffic has reached such proportions in volume and in consequent chaos, it should not be neglected any longer."[24] The commission documented the effect of illegal workers on wage rates in Texas, New Mexico, Arizona, and California, and argued, "That the wetback traffic has severely depressed farm wages is unquestionable."[25] It drew similar conclusions on the subject of "labor competition and displacement," reporting that illegal entrants pushed legal resident farm workers northward since they could not compete with the desperate newcomers. Finally, it presented data on infant mortality, disease, and housing conditions in areas where illegal immigrants were concentrated. The commission reasoned:

> The wetback traffic inescapably postpones effective remedial measures and aggravates these problems. The wetback undergoes no health or physical examination as he illicitly enters the United States. ... Moreover, while he is here ... the wetback will not ordinarily risk the chance of apprehension by seeking medical or health assistance. Reciprocally, the health and medical service agencies that might otherwise be ready to provide assistance for residents will ordinarily be foreclosed to the wetback. ...[26]

Growers and their allies in Congress attacked the report as "ridiculous," biased by union sympathies and driven by a reformist agenda, and likened the commission to the old Farm Security Administration.[27] Despite its powerful detractors, the commission had opened a debate that quickly gathered momentum and ultimately transformed U.S. policy toward illegal immigration for the duration of the Bracero Program.

Immediately after the release of the commission's report, the *New York Times* ran a five-part series on illegal aliens blaming the employment of undocumented workers in southwestern agriculture—which it compared to "peonage"—for depressing wages and contributing to crime.[28] The series triggered an onslaught of media attention to the subject.[29] The press was quick to sensationalize the issue, as in this *New York Times* Service radio broadcast from Los Angeles:

> Illegal immigration from Mexico . . . has reached such over-
> whelming proportions that officers of the United States Immi-
> gration Service admit candidly . . . that there is nothing to stop
> the whole nation of Mexico moving into the United States, if
> it wants to. The numerical equivalent of more than 10 percent
> of the population of Mexico has come in already.[30]

Organized labor stepped up its attacks on illegal immigration, as a
particularly severe recession in 1953 brought renewed warnings that
uncontrolled immigration depressed wages and increased unemployment.[31] Perhaps most influential of labor's efforts to focus attention on
the issue was the detailed exposé, *What Price Wetbacks?* published in
1953. This report, sponsored by the American G.I. Forum of Texas
(an association of Mexican-American workers aligned with organized
labor), compiled statistics on health, infant mortality, crime, immigrant
exploitation, and wage rates, and urged that steps be taken to reduce
the flow of illegal immigrants.

Increasingly, government officials added their voices to this chorus
of concern. A State Department representative told Congress in 1952
that the illegal traffic constituted "one of the most difficult problems
. . . that the agencies of this Government have ever been up against."[32]
California Governor Earl Warren was said to have appealed to his
longtime friend, President Eisenhower, upon receiving a report that
illegal immigration was costing Imperial Valley over $250,000 a year.[33]
Newly appointed Attorney General Brownell made a tour of the Southwest border to view the situation for himself in the summer of 1953,
meeting with local police, mayors, and health and employment officials, all of whom complained loudly of the costs of illegal immigration.[34] Brownell concluded his tour with the proclamation that the
magnitude of illegal immigration was "shocking" and constituted "one
of the nation's gravest law-enforcement problems."[35] The budget re-
straints imposed by Congress on the Border Patrol, warned the new
Attorney General, "was the most penny wise and pound foolish policy
I've ever seen."[36] Brownell figured that, "[f]or every dollar saved
through this Border Patrol economy . . . about $20 has to be spent on
welfare costs and other expenses involving the 'wetbacks.' "[37]

In addition, policymakers pointed to the penetration of illegal immigrants—who, according to the conventional wisdom, had previously
been confined to agricultural employment near the border—into the
interior of the United States and industrial jobs. The President's Commission warned, "Wetback labor is . . . penetrating into the highly
skilled trades. . . ."[38] Three years later, Eisenhower's new Immigration

Commissioner, General Joseph Swing, told the Senate Subcommittee on Immigration and Naturalization:

> The problem now is so much larger. . . . They [illegal immigrants] are doing great harm to our economic situation and industry. . . . In the interior of the country there are thousands who came over here as itinerant farmhands. They very soon learn our ways and our customs, and they infiltrate. They go into industry. . . .[39]

Assistant Secretary of Labor Rocco Siciliano was also disturbed by the movement of illegal aliens into industrial employment: ". . . the wetback influx is no longer limited to farm employment. In the first eleven months of the 1954 fiscal year, we have been informed that the Immigration and Naturalization Service apprehended 40,860 illegal entrants in the industries and trades."[40] The Chief of the Border Patrol, Willard Kelly, was worried not only that undocumented workers were no longer confined to agriculture, but that they might contribute to the industrial labor movement: "Not all wetbacks come to work on farms. . . . Unknown thousands have entered the trades and industries. And, incidentally, many are members of our labor unions."[41]

Last, but certainly not least, was the impact of the Cold War and McCarthyism on attitudes towards illegal immigration. The charge that an uncontrolled border allowed easy access to "subversives" was not new. In 1949, Representative Edward Gossett of Texas had issued a press release urging:

> We should at once tighten up immigration laws and the enforcement of immigration laws. . . . Military intelligence personnel [might] be assigned to the Immigration Service from time to time to help round up illegal aliens. . . . These forces are used to run down enemy aliens in time of war. They should help run down illegal aliens in time of peace. This is especially true since many of these aliens come into the country for subversive purposes.[42]

Senator Pat McCarran, Chair of the Senate Subcommittee on Internal Security and noted cold warrior, alarmed his congressional colleagues in 1951 with his committee's estimate that as many as five million aliens were in the U.S. illegally, including "vast numbers of 'militant Communists, Sicilian bandits and other criminals' " that could "provide an enemy nation with 'a ready-made fifth column.' "[43] The same year, the *Annual Report of the Immigration and Naturalization Service* announced an "increasing strain on enforcement" related not only to the illegal entry of farm workers, but "the crescendo of communism with its devious schemes of infiltration."[44] The report warned that the uncontrolled border "create[s] easy access for non-Mexicans. . . . The danger of such conditions is beyond estimate during these times when alien forces of political and social evil are in violent struggle with the principles upon which our government is established."[45]

By 1953, Cold War rhetoric permeated the debate. The Acting Immigration Commissioner told a subcommittee of the House Committee on Appropriations, "A harvest of dangerous byproducts from the seemingly harmless invasion by illegal aliens is now in the making. Who can say that Communists and subversives do not cross the Rio Grande? . . . [I]t was recently discovered that approximately 100 present and past members of the Communist Party had been crossing daily into the United States in the El Paso area."[46] Other immigration officials reiterated the warning, calling the situation "worse than ever before."[47]

The following year, Senator Hubert Humphrey told the Senate that Mexico was "in almost a death struggle to keep out of Communist control," and that the U.S. might be infiltrated by Communist agents crossing the border. He concluded, "I am shocked beyond words that the Congress, which investigates practically everyone from a baby sitter to a kindergarten teacher, does not impose stringent controls in the case of immigration at the Mexican border."[48] Edmund G. Brown, Attorney General of California, agreed, "The comparatively easy influx that wetbacks now have . . . indicates that the door also is open for potential saboteurs and fifth columnists."[49] Senator Pat McCarran, co-sponsor of the comprehensive 1952 legislation that overhauled immigration policy for Eastern Hemisphere entrants, was more specific in his charges, claiming that communists and spies actually posed as farm workers and went back and forth across the border at will.[50]

In other words, not only did the illegal nature of this immigration intensify the contradictions associated with any large influx of cheap immigrant labor, but this underground, unofficial, and uncontrolled migration fueled Cold War paranoia. On June 9, 1954, with great fanfare Attorney General Brownell announced the administration's commitment to reducing the illegal movement. His statement serves well as a summing up of what were by now perceived to be the intolerably high costs of the unregulated movement:

> A large percentage of illegal aliens now being apprehended in the border districts and elsewhere are not interested in finding agricultural employment except, perhaps, as a stopgap measure. They are heading for our industrial centers to obtain

employment in defense plants and other industries. . . . They are displacing domestic workers, adversely affecting working conditions, contributing to our increasing crime rate, and spreading communicable disease. In addition, the size of the movement may well provide an effective screen for subversives and other undesirable persons to enter. . . .[51]

When Brownell returned from his three-day tour of the Southwest border in August 1953, he initiated a campaign to draw attention to the perils of illegal immigration. At a meeting in Denver, Colorado, he announced the administration's intention to work with Mexico to curtail the flow.[52] In March 1954, Brownell and his Deputy Attorney General met privately in the Attorney General's office with representatives of organized labor to discuss possible solutions to what was now known simply as "the wetback problem."[53]

The next month, General Joseph Swing, a West Point classmate and friend of President Eisenhower, was appointed INS Commissioner. During his trip to the border, Brownell had met with General Swing, who at the time was commander of the Sixth Army in California. According to later Congressional testimony by Commissioner Swing, Brownell told him at that meeting to begin preparations to take 4000 troops to the Mexican border "to stop this horde of invaders."[54] General Swing persuaded the Attorney General that the plan to militarize the border—a plan code-named "Operation Cloudburst"—was both unnecessary and potentially disastrous for U.S.-Mexican relations.[55] When Swing retired from the army in February 1954 and was appointed Immigration Commissioner, regaining control of the border was to be his first order of business.

Commissioner Swing inherited an agency that was the target of increasing criticism and ridicule, making it especially urgent to score a victory. The INS was no stranger to criticism. The Chair of the Senate Appropriations Subcommittee had once denounced the INS record as "the poorest showing that I have ever heard a department make."[56] As illegal immigration continued to increase and drew the attention of the media, the public, and policymakers, a "mounting barrage of criticism" was levelled at the agency.[57] Noting this loss of public confidence in the Immigration Service, Commissioner Swing told the Senate Subcommittee on Immigration and Naturalization that in his visits to the border, he had encountered people who "have questioned the sincerity of my organization in carrying out these [immigration] laws."[58]

Swing feared for the survival of his bureaucracy, given the continuing allegations of incompetence and the periodic recommendations to use the army rather than the Border Patrol to bring illegal immigration under control. According to Harlan Carter, Swing's director of field operations for "Operation Wetback"—as Swing's notorious enforcement drive came to be called—the Commissioner persuaded him to take the post with the warning, "It seems to me that if you knew that the question as to whether there is going to be any Border Patrol in the future depends upon the success of this [Operation Wetback], it seems to me that you'd want to be in charge of it."[59]

As the agency responsible for controlling the borders, the INS bears the brunt of the contradictions surrounding illegal immigration. With the perceived costs of the illegal movement escalating, these contradictions were brought into sharp focus. A *New York Times* reporter summed up the policy dilemma, "The administration's expressed desire to minimize the illegal traffic, involving evils from slave wages to the spreading of diseases, has clashed head-on with the partial reliance of some segments of southwestern agriculture upon cheap Mexican labor. . . ."[60]

One symptom of this dilemma was the indecision and inconsistency of policymakers on the issue of border control, despite their restrictionist rhetoric. Less than a month after Brownell's well-publicized border tour, a front-page *New York Times* article headlined "California Seeks More 'Wetbacks' " informed readers that Vice President Nixon was scheduled to meet with Department of Justice officials to discuss the allegation by California Congressmen that Border Patrol enforcement was "over-zealous."[61] The principal item on the agenda was "the possible tempering of the stepped-up campaign against illegal immigration from Mexico, in the interests of assuring Southern California farmers of a supply of labor."[62]

The Attorney General himself wavered in his position on border control and in any case was hesitant to match his words with action. In December 1953, after having declared to the House Appropriations Subcommittee that the "wetback problem" had never been so bad, Brownell recommended no increase in the Border Patrol budget and asked that the overall INS budget be *reduced* by over $3 million (out of a total budget of approximately $40 million). Citing the need for Mexican farm workers to harvest crops and noting that a new migrant labor agreement with Mexico was in process, Brownell cautioned that the elimination of illegal workers might be premature and that ". . . we should try out the new system [the new labor agreement with Mexico] before we go ahead and indiscriminately increase the number of the border patrol."[63]

The Attorney General's ambivalence was evident in the legislative arena as well. Despite his call for legislation to halt the illegal influx in 1953, and his subsequent promise to organized labor to back such legislation, Brownell's support was at best lukewarm. When S.3660, which would have imposed an injunction on employers of illegal immigrants, was debated in Congress in the summer of 1954, Brownell assured labor leaders that he was "doing everything possible" to get it enacted.[64] But, by August he had reconsidered, displaying such a "sudden lack of initiative" that organized labor expressed "skepticism" about the sincerity of his commitment.[65]

Faced with the well-publicized perils of illegal immigration on one hand, and its clear utility to employers on the other, Brownell's indecisiveness reflected the dilemma confronting immigration policymakers. But the bulk of the fallout from this dilemma was reserved for the Immigration Service itself, in the form of widespread charges of incompetence and complacency. Commissioner Swing was sworn in to an agency that was caught in the middle of a catch-22, and was under attack for the resulting paralysis. With his professional reputation on the line and the survival of his agency at stake, Swing approached Operation Wetback with the determination of a proud man under seige and the tactical mentality of an army general. His strategy was not to launch a frontal attack on the contradiction of illegal immigration, which was clearly a losing proposition, but to penetrate its ranks and wear down resistance from within. Swing understood from the beginning that to win this battle would require careful planning and an element of finesse. Most important, he realized that he needed to enlist the cooperation of the very growers and ranchers whose illegal work force he intended to round up and deport.

Commissioner Swing set the cooperative tone through intensive communication with employers, arranging a "series of cordial meetings" early in the spring and summer of 1954.[66] At these meetings, he assured his audience that he was aware of the importance of Mexican farm labor and promised growers that their undocumented workers would be replaced with legal workers, both Mexican and domestic.[67] Reporting to Congress just before launching Operation Wetback, Swing made it clear that the purpose of his ten-day trip to the border was to spread the message that "*if there is any employer who cannot get legal labor all he has to do is let either the Department of Labor or Immigration know and we will see that he gets it. . . . I am quite emphatic about this because I know I am going to run into some opposition in southern Texas. . . .*"[68]

On June 9, 1954, the Attorney General officially initiated the enforcement drive codenamed "Operation Wetback."[69] The next day, the governors and police chiefs in California and Arizona received notices from the INS soliciting their cooperation in the campaign.[70] The officials enthusiastically agreed to participate, and Operation Wetback quickly gathered momentum. The local Border Patrol, reinforced by units from around the country, set up road blocks, boarded trains, and cordoned off neighborhoods for inspection. Police in the area were instructed to detain suspected illegal aliens on vagrancy charges and then turn them over to Border Patrol agents.[71] The Service launched a buslift, returning apprehended aliens to the interior of Mexico, in order to make reentry more difficult and to encourage aliens to depart on their own to avoid being deported to the interior.

On June 17, Swing assembled a "Special Mobile Force" of 800 Border Patrol officers and conducted a massive roundup in California and Arizona agricultural areas. Two days later, the special force was reportedly making over one thousand apprehensions a day.[72] The drive soon spread to Northern California, and then the rest of the Southwest. By the end of July, the Border Patrol was doing "mop-up operations" of illegal workers in industrial jobs in the interior of the United States.[73] According to the *Annual Report* of the INS, over one million apprehensions were made in fiscal year 1954, most of them during Operation Wetback.[74]

The effectiveness of the drive depended on an intensive publicity campaign designed to convince immigrants of the inevitability of their apprehension and to scare them into "voluntary" departure. Well aware of the limitations of his resources, Swing capitalized on the sensationalism of the media coverage and a few well-placed and highly visible shows of force to create the illusion of a far greater presence than the Border Patrol could actually muster.[75] The tactic seems to have worked, particularly in Texas where it is said that more than 60,000 Mexican immigrants departed on their own in the first thirty days of the drive.[76] By the end of the summer, the INS boasted that "uncounted thousands" had left "of their own accord."[77]

Operation Wetback was declared an unqualified success by Commissioner Swing. There were widespread reports of abuses by the Border Patrol and charges that legal residents and in some cases American citizens had been deported, harassed and/or beaten.[78] Swing was summoned to a meeting with four members of Congress in July 1954, to answer to allegations of "discourteous attitudes [of officers] in their dealings, particularly with United States citizens of Mexican extraction."[79] Nevertheless, policymakers lauded the "efficiency" of the Immigration Service in regaining control of the border. Congress even increased the agency's budget in recognition of the job it was doing.[80]

The following year, Commissioner Swing was able to announce with only slight exaggeration, "The so-called 'wetback' problem no longer exists. . . . The border has been secured."[81]

The roundup and deportation of illegal aliens during Operation Wetback ushered in a new era. At first glance, the crackdown might seem inconsistent with the immigration agency's longstanding attitude that it was their duty to protect the interest of growers. But closer examination suggests that the drive had the effect of buttressing and entrenching a system of contract labor that was uniquely suited to agricultural production. In the first place, Commissioner Swing was true to his promise to supply growers with a substitute labor source. As the number of apprehensions rose in 1954, illegal aliens were replaced with legal braceros. While in 1953, only 201,380 Mexican contract laborers were admitted, by 1955 the number of braceros had risen to 398,650, reaching a peak of 445,197 in 1956.[82]

The increase in braceros was particularly apparent in the lower Rio Grande Valley where illegal immigrants had for years constituted the bulk of the agricultural work force. At the height of the 1953 harvest, growers in the Valley contracted only 700 braceros; one year later, the Reception Center at Hidalgo, Texas, had issued 50,326 bracero contracts to Valley farmers.[83] A Department of Labor report concluded, "The increase is attributable solely to the replacement of illegal workers by contract workers" and "is very dramatically illustrative of the success of the [Operation Wetback] drive."[84] Commissioner Swing went so far as to characterize the removal of illegals and their substitution with braceros as an "exchange."[85]

To understand the advantages to growers of this exchange, it helps to consider the nature of the production process in southwestern agriculture. Max Pfeffer describes the imperatives of agricultural production in California:

> Harvest operations in a geographical area characterized by specialized crop production as well as a number of crops ripening at similar times call for the employment of an extremely large workforce for very short periods of time. . . . The characteristics of the labor process in crop production place constraints on the forms of control growers must exert over workers for profitable completion of the harvest.[86]

While the virtually limitless supply of Mexican migrants—both illegal aliens and braceros—had for years provided growers with the surplus work force with which to enhance the profitability of agricultural production, the contract system was unusually suited in a number of ways to the exercise of *control*. The precise types of control provided by the bracero are best expressed by growers themselves.

An Arkansas cotton grower told the President's Commission on Migratory Labor in 1951, "Cotton is a slave crop, nobody is going to pick it that doesn't have to."[87] Western growers informed Congress a few years later that only those with no real choice in the matter would hoe sugar beets or harvest tomatoes for up to twelve hours a day in desert temperatures of 110 degrees.[88] While illegal immigrants were desperate, they were also mobile. Arthur Watkins, Chair of the Immigration Subcommittee in the Senate during the 1950s, and himself a Utah fruit grower, told an interviewer, "We never picked up any wetbacks if we could avoid it. . . . My son-in-law says 'They won't stay with you. . . . They keep moving on, next thing you know, they're gone.' "[89]

The long hours, sporadic employment, and arduous working conditions of agricultural production made the retention of workers problematic. In this context, the captivity of the braceros was extremely valuable. Unlike domestic workers or illegal aliens, the bracero was *confined by law* to a given crop and employer. As the Chief of the Farm Placement Service of the Department of Labor put it in 1957, "These workers [braceros] are not free agents in the labor market. They do not have freedom to move about as they please and shop for the best job that the labor market could afford."[90] An immigration official in Arizona told the President's Commission the same thing: "The contract worker is tied down to one employer. He is not a free agent to leave whenever he desires and seek more lucrative employment elsewhere."[91] A western grower, speaking to Congress in 1961, listed nine advantages of a bracero work force, the first of which was that the bracero "is not free to leave an employer to seek employment elsewhere."[92]

A Border Patrol report from Yuma, Arizona, underlines the importance of farm worker captivity, and the lengths to which some employers went to ensure this element of control when braceros were, for whatever reason, unavailable. The report notes that in the town of Wellton, Arizona, "officers report that ranchers and farmers in the area are obtaining 'Winos' and negro transients from the Phoenix area by furnishing transportation from Phoenix to Wellton by Company bus or truck. *They more or less force the transients to remain on the farms as no return transportation is available.*"[93] When the Bracero Program was initiated in World War II, other more institutionalized forms of captivity supplemented the contract labor system. In his exposé on migratory farm labor, *The Slaves We Rent*, Moore draws a parallel between braceros and other types of captive labor in use during the war: "As the war progressed, prisoners of war were turned over to growers, along with convicts. Japanese-Americans, impounded in concentration camps, were released to the custody of the big growers. Armed guards patrolled the fields. When the war ended the POWs went back to Italy and Germany, and the convicts went back to their cells" but the braceros stayed in the fields.[94]

The piece rate system of payment, in wide use in western agriculture, put an additional premium on captive labor. Piece rates maximized profitability in the face of unpredictable labor needs, but at the same time contributed to high turnover, at least among workers who had the freedom to migrate in search of a full day's wage. Henry Anderson[95] described the role of a bracero work force in this context as growers shifted the costs of the unpredictability of production onto the workers themselves: "They [growers] want enough workers to meet any conceivable contingency. . . . Under the piece rate system of payment which prevails in most harvests, it is no disadvantage to growers if there are so many workers each only works half of the time. Labor costs are exactly the same as if half that many workers work full time."

If the arduous nature of the production process, together with the piece rate system, made labor availability and dependability problematic, the urgency of that production process and the limits imposed by nature made a captive labor supply all the more valuable. Senator Arthur Watkins, drawing on his own experience as a grower, pointed out, "The real Mexican [by which he apparently meant the bracero], not the 'wetback' . . . would be a much more dependable worker. . . . And the very fact that the crops with which they're working are highly perishable. . . . You can see how desperate a farmer . . . would be."[96]

The drawbacks to the employer of the relatively haphazard nature of illegal immigration and the illegal workers' comparative mobility were exacerbated by the relatively wide range of wages and working conditions in agriculture. A Border Patrol report from Brownsville, Texas, underscored the difficulties of retaining a work force in this context.[97] Pointing out that the cotton harvest had unexpectedly begun sooner than usual, the report warned:

> these people [illegal aliens] would much rather go to the northern areas of the state where the cotton harvest is at its peak . . . than to work in the fall vegetable seedings and transplantings here in the lower valley. The preparation of the field and the planting . . . is getting under way and will offer employment to many field laborers for a very short period.

These fields must be irrigated, weeded, and cared for for the next thirty to forty-five days if the harvest is to be expected as usual in November. Reportedly many people who ordinarily seek employment in these crops are traveling to the coastal bend areas and from there to the northern part of the state as the cotton harvest progresses northerly.

The bracero, operating outside of the free labor system, contracted for short periods of time, and delivered to the employer to do specific tasks as the need arose, provided an important element of predictability, stability, and—above all—control, in what was otherwise an unpredictable production process.[98]

Another element of control was provided by the reduction of bracero desertions following Operation Wetback. Commissioner Swing paraphrased a representative of the Growers Farm Labor Association in Salinas, California after Operation Wetback, "Fewer skips are reported by his association's members, which he attributes to the increased likelihood of Mexican nationals being apprehended if they are not in a legal status."[99] It was even reported that braceros who had "skipped" their contracts prior to the drive had returned to their employers because they could not find work as illegal immigrants.[100]

If braceros could be counted on at the moment of need and could be coerced not to "skip," this highly regulated supply of labor had the additional advantage that once the need had subsided, the workers could be sent home. Operation Wetback emerged in part in response to the perceived costs of a large, impoverished illegal population, many of whom experienced periods of unemployment and underemployment. Braceros minimized the costs associated with the highly irregular labor demands of southwestern agriculture not only because large numbers arrived promptly as the need arose, but because they equally promptly disappeared when the job was done. A critic of the system bitterly compared this commodification of labor to the other central component of the agricultural infrastructure in the arid Southwest, "Like the sprinkling systems of mechanized irrigation, braceros could be turned on and off."[101]

Finally, as Commissioner Swing put it, "Under the Bracero Program [growers] are free of the troubles inherent in bootleg labor."[102] Specifically, "When using legal labor [growers] do not run the risk of having the laborers taken from them by arresting officers. They can feel confident that they will have legal laborers of a good quality when and where needed."[103] The Department of Labor, summarizing the successes of Operation Wetback, also claimed that the elimination of "bootleg labor" had substantially improved the quality of workers. Using data from the lower Rio Grande Valley in Texas where cotton farmers had traditionally hired undocumented workers, the Labor Department pointed out that 318,219 bales of cotton had been picked by August 5, 1954, with an entirely legal work force, compared to 255,161 bales the year before. Furthermore, whereas in the past, a work force of 150,000 illegal workers—including children—was needed for the harvest, a far smaller number of "physically able, adult male" braceros was sufficient.[104]

While earlier episodes of Border Patrol enforcement elicited outrage from employers, Operation Wetback was generally applauded. Although Texas growers initially launched a "campaign of protest and vilification" against the Immigration Service,[105] they too were soon converted. Indeed, it was understood by government officials that the operation could not have succeeded without the active cooperation and support of agricultural employers.[106] Commissioner Swing used every opportunity to praise growers for their role in the enforcement drive, emphasizing that "accomplishment of this task [Operation Wetback] would have been impossible without the generous cooperation extended to the effort by ranchers, farmers, and growers."[107]

It is difficult to determine the percentage of growers who actually refused to hire illegal aliens after Operation Wetback. However, anecdotal evidence, apprehension statistics, and the wide availability of legal braceros, suggest that the employment of undocumented workers was substantially reduced. A Border Patrol report from El Centro, California, revealed the desperation of one illegal worker in search of employment: "When farmers in the Bakersfield area had refused to hire him because he did not have papers . . . he had been able to work several days a week by being hired by braceros, usually on night irrigation in cotton fields, to replace them. . . ."[108]

Fundamental to employers' receptivity to Operation Wetback was the understanding that the enforcement campaign would uniformly remove illegal farm workers, and hence eliminate competition from growers who used the sometimes cheaper, but less predictable and stable, illegal labor supply. As long as the Border Patrol crackdown was uniform, consistent, and effective, it had the potential to stabilize an otherwise chaotic and competitive labor market, allowing growers collectively to reap the benefits of the more dependable bracero supply. While Operation Wetback was still in its planning stage, the Secretary of Labor wrote the Attorney General that "farmers who employ legal workers are constantly expressing their resentment at competition by farmers employing cheap illegal labor."[109] After the drive, the head of the California Farm Placement Service described the reaction of California growers, "Employers using legally contracted Mexicans welcomed 'Operation Wetback'. It relieved them from the unfairness they had felt in adhering to the wage, housing, and other regulations governing the legal use of Mexicans, while their neighbors using wet backs [sic] were not subject to such regulations."[110] A Department of Labor document highlights the importance of the elimination of competition in growers' decisions to cooperate with the Border Patrol: "One large Gin Association prior to the drive indicated they were willing to contract labor, but stated they would not contract and pay the higher rate until they were sure that other farmers in the Valley would not be able to pick their crop with the cheaper wetback labor."[111]

In 1957, the Immigration Service conducted a public opinion survey of growers, ranchers, businessmen, and community officials in the areas that were affected by Operation Wetback. The responses of agricultural employers to this survey reveal their unanimous appreciation of the INS for its role in replacing illegal farm workers with braceros. A bracero camp manager for the Farmers Gin Association in Texas told the government interviewer that "prior to the 'wetback drive' of 1954, he used illegal aliens for almost all of his required labor needs . . . [He] stated that . . . he had no desire to return to using them. [He] stated that the farmer is now receiving a better type of farmhand."[112] A grower in the Rio Grande Valley of Texas, a region that had depended almost entirely on illegal immigrants, "stated that the farmer today actually gets more labor from the bracero . . . for the money he spends than he did from the wetback. . . . [H]e now considers the border patrol as an organization of fine people and something that is absolutely necessary in the Rio Grande Valley."[113] A Texas farmer and businessman reported that bracero labor was cheaper than illegal labor because the contract worker was confined to one employer. "The biggest trouble with the wetbacks," he told immigration officials, "was that you could not demand a day's work for a day's pay because if you did, the wetback would leave and go to work for someone else."[114] The Director of the Yuma Producers Cooperative Association in Arizona emphasized predictability: "Farmer-members have learned that alien labor obtained through the farmers' association from the United States Employment Service is . . . more reliable in that this method permits each member to plan ahead with assurance that his crop demands for labor will be taken care of. The Yuma Producers Cooperative Association membership unanimously agrees that a return to the old method of obtaining farm labor would be most undesirable."[115]

Operation Wetback, and the expansion of the bracero system that it triggered, had a long-term impact that went well beyond the profitability of individual farms and ranches. Because it was more convenient and cost-effective to contract workers collectively, Operation Wetback precipitated a dramatic increase in the size of growers' associations and in the percentage of employers belonging to these associations.[116] So rapid was this increase that the Department of Labor called it "the most immediate effect of the Immigration and Naturalization Service operation."[117] In September 1954, Commissioner Swing recommended that in order to facilitate bracero contracting, "Growers should be encouraged to band together in associations or organizations according to common interests or area."[118] Three years later, immigration officials were able to report that "association membership has been steadily increasing;" in some areas it had tripled.[119] This trend was particularly pervasive in California, where by 1959 over 99% of the 11,629 employers of braceros were members of growers' associations and contracted their braceros through those associations.[120] Thus, not only was growers' power over their work force enhanced by the Border Patrol crackdown and the subsequent entrenchment of the bracero program, but the labor system imposed a degree of organization on growers that ultimately enhanced their collective power *vis a vis* the rest of society as well.

If the successes of Operation Wetback and the expansion of the labor importation system had beneficial effects for growers, the Immigration Service reaped benefits as well. In the kind of self-conscious concern with their image that is typical of bureaucracies plagued by public criticism, the INS public opinion survey was conducted for the purpose of gauging the public relations impact of Operation Wetback. According to the regional officers who were responsible for carrying out the survey, the drive was a public relations coup. Basking in the afterglow of victory, the Assistant Commissioner of the Southwest region concluded, "Public opinion toward the Border Patrol has become increasingly favorable. ... We have gained considerably in prestige."[121]

PL 78 and Operation Wetback together institutionalized and stabilized the Bracero Program and injected increased control in a farm labor system that had been largely informal and haphazard. Institutionalization did not make the system rigid, however, nor did it reduce administrative discretion. Rather, INS implementation ensured that the newly entrenched program would retain the flexibility that had always been a central feature of its utility to growers.

ANOTHER "WALK AROUND THE STATUTE"

As institutionalized by PL 78 and the bilateral agreements with Mexico, the Bracero Program in the mid-1950s operated in the following way. Once the Department of Labor had certified a particular grower's (or grower association's) need for labor, Mexico was given a thirty-day notice as to how many workers would be required. Aspiring braceros had to obtain a permit from municipal Mexican officials, for which they often had to pay a "mordida."[122] Those who obtained these permits were sent to central recruiting centers, where there were sometimes ten workers for each bracero vacancy. At the recruiting centers, workers frequently had to pay another bribe in order to be considered.[123] It was from this pool that Department of Labor officials selected braceros to be sent to the border reception centers. One immigration agent with a narrative flair described the workings of the recruiting center in Chihuahua, Mexico:

> The grist for this mill consists of some 4,000–5,000 braceros gathered outside the head-high stone wall of the Compound where the processing is conducted. The outside area has several rows of "loncherias" [lunch counters], sanitary accommodations, and in the town and nearby are dormitory facilities. . . . The guardians of the gate to the Compound are the typical nondescript military of our sister republic. A general commotion among these braceros develops periodically during the day when the [Mexican government representative] announces by loud speaker the municipality whose registrants will be called. If the number is large, the gate is soon blocked, and the wall is surmounted by a line of braceros who race to the announcing booth. As the names are called, and checked against the list, each bracero is issued a numbered colored slip, 4" x 6", known as the *ficha*. They then queue up before the Department of Labor screening team, presently three in number. Each by this time has extracted an array of documents of varying size which thereafter continually get out of hand, being dropped, overlooked, picked up, folded, assorted, waved, clutched, and crumpled at various stages in the process. One skeptic carried his collection thru [*sic*] his physical inspection. A truly inventive character extracted his folded dossier from a Prince Albert tobacco can.[124]

After security screening and medical examinations, the braceros were dispatched to border reception centers where they signed contracts (which were countersigned by the two governments) with employers' representatives. Workers technically had some freedom of choice in this contracting process. Indeed, this freedom to negotiate a contract had been advertised by growers' allies in Congress as one of the primary virtues of PL 78.[125]

The "freedom of contract" provision, lauded in Congress, remained largely an abstraction. Those who turned down their first offer of employment for whatever reason[126] were often blacklisted by subsequent employers and sent home empty-handed.[127] Those who were "lucky" enough to secure employment after the degradation and bureaucratic delays at the recruiting stations and reception centers, risked physical injury as well. A Border Patrol memo from Yuma, Arizona, told of braceros being "fumigated prior to their departure to the United States . . . by spraying them by use of airplanes, much in the same manner as agricultural fields are sprayed."[128] Working conditions were often so strenuous and the braceros' hands so "badly scratched" that efforts to obtain the fingerprints required for FBI clearance frequently failed, with the incomplete forms stamped "unclassifiable" and returned to Washington.[129]

Once the contract was signed and the braceros admitted, the implementation of the program guaranteed that it would remain accommodating to the needs of growers. Until the late 1950s, the "prevailing wage" was determined by growers themselves, much as it was before the enactment of PL 78. While the Bureau of Employment Security (BES) in the Department of Labor was in theory responsible for certifying that domestic labor had been sought at "prevailing wages," growers took the lead in establishing what that wage was, with the BES cast in a reactive role. Having offered employment to domestic workers at a given wage rate and finding a "shortage of labor" at that rate, growers were then free to contract braceros at the same wage that had been unacceptable to domestic workers.[130] A 1955 amendment to PL 78 required that domestic workers be consulted in determining prevailing wages.[131] However, employers and the Department of Labor were free to ignore the workers' recommendations, which they frequently did. In addition to the issue of wages, the determination of a "shortage of labor" was complicated by the fact that there was no provision for the transportation of domestic labor, as there was for braceros. So that a "shortage of labor" meant that domestic workers were not available *on the spot,* or could not get there on their own. The result was that braceros were transported from Mexico even when there were unemployed farm workers elsewhere in the United States, or even in the same state.

"Adverse effect" was a similarly vague term and was integrally related to the definition of the prevailing wage. In a statement to Congress, Henry Anderson, a researcher and active opponent of the bracero system, pointed out that the annual infusion of almost 400,000 Mexican farm workers *necessarily* had an adverse effect on wages and working conditions and likened the Bracero Program to "farm labor colonialism."[132] It was not enough, he said, that PL 78 and the international agreements included abstract protections for domestic workers and braceros:

> If Congress passed a law repealing the law of gravity, we might reasonably expect it to include some indication of how this difficult form of repeal was to be carried out. Having passed a law which repeals the law of supply and demand (the supply of labor is to be increased without effect upon the price of labor), it is incumbent upon Congress to demonstrate how this equally difficult form of repeal is to be administered.[133]

If this "repeal of the law of supply and demand" was an inherent component of the contract labor system, lax enforcement of the terms of the contract redoubled the advantages to employers. While it was the duty of the Department of Labor to oversee contract compliance, the Immigration Service was responsible for removing braceros from employers who violated the terms of their contracts, and for reporting employers who used illegal aliens. In both activities, the agency was notoriously lenient. The international agreements of the late 1940s, PL 78, and all subsequent accords with Mexico, specified that employers of illegal workers were ineligible to receive braceros. Since it was generally the INS that apprehended undocumented workers in the course of its border patrol and investigations activities, enforcement of this provision depended on the agency reporting the aliens' employers. One well-publicized episode of non-enforcement occurred in 1951. The National Farm Labor Union (NFLU), centered in California and affiliated with the AFL, was gearing up for a strike in the Imperial Valley. Struggling for survival as one of the few labor organizations representing farm workers in this period, the NFLU notified officials that a large vegetable farm in the Valley was using a mixed work force of braceros and illegal immigrants (the farm was co-owned by Frank O'Dwyer, brother of the U.S. Ambassador to Mexico). The Border Patrol was prodded by the union into rounding up 300 illegal workers on the farm, but no braceros were taken from the employer.[134]

One INS district was particularly imaginative in its efforts not to deny braceros to employers who were caught with illegal workers.

According to a Border Patrol Report from Marfa, Texas, in June 1957, an employer in that sector "persisted" in hiring illegal workers along with his braceros, despite repeated "warnings."[135] Unable to ignore the flagrant violations any longer, the Border Patrol rounded up the illegal aliens and removed the braceros.[136] However, the employer was allowed by El Paso District Director Neelly to post a "compliance bond" of $2000, with $300 to be deducted for each illegal worker discovered on his farm in the future, rather than suffer ineligibility for bracero contracting. This tactic was apparently institutionalized in the El Paso District—where the Marfa Border Patrol sector was located—and was considered so satisfactory that the Chief of the Marfa Sector urged that "it might be considered for general application where difficulty is had with authorized [bracero] employers who persist in violating that portion of their agreement."[137] Commissioner Swing's handwritten comment in the margin of the report noted approvingly, "Mr. Neelly's fine support."

The immigration agency was even more accommodating with violators of the wage and working conditions provisions of bracero contracts. The *INS Information Bulletin*[138] described an alternative to denying braceros to employers guilty of such violations. Reporting that "[a] practice exists in the Rio Grande Valley whereby employers require workers to accept less pay than the minimum wage in their contracts in order to retain their jobs,"[139] the *Bulletin* announced that the District Director had instituted a system to deal with the violators without depriving them of their braceros. Employers under this system were permitted to retain their braceros after signing "pledges" with the Border Patrol that they would comply with their contracts in the future.[140] District Director Sahli sent an open letter to bracero employers in the area "warning" them that "when further violations are found, similar action will be taken."[141] It can be safely assumed that such "warnings" were at best meaningless, at worst counterproductive.

The bargaining edge that Mexico enjoyed during negotiation of the 1951 accord as the Korean War escalated was steadily eroded, precluding Mexican officials from pressing for more effective implementation of the provisions of the bilateral agreements. An open border incident in early 1954 and several weeks of unilateral recruitment on the part of the United States confirm Mexico's weak position and subordinate status as a negotiator—a status it retained for the duration of the program. In January 1954, U.S.-Mexico negotiations for a new bracero agreement broke down over the issues of border recruitment centers, which Mexico continued to resist; how the prevailing wage was to be determined; and the amount of subsistence payments to be provided to unemployed braceros. For several months, U.S. officials threatened to import braceros on a unilateral basis if Mexico did not give in to U.S. demands.[142] By January 15, when the existing bilateral agreement expired, no new accord had been reached, despite a 15-day extension designed to buy additional time. The following day, the Department of State, Labor, and Justice announced that Mexican farm workers would be unilaterally contracted at the border on a first-come, first-served basis.[143]

The result was a kind of international hiring hall, as U.S. officials stood at the border and called out the number of workers needed each day. Aspiring braceros rushed the gates, where Immigration Service and Labor Department representatives selected and processed the workers. The *New York Times*[144] carried pictures of the mayhem, as rioting Mexican farm laborers were met by American police using tear gas and fire hoses to control the crowd. Mexican officials often joined in. A picture of one incident shows a Mexican worker straddling the border, with a Mexican agent tugging at him from one side and a U.S. official pulling from the other.[145]

In early February 1954, the U.S. Comptroller General informed the Department of Labor that funds appropriated under PL 78 for the administration of a bilateral program could not legally be used for continued unilateral recruitment.[146] Several days later, the unilateral program ended, and a new agreement was reached with Mexico on March 10. However, Congress passed Public Law 309 for safe measure, specifying that in the future, if bilateral negotiations reached an impasse, unilateral recruitment could be resumed. The unilateral episode in the winter of 1954 lasted only a few weeks, but its impact endured. Mexico's ability to press its interests in international negotiations or to contest implementation policies was effectively curtailed for the rest of the Bracero Program.

THE TEXAS PROVISO: A TEXTBOOK CASE OF ADMINISTRATIVE LAWMAKING

We have seen here that administrative discretion was used to circumvent Mexican demands and to implement informally procedures or policies that Congress and State Department negotiators—with their highly visible profile and formal rule-making procedures—found it impossible or undesirable to establish officially. Perhaps no single set of developments better illustrates this pattern than the political and bureaucratic maneuverings surrounding the passage and implementation of the "Texas Proviso."

In the spring of 1951, Democratic Senators Paul Douglas of Illinois, Wayne Morse of Oregon, and Hubert Humphrey of Minnesota, attempted to amend S.984 (later to become PL 78), in response both to Mexican demands to reduce illegal immigration and to the recommendations of the President's Commission on Migratory Labor. Most controversial was the amendment introduced by Senator Douglas that provided:

> Any person who shall employ any Mexican alien . . . when such person knows or has reasonable grounds to believe or suspect or by reasonable inquiry could have ascertained that such an alien is unlawfully within the United States . . . and shall fail to report such information promptly to an immigration officer, shall be guilty of a felony. . . .

The amendment passed the Senate by a narrow margin, but was deleted from the bill by the Conference Committee. Senator Allen Ellender (D-Louisiana), Chair of the Senate delegation to the Conference Committee and champion of agricultural interests, explained the deletion saying that the measure was "not germane to the purpose of this bill"—which was to provide for foreign contract labor—and that in any case the provision should go through the Judiciary Committee, rather than the Committee on Agriculture.[147] Having assured the success of PL 78 by channeling it through the Agriculture Committees and bypassing the less friendly Judiciary Committees, growers' allies now scuttled the Douglas Amendment by arguing that all immigration matters had to be routed through the Judiciary Committees.

Pressure from Mexico continued to mount. Mexican officials had already registered concern with the State Department when the initial version of S.984 contained no penalty for employers of illegal aliens.[148] Following enactment of PL 78 and rejection of the Douglas Amendment, they threatened to close down recruitment centers unless evidence was provided that "the subject of sanctions would not be dropped as a dead issue."[149] State Department promises that employer sanctions legislation was under serious consideration, and President Truman's apparent support for the measure,[150] momentarily sufficed to bring Mexico to the bargaining table to sign a new bilateral agreement.

Seven months later, with the expiration date of this Migrant Labor Agreement fast approaching, the Senate hastily addressed the "anti-wetback legislation" which Mexico required to extend the pact. But in place of the Douglas Amendment's explicit prohibition of illegal alien employment, the bill introduced by Senator Harley Kilgore of West Virginia (S.1851) made it illegal only to "harbor, transport, and conceal" illegal entrants. The debate in the Senate on February 5, 1952—exactly six days before expiration of the Migrant Labor Agreement—made it perfectly clear that the legislation was a way to appease Mexican negotiators and thus secure the continuation of the contract labor system. Prefacing his remarks with the assurance that his bill "was accepted by the Department of Agriculture and representatives of the agricultural organizations," Senator Kilgore introduced S.1851 with the warning that there was "a dangerous situation in the southwest. There is a legal means of getting labor over the international boundary if the agreement is renewed. But the agreement cannot be renewed . . . until the Senate passes this bill and the bill goes to the House."[151]

Senator Humphrey and others complained of the absence of hearings on the bill and the lack of time for debate.[152] Nevertheless, even those who protested seemed to share Senator Humphrey's sentiment when he remarked candidly, ". . . I recognize the difficulty which our government has encountered in the renegotiation of the agreement with the Republic of Mexico, and if this is a part of the means to get the agreement renewed . . . then I shall not object."[153] As the debate proceeded, Senator Ellender lobbied hard for the measure and reminded his colleagues that "the enactment of this [bill] is necessary . . . because the Mexican Government refuses to enter into another contract . . . unless we strengthen our immigration laws."[154]

Repeated warnings of this kind left little doubt about the motivation for the legislation. Less clear was its actual meaning. Central to the confusion was an amendment known as the Texas Proviso, named after the Texas growers who fought for it. The Texas Proviso stipulated that "for the purposes of this section, employment (including the usual and normal practices incident to employment) shall not be deemed to constitute harboring."[155] The amendment was ostensibly introduced as a way to protect employers who were *unaware* of their workers' illegal immigration status, from prosecution under the harboring clause. Senator Hubert Humphrey (D-Minnesota) challenged its sponsors, "What is the purpose of that particular proviso if the purpose of the bill is to stop the tragic wetback situation?"[156] Senator Harley Kilgore (D-West Virginia) responded, "Many wetbacks have been in the country for years. They are frequently mistaken for American citizens."[157] Later he added, ". . . it is very difficult for an employer to know which ones are in the country illegally."[158] Senator Dennis Chavez (D-New Mexico) agreed with Kilgore, asking rhetorically, "Why should a man be punished . . . if he has not acted willfully and unlawfully [*sic*]? If he acts as a matter of course, by mistake, because he does not know whether a person is a citizen or not; if he does it in an innocent manner . . . why should he be punished?"[159]

It was left ambiguous as to whether "*knowing* employment" would be considered harboring. When a few senators who were interested in a strict employment prohibition pressed their colleagues on this issue, sponsors of the Texas Proviso assured them, "Once he [the employer] finds out the real situation, he is knowingly and willfully harboring the man, and the authorities can go after him."[160] In a similar exchange, Senator Paul Douglas (D-Illinois), an opponent of the employer exemption, stated his interpretation of the Texas Proviso:

> . . . the committee proposes a specific exemption for employment. It specifically provides that employment shall not constitute harboring. In other words, under the committee proposal it is not illegal for an employer knowingly and willfully to hire a wetback who has illegally entered the United States.[161]

Senator Kilgore, the Texas Proviso's sponsor and tireless spokesperson, intervened, ". . . the Senator from Illinois misinterprets the bill."[162]

Despite assurances by Texas Proviso advocates that it did not provide a loophole for knowing employment, they rejected by a margin of 69 to 12 an amendment proposed by Senator Douglas specifically stipulating that knowing employment would be penalized.[163] Senator John McClellan (D-Arkansas) claimed that such a provision would "victimize" the farmer.[164] Senator Herman Welker (R-Idaho), who owned farm land himself, called Douglas's proposal "vicious" in its focus on farmers.[165] Others argued that consideration of the amendment would complicate the passage of S.1851 and hence hold up negotiations with Mexico.[166] Within days, the Senate had passed the bill with the Texas Proviso intact. The House quickly followed suit, and the bill was signed into law in March, 1952.[167]

Richard Lyon[168] notes the double-talk in the arguments of Texas Proviso proponents, as they repeatedly assured their skeptical colleagues that the bill would penalize those who *knowingly* employed illegal immigrants, but strenuously resisted building any such specification into the law. Introducing his discussion of the bizarre congressional debate, Lyon quotes the ditty:

> "Mother, may I go out to swim?
> "Yes, my darling daughter,
> Hang your clothes on a hickory limb,
> But don't go near the water."[169]

Broadly interpreted by the INS to mean that illegal alien employment was altogether excluded from the category of "harboring," the Texas Proviso served as a *carte blanche* for the continued use of undocumented workers. Despite the potentially controversial nature of this interpretation and the ambiguity of the Congressional debate, the Immigration Service acted quickly—so quickly in fact that the regulations were drawn up and published in the *Federal Register* without the required period of advance public notice and comment. One sentence of explanation accompanied the move: "Compliance with the provisions of section 4 of the Administrative Procedure Act[170] relative to notice of proposed rule-making and delayed effective date is impracticable and contrary to the public interest in this instance. . . ."[171] In one stroke, the agency established in practice a policy that Congress was unwilling or unable to make explicit, and ignored normal administrative procedures in the process.

Congressional passage of S.1851 was designed to satisfy Mexican demands for a law against the hiring of illegal aliens. Together, growers' demand for cheap immigrant labor and Mexican pressure to curtail illegal immigration required that legislative intent be left ambiguous. Revealing it for what it was—one Senator called the Texas Proviso an "escape clause" and another characterized the bill as "little more than a gesture"[172]—would have jeopardized its utility to State Department negotiators for a renewed Migrant Labor Agreement.[173] To explicitly prohibit the employment of illegal aliens would have deprived southwestern growers of a continuing source of labor and was unacceptable to members of Congress who, in the years before Operation Wetback and the increased availability of legal braceros, called such measures "employer harassment."

A GROWER'S DREAM

Growers initially feared that the regulations and red tape of the government program launched by PL 78 in 1951 might constitute an undue burden on their labor recruitment efforts.[174] However, protections built into the Bracero Program came to naught in the absence of rigorous enforcement. In fact, during its peak years in the mid-1950s, the program could not have been better suited to growers' needs. As one observer put it, "United States employers benefitted from a risk-free pool of menial labor. . . . And they determined all the working conditions, hours, wages, and living accommodations."[175]

Wherever braceros were concentrated, wages tended to stagnate or even fall. According to a Department of Agriculture report, farm wages as a whole increased 14% between 1953 and 1959, but remained the same in regions with braceros.[176] In California, domestic farm workers earned *less* per hour in 1955 than they had in 1950.[177] A telegram from a large Texas growers' association to the Secretary of Labor in 1954 suggests that the wage reductions were no accident. "The present minimum wage of Mexican national contract [*sic*] is causing an *undue stabilization* of farm wages," the telegram read. "We need very much to have it lowered 40 cents per hour and 1.25 CWT as a minimum weight. . . ."[178] A study conducted by the California Reference Service, a research unit attached to the California legislature, reported that the Bracero Program was used deliberately to lower farm wages.[179] While growers insisted that "stoop" labor was inherently unacceptable to domestic workers, researchers at the Institute of Industrial Relations at the University of California, Los Angeles, linked the inability of growers to find willing domestic workers to the low wage rates resulting from the influx of foreign labor.[180]

Mechanization continued at a rapid pace, reducing the total number of farm workers by an unprecedented 41% between 1950 and 1960, while agricultural output expanded.[181] Citing high unemployment rates among domestic farm workers and quickly accumulating agricultural surpluses, *New York Times* reporter Gladwyn Hill questioned the Alice-in-Wonderland logic of importing foreign labor: " 'What are these people doing?' asked Alice, surveying a vast, fertile southwestern valley. 'They're cultivating surplus cotton and lettuce,' replied the Red Queen. 'Who are they?' asked Alice, tactfully ignoring the matter of why anyone should produce surplus crops. 'They are Mexicans imported because of the labor shortage,' explained the Red Queen."[182]

A handful of persistent and well-organized unionists, first in the National Farm Labor Union (NFLU) and then in its successor, the National Agricultural Workers Union (NAWU), made the Bracero Program their main focus of attack. Ernesto Galarza, researcher and union activist, documents the slow and difficult process of farm labor organizing in this period, and describes the efforts of the NFLU to fight the bracero system beginning in 1947. Galarza writes that, by 1952, "the problems of organization . . . centered on Public Law 78 and its multiple effects. Without opposition, the bracero system would have a drastic effect on the hiring of domestic agricultural laborers, except as needed as standbys for emergencies."[183] Launching investigations, testifying to Congress, prodding the Department of Labor into enforcement, and organizing collective actions against abusive employers, during the 1950s these unionists fought a losing battle against the labor importation system.[184] Despite the efforts of farm worker unions, the

Bracero Program expanded and grew. Over 2 million braceros entered between 1952 and 1958, with more than 445,000 coming during the peak year 1956 (see Appendix B). In California, braceros comprised approximately 34% of the seasonal agricultural workforce in 1957, and in some California counties they made up over 90% of the total farm work force.[185]

The *INS Information Bulletin,* speaking of the Bracero Program in Imperial Valley, described the effects of the system: "Imperial Valley's agriculture could not have boomed in the postwar years without a strong labor supply. One of the most significant developments in the decade here since the war has been the steady building of the biggest and most stable farm labor program of its kind in the history of the U.S."[186] Commissioner Swing continued to praise employers for asserting their own self-interests, as he summarized the successes of Operation Wetback and the advantages of the Bracero Program: "Net results of farmer-grower cooperation [with the INS] include a shoring up of the agricultural economy of the Southwest, and establishment of a dependable source of qualified agricultural labor."[187] The following chapter examines the precise nature of this alliance between growers and the Immigration Service.

CHAPTER 4

LET'S MAKE A DEAL

The Bracero Program owed its very existence to the broad exercise of administrative power. Invented and put into place in the pre-war years by federal agencies, it was sustained by administrative fiat whenever Congress failed to act or when negotiations with Mexico stalled. Beyond that facilitative function, the INS used its front line position to provide growers with workers whenever bracero supplies were threatened. Paroling illegal immigrants to their employers, periodically opening the border to aspiring braceros who were documented on the spot, and collaborating with the Department of Labor on unilateral recruitment, the Immigration Service used its discretion to paste together an uninterrupted system of imported farm labor for over two decades. Noting the advantages of this system to agricultural employers in the Southwest, Ernesto Galarza cited a remark by the Assistant Secretary of Agriculture, casually comparing the state's relationship to growers to a "hired hand on the farm."[1]

Though vivid, this "hired hand" analogy is misleading. While immigration operations generally favored growers, agency-centered interests were never identical to, nor completely submerged by, those of bracero employers. This chapter, in examining the enforcement tools and administrative inventions developed by the Immigration Service in the 1950s, continues to document the ways the agency used its extensive powers to the advantage of growers. More importantly, however, the chapter reveals the nature of the agency's *own* bureaucratic interests and the centrality of those interests to policies that expanded and entrenched the contract labor system. We will see that the INS was capable of substantial independent action, often taking the lead in policy formation and then aggressively persuading growers to cooperate. We will even see evidence that the immigration agency occasionally *ignored* the demands of growers when those demands jeopardized agency priorities. These findings are clearly incompatible with the hired hand analogy, and the essentially instrumentalist model of state action that it implies.

By the end of this chapter, the picture that emerges is not of a hired hand or puppet agency responding at every turn to the whim of employers, but rather of a state bureaucracy with needs and interests of its own—interests that were clearly interwoven with, but not identical to, those of bracero users. The realization of those agency interests subsequent to Operation Wetback was contingent on a delicate and sometimes rocky alliance with bracero users, who continually threatened to return to using illegal labor. While this alliance with powerful southwestern growers and ranchers was admittedly an asymmetrical one, it should not be concluded from this asymmetry that the Immigration Service was without an agenda of its own, or that it was unwilling or unable to contradict employer interests in pursuit of that agenda. Before turning to this evidence of relative agency autonomy, the following sections discuss generally the importance of control over the agricultural work force, the role of captive braceros in that control, and the ways the INS maximized bracero captivity.

BRACEROS AS A CAPTIVE WORK FORCE

Commissioner Swing, in his meetings with growers and ranchers prior to Operation Wetback, had emphasized the advantage of control to elicit their cooperation in the enforcement drive. Not only would the elimination of illegal "bootleg labor" increase predictability, Swing told them, but using workers whose legal status was contingent on their staying with one employer would reduce the turnover of workers attracted to better wages or working conditions elsewhere, and ultimately stabilize or even reduce labor costs. INS enforcement policies were fashioned to enhance the advantages of an effectively captive workforce, and thus ensure growers' continued preference for braceros over illegal workers.

In 1955, Commissioner Swing reorganized and decentralized the bureaucratic structure of the Immigration Service. Four regional offices were created, each headed by a regional commissioner with substantial authority to oversee and supervise operations in the area. Beneath these regional offices were local districts, managed by district directors who reported directly to the regional commissioners.[2] The twenty sectors of the Border Patrol, a separate branch of the Immigration Service with its own organizational structure and geographic jurisdictions, were linked through the regional commissioners to the central office in Washington. Despite the ostensible decentralization, Commissioner Swing ran a tight ship, involving himself in every aspect of policymaking and keeping a close eye on field operations.

In his hands-on style, Swing introduced monthly "sector activity reports" in which Border Patrol officials in each region detailed their enforcement activities—reports that he personally perused, as evidenced by his extensive handwritten notes in the margins. These reports were prepared for internal consumption only and, while they were no doubt written with an eye for pleasing "the General"—as Swing was called by his troops in the agency—they serve as a good barometer of agency priorities. Taken together, these four to five-page monthly reports from each field office suggest that, in the Southwest region where the Bracero Program operated, the reduction of illegal immigration was a primary goal. The reports began with information on "Potential Illegal Entrants Outside the United States" (focusing on concentrations of potential illegal immigrants on the Mexican border), then covered "Strategic Factors Influencing Illegal Entry" (emphasizing agricultural conditions and employment opportunities), and concluded with statistics and details on apprehensions and "Miscellaneous Remarks" related to enforcement. In a radical departure from the laissez-faire approach prior to Operation Wetback, the agency now took a decidedly aggressive posture in the detection and removal of illegal workers.

A close look at the day-to-day enforcement activities described in these reports reveals that efforts to control the border went hand-in-hand with enforcement strategies designed to maximize the control of *braceros*. One area of control emphasized by the Border Patrol involved the apprehension of "skips," an activity that was covered regularly and in detail in the monthly sector activity reports. The centrality of this function was due in part to the fact that in the years following Operation Wetback, bracero "skips" made up a large proportion of the "illegals" to be apprehended. As the success of Operation Wetback and the corresponding entrenchment of the Bracero Program increased the number of braceros relative to illegal entries, the attention given to apprehending deserters was part and parcel of the Border Patrol's regular enforcement duties.

At least as important, however, rounding up "skips" was a service to growers, and a central ingredient in the control structure of the contract labor system. After all, it was the predictability of the bracero that made him preferable to the illegal worker. To realize this advantage, the bracero's captive status had to be rigorously maintained. Border Patrol reports of "skips" and their reasons for desertion serve as a reminder both of the arduous conditions and erratic nature of agricultural production, and the role of a captive work force in that production process. In areas like Tucson, Arizona, and El Centro,

California, where temperatures during the cotton harvest hovered around 100 degrees, braceros regularly deserted to go back to Mexico or to seek work elsewhere.[3] And when temperatures exceeded even these normal highs, the desertion rate rose precipitously. A report from the Southwest region described one particularly hot summer: "In one three-day period in June of this year, temperatures reached 117 degrees and over 500 Mexican braceros left the fields and returned to Mexico leaving the crops to spoil."[4] In other instances, uneven conditions and staggered harvests attracted braceros to "greener pastures."[5] As one Border Patrol official explained, noting a larger than usual number of "skips" in his sector, "This is attributable, so a number of aliens have stated, to their desire to work for a few days in the 'big pay' crops being harvested at this time."[6]

The most common reason for desertion was not heat, but lack of work. When crops were poor or weather conditions were bad, braceros—most of whom worked on the piece rate system—found it hard to break even, after room and board had been deducted from their pay. The lack of work was sometimes the consequence of deliberate employer tactics. One tactic, designed to ensure that enough workers were on hand to meet any conceivable need, was to contract more workers than actually required, since under the piece rate system, workers were paid only for what they produced. Another strategy was to extend the contracts of workers who were not needed immediately, to make sure that they would be available when the need arose. In both cases, workers who were bound by law to their employers were used as a way to compensate for the vagaries and uncertainties of agricultural production.

The apprehension of "skips" fit well into this scheme of things. Border Patrol reports kept careful tabs on the conditions of employment, the supply of braceros relative to the labor need, and the potential number of deserters. One report from Yuma, Arizona, told of growers who planned to keep braceros on hand without employment, and the potential for an upswing in the number of deserters seeking full-time work elsewhere:

> The Yuma Producers Cooperative Association are requesting the extension of contracts for some 2,500 braceros presently assigned to that association. Although there will be only moderate needs for their services during middle July to middle August, extension of these workers' contracts is being requested at this time in order to ensure a sufficient labor pool for the start of the cotton harvest in late August.[7]

It was the Border Patrol's task to apprehend deserters, thereby shoring up this reserve pool of braceros.

Efforts to control "skips" were intensified during the recession of 1958. As unemployment in the United States increased and the Department of Labor was hard-pressed to certify that domestic farm labor was unavailable, the number of braceros admitted went down for the first time since Operation Wetback.[8] The recession, combined with the temporary reduction of braceros, had two effects. First, as unemployed domestic workers entered the farm labor market in the place of braceros, farm wages in some areas began to rise. In northern Texas, wages went from the guaranteed bracero rate of 50 cents an hour up to 75 cents on the open market,[9] triggering a "skip alarm" by the Border Patrol. Worried that braceros would be attracted to higher wages outside the contract system, officials in Del Rio, Texas, warned, "This situation could result in an increase in bracero-skips and is being closely watched."[10] Second, not only did the number of potential deserters increase as wages in the open market went up, but with the reduction of new bracero contracts, it was more important than ever to keep them from deserting. In response, several Border Patrol sectors announced stepped-up efforts to track down deserters, including soliciting detailed information from employers' associations, reception centers, and any other possible lead.[11]

There was a neat compatibility between the INS mission of apprehending illegal aliens—who during this period were increasingly bracero deserters—and the growers' interest in control. This was particularly apparent in Arkansas where, in the late 1950s, there were no permanently stationed Border Patrol officers.[12] Teams of Border Patrol agents were periodically dispatched to the state as necessary to round up deserters. In 1960, it was reported that there were approximately 30,000 braceros in Arkansas, and that four officers had been sent there on detail from the Southeast region in response to complaints of an increase in desertions. A Border Patrol officer described these assignments: "During the 1959 cotton picking season there were 100 alleged desertions in the State of Arkansas. . . . In the event desertions increase in the State of Arkansas, up to 18 additional officers from the Southwest Region will be detailed immediately to help control the area."[13]

A second dimension of control pursued by the Immigration Service involved the elimination of "subversives" or "labor agitators." According to the INS *Annual Report* in 1955, the agency assigned top priority to enforcing the McCarran-Walter Act provision excluding "subversive" aliens. The intensity of the agency's efforts in this regard was clear: "Increased emphasis was given investigation of cases where even a trace of subversive activity, however remote, had occurred within the past 10 years."[14] In May 1956, David Carnahan, the Regional Commissioner of the Southwest region, alerted his district directors to the need "to prevent the infiltration into the Bracero Program of aliens who may be excludable or deportable on subversive grounds." To this end, he instructed his directors:

> Any officer or employee who receives any information, *however trivial*, touching upon this subject matter shall immediately transmit it by the fastest means to the appropriate Division Chief in the Regional Office. Particular interest shall be given to any information emanating from a labor camp or other place where laborers congregate. . . .[15]

Agents were told to "use their ingenuity and resourcefulness to the fullest" in dealing with the troublemakers.[16]

Growers were encouraged to participate in the effort to purge the Bracero Program of "agitators." According to the Chief Border Patrol Inspector in McAllen, Texas, "Farmers and field men have been contacted in connection with the agitator program and it is reported that the officers have received excellent cooperation."[17] One incident involving such cooperation reveals the urgency with which the INS approached the routing of so-called agitators. When eleven braceros near the northern California town of Marysville were reported to the INS by their foreman in the summer of 1956 for refusing to work, two agency investigators rushed to the scene to determine if the workers were "professional agitators or possibly communists."[18] According to the report that the investigators sent to the regional office, the Mexican foreman had overheard several braceros "talking about something" in their barracks the night before the work stoppage, but was unable to decipher what they were saying. Of the three workers subsequently interrogated, the investigators believed that one "might be a Communist," but they "were unable to develop any evidence to substantiate that belief."[19] When the regional commissioner was told that all three workers were deported to Mexico but that only the one suspected of being a communist was barred from future contracts, he handwrote a memo to Commissioner Swing: "Please note—I believe there should be a stop order on all three who returned to Mexico and not just the one." Swing scribbled at the bottom, with typical decisiveness, "You bet."[20] Despite the continued Cold War rhetoric about communist instigation, one brief report of the "Marysville incident" noted that "nothing was revealed during the inquiry to indicate that it was inspired by subversives." The report concluded that "not in a single instance has there been evidence of subversive influence in the incidents of dissatisfaction among the workers."[21]

Later that month, Commissioner Swing outlined a new enforcement program in response to what he continued to call the "Infiltration of Bracero Program by Agitators."[22] "In furtherance of our program to more vigorously combat infiltration by these elements," Swing wrote his first in command in the Southwest, "[a]ll officers in the field should be alerted, and instances of agitation reported to the Region, by telephone, promptly upon discovery." The Department of Labor was to report to the INS any "work stoppage or slow-down" by braceros so that it could carry out a full investigation to determine if the "agitators" belonged to any "Communist, Communist-front, splinter and sympathizer organizations in Mexico." In any case, Swing advised, "Our officers should bear in mind that establishing agitators' membership in a group or organization is *not* absolutely essential to establish that agitation was subversive-inspired [and, therefore, a deportable offense]."[23] The memo concluded emphatically, "Service interest in this matter transcends organizational lines. A concerted effort of the entire Service is necessary to achieve our objective."

The language of these intra-agency communications and the sense of mission in apprehending "Reds" and "Communist sympathizers" suggest the impact of the Cold War and McCarthy propaganda on INS policies. But the primary effect of these polices was not to deport communist braceros, of whom there were few even according to INS accounts, but to control bracero *activism*. The right of braceros to organize and make demands on their employers was already severely limited by the terms of the labor agreement. The role of the Immigration Service in investigating complaints by foremen and growers, and its ability to deport anyone suspected of subversive tendencies, eroded whatever rights to organize were theoretically left to these farm workers. While the International Agreement specified that braceros could name representatives to bring complaints to their employers, such complaints were often taken as evidence of communist sympathies. Anderson described the *de facto* nullification of braceros' rights: "When workers try to uphold their right of representation, by selecting spokesmen from among their own crews, they . . . find their spokesmen are deported as 'troublemakers,' 'Reds,' and 'agitators.' "[24] While few braceros were formally deported on political grounds, the threat of deportation and exclusion from future contracts was a powerful instrument of bracero control.[25]

Substantial evidence suggests that the INS worked to round up both agitators and deserters not just because this happened to be its enforcement duty, but also because it was general agency *policy* to enhance growers' control over braceros, in the interest of preserving grower satisfaction with the contract system. The broad interpretation of what constituted a "subversive" bracero to include anyone even suspected of being a labor activist is indicative of the agency emphasis on worker control, above and beyond its more narrow enforcement duties.

That INS policies were designed to maximize grower control is further confirmed by the agency's approach toward the permanent immigration of Mexican braceros. There was no per-country quota for Western Hemisphere countries in U.S. immigration law until 1976.[26] Instead, immigrants were admitted on a first-come, first-served basis (up to the 120,000 limit for the hemisphere), upon joint determination by the Department of State and the Immigration Service that they were eligible for permanent residence status. While immigration officials periodically advised employers who had lost their bracero eligibility or who were disgruntled over Department of Labor regulations that they could attempt to get permanent residency for their favored braceros, generally the INS was opposed to granting immigrant visas to Mexican farm workers in the years following Operation Wetback.

A series of events in 1955 reveals that opposition to the permanent immigration of Mexican agricultural workers was integrally connected to the vulnerability inherent in bracero status, and the desire of the INS to preserve that vulnerability. In September 1955, one of the largest growers in Southern California complained to Congressman James Utt and Senator Thomas Kuchel of California that one of his workers—a former bracero—had obtained a permanent visa and was disrupting his bracero workforce. The complaint was forwarded to the INS. According to an internal INS memo,

> [the grower] complained that the alien who was successful in immigrating appeared in his labor camp and there bragged about being able to take employment anywhere he desired, thereby causing a great deal of unrest among the balance of the contract laborers, and even causing an excessive amount of absenteeism by a number of these agricultural laborers who proceeded to Tijuana endeavoring to likewise secure immigrant visas. [The grower] complained that a number of other employers of agricultural contract laborers in the San Diego County area were experiencing the same difficulties. . . .[27]

Six weeks later, a secret meeting between top State Department and Immigration Service officials was held in El Paso, Texas at the request of Commissioner Swing. Their purpose was to devise ways to reduce the number of permanent Mexican visas.[28] Assistant Immigration Commissioner, Albert Del Guercio, chair and moderator of the meeting, called attention to "the alarming number of Mexican immigrants who have been issued visas and admitted to the United States for permanent residence," citing figures that showed a 690% increase in Mexican visas—from 6,372 in 1951 to 50,772 in 1955—with 42% going to "agricultural laborers."[29] The need to reduce the number of Mexican visas was tied to the concern that if Mexican farm workers were able to obtain permanent visas, it could cut down on the supply of braceros and stir up dissatisfaction among contract workers. Del Guercio summed up the solution as he saw it: "The Immigration Service, under the immigration laws, may be able to control the situation by excluding from admission [with visas] so-called braceros or agricultural workers." The State Department representative from the Office of Mexican affairs added that both the State Department and the INS would "make this separation—*braceros would not be regarded as prospective immigrants.*"[30]

The officials were well aware that their agreement to bar Mexican agricultural workers from obtaining permanent immigrant status, despite the absence of a statutory quota, was potentially controversial. The Administrator of Consular Affairs for the State Department opened the meeting by highlighting the importance of resolving matters in private: "I am convinced that the proper way to handle these border problems without exciting either the Congress or the public is by means of these meetings. . . ." Another State Department representative stressed the political importance of not tampering with the official no-quota policy for neighbors of the United States, noting, "We should delay this evil until the very last" because of its potentially negative impact on foreign relations. The way to limit Mexican visas, he cautioned, was to do it behind the scenes through inter-agency agreements—whereupon Del Guercio reminded everyone, "THIS MEETING IS STRICTLY CONFIDENTIAL. There will be no publicity. All discussions here are within the family and will be treated as such."[31] The secret agreement to deny visas to Mexican agricultural laborers resulted in a substantial decline in the number of Mexican visas granted in 1957, 1958, and 1959 (see Appendix C).

The El Paso conference and the policies agreed to there are important for at least two reasons. First, they serve as another illustration of how administrative discretion is used to circumvent official channels of policymaking. Second, the secret policy of denying visas to Mexican farm workers highlights the priority the INS placed on securing a plentiful supply of captive, and therefore docile, braceros. One might conceivably argue that in the case of labor activists and deserters, the agency was simply fulfilling its enforcement duty of apprehending "subversives" and illegal aliens, and only coincidentally advanced growers' interests in the process. The agency position on withholding visas from Mexican farm workers, however, provides clear and dramatic evidence of an INS interest in maximizing employers' control over braceros, beyond what its more narrow apprehension duties called for.

If the agency's pursuit of growers' interests in a captive work force was not simply a by-product of its apprehension functions, neither was it unrelated to those functions. Rather, as we will see in the following sections, shoring up a docile labor force for agriculture was an integral part of the Service's strategy to cope with its own enforcement dilemmas, especially those arising from the underlying contradictions of immigration. The architects of Operation Wetback had understood that resolving the dilemmas that subjected their agency to ridicule and bureaucratic paralysis required enlisting the cooperation of growers and ranchers in exchanging their illegal workers for braceros. In the aftermath of the enforcement drive, immigration officials were painfully aware that the continued viability of that fragile resolution was contingent on preserving growers' satisfaction with the quantity and quality of the bracero workforce.

KEEPING THE SUPPLY FLOWING

Border Patrol reports in the years following Operation Wetback read like farm trade journals, with agricultural conditions traced in detail and the supply and demand for labor carefully calculated. Each month, the Southwest sectors estimated whether or not the number of braceros would be sufficient to satisfy employers' demands. Typical entries read, "Braceros continue to arrive in sufficient numbers to keep the labor supply slightly ahead of demand for those farmers eligible to use bracero labor," and,

> Demand for labor and supply of same is pretty well balanced.
> . . . The Yuma Producers Cooperative Association report they
> have a sufficient number of bracero labor to adequately fill
> their needs with the 5,927 assigned. The Blythe Growers Incorporated and Colorado River Cotton Growers Association also
> report a sufficient number of braceros, with 2,770 and 1,000
> assigned respectively. . . . Lettuce thinning is about to com-

mence, which will divert some labor from the cotton harvest, but not in quantity to seriously retard the cotton harvest.[32]

Border Patrol officials knew that any shortfall in the number of braceros would result in the employment of illegal aliens. From Del Rio, Texas, to El Centro, California, the message was the same: "Should Public Law 78 be repealed or a restriction placed on the number of braceros allowed to enter the United States, we can look forward to a large increase in the number of illegal alien entrants into the United States."[33] When the labor demand exceeded the supply of braceros, it was simply assumed that growers would attempt to use illegal aliens to fill the gap. During the 1958 recession and the decline in the number of braceros certified by the Department of Labor, the Border Patrol in Del Rio, Texas, reported:

> The cotton harvest this year is predicted as the largest in history and a large labor demand is anticipated when the harvest gets into full swing. More citizen and local labor is planning to participate in the harvest this year [due in part to the recession, as discussed above], but combined with anticipated numbers of contract laborers, will be insufficient to meet the labor demands. This situation will attract illegal entrant labor from Mexico. . . .[34]

If the Immigration Service was aware that the realization of its mandate to control illegal entry depended on employers' access to a plentiful bracero supply, so were growers—and they were not reluctant to capitalize on this trump card. Bracero users periodically let it be known that should their supply of Mexican contract labor be curtailed, they would not hesitate to employ illegal aliens. During the recession of 1958, representatives of one large Arizona grower told the Border Patrol, in a thinly veiled threat, that if they did not get permission to hire 100 braceros to harvest the melon crop, ". . . they will hire any and everybody who comes along looking for farm work."[35]

Sometimes the threats were more explicit. When braceros were withheld by the Department of Labor from cattle ranchers in Southern California, a lawyer for the biggest cattle ranchers in the region— himself a rancher—warned Commissioner Swing, "Certainly the Immigration Service ought to be interested in helping agriculture get legal Mexicans because it is obvious that farmers . . . are going to employ illegal Mexicans if they cannot get legal help."[36] Two years later, the President of the huge Texas Sheep and Goat Raisers' Association complained to Commissioner Swing about the impending exclusion of ranch work from the Bracero Program. In the past, the rancher wrote, "Mexican Nationals or 'braceros' have been the source. Unless a supply of legal labor is available we will be faced with the wet back problem again and costs of deportation of illegal aliens will greatly increase." He concluded pointedly, "None of us wants this to happen."[37] Farmers near Brownsville, Texas, threatened local Border Patrol officials that if they could not get the braceros they needed, "they will have to start hauling illegal aliens again and that the Border Patrol can haul them back to Mexico."[38] In the margin of the report, Commissioner Swing jotted, " 'Political' talk—but situation watched closely," suggesting that while he understood the political utility of such threats for farmers who were lobbying to receive as many braceros as possible, nonetheless those threats could not be discounted.

While the INS did not have direct control over the number of braceros admitted (this depended on Department of Labor certifications of need), immigration officials did what they could to keep the supply flowing. Whenever the Department of Labor or the Mexican government suggested tightening the bracero supply or barring certain abusive employers from participation, immigration officials voiced their opposition. For example, when the Mexican government requested that the largest farm association in the Rio Grande Valley be barred from receiving braceros due to a history of contract violations, the Border Patrol objected, "It [the farm association] has about 1,700 members in the four Valley counties which it supplies braceros and has handled an estimated 35,000 braceros during the current season. Revocation of this association's certificate would result in an acute shortage of agricultural labor and offer employment to illegal entrants."[39]

Immigration officials regularly appeared before Congress to testify against the termination of the Bracero Program.[40] The content of this testimony underlines both the enhanced prestige and political mileage the agency gained from the reduction of illegal immigration after Operation Wetback, and the centrality of a generous contract labor system to their continued success. One exchange between James Hennessy, Executive Assistant to Commissioner Swing, and the House Committee on Agriculture in 1958 is illustrative. Hinting at the importance of maintaining a steady supply of bracero labor despite the lingering recession, Hennessy began, "The wetback situation . . . will continue to exist as a potential," hastening to add, ". . . the Immigration and Naturalization Service at the present time has it under control."[41] Citing figures to document the decrease in illegal entry, Hennessy won praise from Representative Gathings of Arkansas, himself an employer of bracero labor: "That is a fine record. I wondered how do you account for doing the job in such a splendid fashion?"[42] While Hennessy at first insisted that INS enforcement policies be given full credit for both the reduction of illegal aliens and the subsequent expansion of the Bracero Program, he was ultimately forced to admit that control of the border was in large part the *consequence* of an ample supply of bracero labor. Hennessy was stuck between wishing to credit his agency for reducing illegal immigration beyond what had been the natural consequence of an expanded Bracero Program, and needing at the same time to lobby for the continuation of a generous supply of braceros to ensure continued border control. He agreed with Gathings that "Public Law 78 is an antiwetback program . . . ," but continued to insist that it was the INS elimination of illegal aliens that had made possible the expansion of the program, not vice versa. Finally, asked what would happen to the agency's enforcement successes should the contract labor program be terminated, Hennessy concluded, "We can't do the impossible, Mr. Congressman."[43]

ADMINISTRATIVE INVENTIONS

In the decade following Operation Wetback, the INS used its extensive discretion to avoid having to "do the impossible." Analyzing employers' needs and processing their complaints with an unwavering eye to maximizing satisfaction with the contract labor system, the Service assiduously adhered to its side of the bargain struck during Operation Wetback. The slightest evidence of grower discontent with either the quantity of braceros or the conditions of their employment was of concern. When contracting fees were raised in 1958 just as the recession was reducing the number of bracero certifications and increasing desertions, Border Patrol reports across the Southwest echoed the fears of officials in Brownsville, Texas: "The mounting resentment to the ever-increasing cost of the Bracero Program may cause some small independent farmers to abandon the Program entirely, thus offering employment opportunities to illegal entrants."[44] Agency officials even occasionally took it upon themselves to launch investigations into *rumors* of employer dissatisfaction, tracking down their sources, and doing their best to address the complaints.[45]

The policy recommendations advanced by the INS to other state agencies consistently focused on eliminating red tape, minimizing regulations, and increasing the direct role of growers and ranchers in the recruitment process. In his 106-page report to the inter-agency American Section of the Joint Commission on Mexican Migrant Labor in

September 1954, Commissioner Swing spent over 70 pages congratulating himself and his agency on the "Wetback Drive" just completed. The last 30 pages were devoted to urging a greater consideration of the needs of growers in the Bracero Program. He concluded,

> The employment in the United States of Mexican laborers lawfully admitted temporarily for agricultural labor should be made as attractive as possible to employers and the employees by means such as (a) giving the employers the types of workers they need in the amount needed, and precisely when needed; (b) making that process as simple as possible . . . ; (c) making the working and living conditions of these imported workers equal to (but not superior to) domestic workers in the same job.[46]

The following year, an untitled INS document linked the continued control of illegal entries to a generous Bracero Program and recommended that the renewed agreements with Mexico include "provisions which would permit the grower to have greater participation in the recruitment and selection of workers."[47] The document encouraged Congress to pass legislation "to permit the importation of temporary [agricultural] workers from certain other countries," pointing out, "If we were not in the position of having to rely almost entirely on Mexican labor for help in some of our agricultural areas, we would be able to negotiate a more workable agreement with Mexico."[48]

These and similar policy recommendations by the immigration agency, which would have relinquished much of the control over the Bracero Program to growers, were never adopted. In part, the reluctance to hand over the reins to employers was related to the foreign policy priorities of the State Department. The role of the State Department, as the official negotiator with Mexico, was to bargain on behalf of U.S. agricultural interests, while at the same time trying to preserve friendly international relations. The State Department commitment to smooth international relations—a commitment grounded in its particular institutional location within the state—meant that it periodically had to give in to Mexican demands, despite the potentially negative repercussions on bracero employers. One such concession had to do with recruitment at the border rather than in the interior of Mexico. Mexico continued to be convinced that border recruitment would encourage illegal immigration and draw workers away from agricultural jobs in the northern regions of Mexico where unemployment was low compared to the interior. However, for bracero employers, border recruitment meant significant savings in time and transportation costs.

In addition, Mexican officials always insisted on having the authority to select bracero candidates in order to maximize the regional economic utility of the labor export program and to minimize the number of repeat braceros who effectively became U.S. residents. Growers, on the other hand, preferred to select workers for themselves and showed a strong preference for experienced braceros. Despite their efforts, State Department negotiators had only limited success on the issue of border recruitment[49] and were never able, within the confines of diplomacy, to wrest from Mexico official control over the bracero selection process.

Immigration officials were undaunted by their lack of success in the official policy arena. Instead, they devised a number of administrative procedures to achieve their goals. Two inventions in particular—the I-100 card system and the "Special" Program—accomplished administratively what had been impossible to negotiate. In addition to cutting the costs and red tape associated with recruiting braceros in the interior of Mexico, the cumulative effect of these administrative inventions was to increase bracero vulnerability and powerlessness. Just as enforcement activities against "subversives" and deserters ensured bracero subordination, these inventions were carefully crafted by the Immigration Service to increase employers' control over bracero workers.

The I-100 card was introduced by Commissioner Swing in 1954 as Operation Wetback was winding down. Issued to braceros at the end of their contracts, the card designated workers as "special" or skilled "key men," as well as "satisfactory," meaning that they had completed their contract without deserting and that the employer was satisfied with their performance. If the bracero was "unsatisfactory" or a "skip," a record was made of it, and no I-100 card was issued. Both of these determinations (whether workers were "special" and/or "satisfactory") were made by the employer. Swing instructed his district directors to let growers know that this was "the opening step in the campaign to facilitate (1) [that] the employer gets the man whom he critically needs . . . (2) that the workers he does receive are satisfactory, and (3) that the unsatisfactory workers . . . will not again be contracted."[50] The Commissioner was not shy about advertising his unilateral action. Writing to Congresswoman Bolton, he explained, "I have recently modified the Bracero Program to permit the issuance of laminated identification cards to braceros who have proved to be satisfactory workers. This will provide a pool of reliable, competent, security screened workers and will, therefore, materially assist the farmers participating in the program."[51]

The procedure did "materially assist the farmers." As implemented by the INS, it allowed growers to circumvent the interior recruitment

Mexico had insisted on, and instead contract workers at the border. This was clearly Swing's intention. Two weeks after he launched the I-100 program, he proposed to the American Section of the Joint Commission on Mexican Migrant Labor (the U.S. delegation of which was comprised of representatives of the federal agencies responsible for the Bracero Program), "Those workers who have returned to Mexico and who have in their possession I-100 cards . . . should not have to obtain letters of reference from local Mexican government officials. . . . They should not have to go to the recruitment center at all but should be handled entirely at a reception center at a point of entry."[52] Swing reasoned that with his new system, the " 'red tape' in Mexico in processing laborers at the recruitment centers there" would be reduced, at enormous savings to employers in turnaround time, expense, and predictability.[53] Swing's Assistant Commissioner explained the plan to a grower: "A procedure has been provided whereby an employer seeking to recontract a Mexican worker who was previously contracted by an employer in the United States may do so without the need of the worker passing through the migratory center in Mexico."[54]

When officials of the State Department and the Department of Labor pointed out that both the letter of the law and friendly international relations prohibited unilaterally establishing border recruitment, semantic ingenuity came to the rescue. Swing explained to Senator Fulbright, "Public Law 78 . . . does not provide for border recruitment but requires that Mexican agricultural workers be recruited through migratory or recruiting stations in the interior of Mexico. Workers recontracted under the I-100 program, *having been previously recruited, are not considered to have again been recruited*."[55]

While Swing invented the distinction between recontracting, which could go on at the border, and first-time contracting over which the Mexican officials retained control, his long-range plan was to reduce the number of braceros who had not been previously contracted and thus could not be "recruited" at the border. In December 1955, the central office wrote to the Southwest regional office, "Effective immediately braceros contracted at reception centers who are holders of micas [I-100 cards] . . . shall be given priority over all other workers when being processed for admission to the United States. Mica [I-100 card] holders shall be singled out for such purposes from among the available braceros."[56] In 1958, the agency considered a plan to *refuse* admission to any bracero who did not already hold an I-100 card. Aware of the politically controversial nature of the scheme, which would have given the INS (and through them, employers) virtually exclusive authority over bracero selection, a senior official of the Southwest region telephoned the central office warning, "Just as soon as this is placed in effect everybody is going to know; [it] can't be just slipped into operation."[57] The official went on to suggest trying to sell the plan as an enforcement measure, arguing that "no one can challenge it if that is what our decision is. . . . This is an inspectional thing." Since immigration inspection is the exclusive jurisdiction of the INS, defining the plan "an inspectional thing" was explored as one way to buttress the legitimacy of the procedure. That summer the plan was dropped, "in view of certain developments," presumably having to do with continued resistance from the Department of Labor and the State Department.[58] Yet, the Service continued to give priority to I-100 card holders and kept the expansion of the I-100 card system as a major goal. By July 1958, the Southwest regional Commissioner could report, "The mica [I-100 card] program has been firmly established, as indicated by statistics showing 75 percent of all entrants in possession of micas."[59]

In addition to allowing for border recruitment, the I-100 program increased grower involvement in the selection of their workers. By eliciting the employer's evaluation of the bracero and recording that evaluation on the I-100 card (which was increasingly required for admission), the Immigration Service in effect handed over to growers substantial control over which braceros were readmitted, and hence ultimately increased growers' control over the workers themselves. The INS Information Bulletin was straightforward in this regard, " . . . any worker found to be satisfactory by his American employer, and issued such a card [an I-100 card], will be permitted to return to the U.S. each year for agricultural employment under the Mexican Agreement."[60]

Immigration officials did not hide their desire to enable growers to select braceros. In their report to the American Section of the Joint Commission on Mexican Migrant Labor, the agency made a case for replacing government officials at recruiting stations with growers' representatives. They concluded the "Recruitment" section of the report, "It is our view that as a long-range objective, Federal assistance should be given only as needed and wanted; that the Federal Government should get out of the 'hiring hall' business. . . ." In the short term, "It is believed that growers should be permitted to have some choice in selecting employees. . . . They are willing for the government to supervise but they do definitely want to participate in the selection of workers. . . . The new procedure for the retention of good workers of their Forms I-100 when they return to Mexico . . . should lay a find groundwork."[61]

In addition to giving growers the authority to determine which braceros would be recontracted, the employer evaluation procedure weeded out what Commissioner Swing called "misfits" who "continue to plague the farmers." Sympathizing with growers who, he said, "do have a real problem in coping with 'problem' laborers such as misfits, malingerers, sloths, 'slow-downers,' 'kleptos,' and similar inept individuals," Swing promised to resolve the problem with the I-100 procedure.[62] Proud of the contribution his new system made to bracero "discipline," the Commissioner informed the Senate Subcommittee on Appropriations in 1956 that a bracero would be able to retain his I-100 card only if "he doesn't break up a lot of equipment and he doesn't skip and he behaves himself properly."[63]

The discipline aspect of the I-100 card system was a central component of bracero control. Nowhere is this more apparent than in the way the system was advertised to workers. A flier disseminated to braceros by the INS announced, "The only purpose of this card is to identify you as a good worker." And then, in capital letters, "THIS IDENTIFICATION CARD IS WORTH A LOT TO YOU. TRY TO EARN ONE. . . ."[64] Growers were quick to capitalize on the control advantages of the rating system. The warning of a representative of a large citrus growers' association, as he selected braceros in the "bull-pen" of a reception center, appears to have been typical:

> If you do a good job and keep out of trouble, we'll give you a good rating, and you will have a better chance of getting another contract some day. The person who will give you your rating will be your foreman. See that you do what he tells you to. . . .[65]

The rating system was used to bar not only slow workers and "agitators," but those who caused any kind of trouble to the employer. Henry Anderson, scholar and noted critic of the Bracero Program, tells of one worker who was rated "satisfactory" and "diligent" after working for eighteen months picking lemons, but whose evaluation changed abruptly to "highly unsatisfactory" and "most uncooperative" after falling ill and requesting to see a doctor.[66]

Despite complaints by the Department of Labor and Mexican officials that the rating smacked of a "blacklist,"[67] its institutionalization quickly became a top INS priority. A memo from officials in the Southwest region after the introduction of the I-100 form assured Commissioner Swing that "nothing will be permitted to hinder its successful operation." The memo referred somewhat obliquely to potential hurdles, but reconfirmed the region's commitment to the procedure. Swing was notified that regional officials had been instructed that "the plan must be put into operation, and that it would be necessary to work out means of overcoming any difficulties, and to take all steps necessary to ensure the success of the program. Proposals advanced to 'water-down' the plan . . . were vetoed."[68]

One difficulty the officials faced in implementing the system was that braceros did not always check out through the reception center, or came through at night or on holidays when no one was on duty, and therefore could not be issued their I-100 cards as they departed. The Acting Regional Commissioner pointed out that since "it is anticipated that their employers will nevertheless request that these workers be recontracted to them at a future date . . . [it may be] desirable and advisable . . . as a matter of cooperation with employers, to have laminated cards mailed to this group."[69] Swing noted emphatically in the margin of the memo, "Do it."

Another difficulty involved Mexico's resistance to the system. In theory, Mexican officials informally agreed to the evaluation procedure. In practice, however, they were understandably reluctant to concede their authority for selecting braceros to a system which, they correctly maintained, had been "installed unilaterally" by the INS.[70] In part, this resistance was related to the desire to shape the Bracero Program in accordance with Mexico's own economic and employment needs. However, other factors were involved as well. One INS memo attributes the reluctance of Mexico to go beyond "lip service" support of the I-100 procedure to the lucrative system of bribes through which Mexican officials effectively sold bracero selections.[71] Expansion of the role of the INS and employers in recontracting braceros reduced the number of braceros recruited from the interior of Mexico and limited the discretion of Mexican regional officials, thereby interrupting a profitable arrangement involving kickbacks and bribes for favorable treatment.

Growers of course were enthusiastic about the initiative. The *Newsletter* of the Agricultural Producers Labor Committee, dated two days after the memo from Swing to his district directors that launched the I-100 program, informed subscribers of the development:

> According to information recently received from Immigration Officials, the new Commissioner, General J.M. Swing has made a very helpful and progressive move in connection with the Agricultural Labor Program, PL 78. We feel this is just another fine example of the splendid cooperation we receive from the U.S. Immigration Department and particularly under the administration of General J.M. Swing.[72]

Individual farmers wrote the agency directly to applaud the new system. A grateful Missouri planter wrote, "The Program [the I-100 card system] made so much sense to me that I wanted to write to tell you how much I appreciate [it]. . . . Please accept my thanks and appreciation for a job well done."[73]

The Special Program for skilled workers ran parallel to the I-100 system and served similar purposes. Invented in the summer of 1954 as Operation Wetback rounded up illegal farm workers for deportation, the Special system allowed farmers and ranchers to designate certain of their skilled illegal workers "Specials." These men were then taken to the border by immigration officials, where the employer could contract them back as braceros, much as illegal aliens had been "paroled" or "dried out" by the Border Patrol a few years earlier. Initially designed to offset the temporary inconvenience of Operation Wetback, the system became a more or less permanent feature of the Bracero Program, whereby employers could be assured of retaining braceros with critical skills.

The Special system was originally conceived as part of the I-100 program. When the I-100 card system was introduced, "Special" status for skilled workers was indicated on the card along with the "satisfactory" determination. Commissioner Swing explained the Special system to Senator Fulbright:

> An employer seeking to recontract the workers whom he had previously contracted or who had been previously contracted by another employer simply supplies a list containing the names of such workers to the Manager of the U.S. reception center who, after approval, furnishes it to the Mexican Consul for approval. The worker then goes to the reception center and is contracted without the need of going through the recruiting or migration center in Mexico.[74]

Thus, not only were "unsatisfactory" workers filtered out through the I-100 card system, but employers could designate precisely which skilled workers they wished to retain. As explained in Swing's letter to Senator Fulbright, this allowed growers both to get their workers at the border and to name specifically which braceros they wanted to recontract, with Mexican officials consigned to after-the-fact "approval." The President of the local Farm Bureau in Laredo, Texas, wrote Senator Lyndon Johnson to explain the advantages of the Special system and to complain of the Labor Department's efforts to confine it to farm hands, thereby excluding Texas ranchers:

> This procedure [specials] was much simplier [*sic*] than the
> method devised by [the Department of Labor] which is
> clumpsy [*sic*], wasteful, and expensive. . . . At a prearranged
> time we take our men to the Bracero Center in Eagle Pass,
> Texas, the men receive a voluntary departure slip, leave for
> Mexico over the International Bridge, return to the American
> side and are taken back to the Bracero center where they enter
> into a new contract. Very simple, inexpensive and no time
> wasted.[75]

After its introduction through the I-100 form, the Special system
quickly evolved into its own separate program, and ultimately became
even more popular with employers than the more general I-100 system,
which, while allowing employers to rate workers, did not by itself
allow them to recontract specific workers. So useful was the Special
Program to growers and ranchers that the Immigration Service repeatedly attempted, with only partial success, to redefine it as a "predesignated worker" system, eliminating the original requirement that Specials be *skilled* workers, and opening it up to any employer who wanted
to recontract the same workers year after year.[76] In INS lingo, the
"Special" worker became the "predesignated" worker, or simply the
"turnaround."[77] The predesignated worker system, in conjunction with
the I-100 program, was hailed by Commissioner Swing as a "workable
labor program" which "served to eliminate the situation under which
the busy farmer and grower was faced with the prospect of using
anonymous workers selected for him by a government agency."[78]

As it turned out, the system was the focus of enormous controversy.
For one thing, Mexican officials preferred to contract out unskilled
labor, rather than the skilled Specials. For another, they feared that
the program would result in the more or less permanent migration of
workers who were continually recontracted to the same employer.
Having viewed the Bracero Program (and their control over who participated) as a way to rotate a large number of farm workers in and out of
the system, Mexican policymakers strenuously resisted the increasingly
quasi-permanent nature of bracero migration. As a result, they never
officially endorsed the Special Program and always refused to include
provisions for it in the international accords. Instead, the system was
decentralized and arranged on an *ad hoc* basis, with Mexican and U.S.
officials at each reception center negotiating over conditions. Mexican
officials in some regions periodically suspended the contracting of
predesignated workers, or Specials, to protest local INS procedures. In
1956, Mexican officials in Hidalgo, Texas, complaining that lists of

predesignated workers were not even submitted to them for prior approval, prohibited recontracting altogether thereby interrupting not only the Special system but the I-100 card program.[79] During the same period, the Mexican Consul at the El Centro, California reception center temporarily stopped processing Specials in response to build-ups of unemployed braceros in the border regions of Mexico, as they waited, sometimes for weeks, to be recontracted.[80]

The decentralized nature of these negotiations and the unpredictability of the system, together with the appeal of Specials to employers, opened the program up to systematic corruption. To obtain permission to rehire Specials at the reception centers, employers often paid Mexican officials a bribe of $12 to $25 per bracero.[81] This "mordida" was sometimes paid directly by the grower to the officials. More often, the grower deducted the bribe from the bracero's future wages, funnelling it through insurance representatives (who handled bracero benefits, such as medical and disability insurance), who took a cut before passing it on to Mexican immigration officials at the reception center. The mordida system was apparently so well entrenched that when a new Mexican chief of immigration at the Piedras Negras reception center refused to become involved in it, Mexico City officials terminated all recontracting of Specials at the center. The INS interpretation of the move was that Mexican officials were worried that growers might continue to extract the now unnecessary mordida from braceros.[82] Whatever the actual motive for the abrupt suspension of Specials contracting, it triggered efforts to establish more predictable ground rules.

In 1956, a group of Mexican and U.S. officials convened in Mexico City to negotiate a uniform and reliable Special Program. The agreement that was reached after prolonged haggling and more than one deadlock, was to limit the number of Specials to 5% of a given employer's workforce, or three workers, whichever was more.[83] Despite this agreement, in the face of continued employer demands, the enticement of the mordida, and the relatively powerless position of Mexico in bracero negotiations, the limitations were rarely observed.

The Special Program was gratefully received by ranchers and growers of specialized crops who had a skilled work force delivered to them at bracero wages. Its popularity with growers was illustrated by the bind the INS found itself in when the Special Program was temporarily suspended in 1958, following protests from Mexican officials and Department of Labor opposition.[84] The District Director at El Paso was apparently "fearful that if he does not continue to arrange for specials to enter at El Paso his relationship with the farmers in that area will be injured."[85] The system was soon reinstated, and immigration officials were spared such negative fallout from the extraordinary success of their own administrative creation.

The I-100 card and the Special system were put in place by the INS as a way to enhance grower control over the government-to-government program established by PL 78. The system allowed for border recruitment and the direct input of employers in selecting workers despite the prohibition of such practices in the bilateral accords, and provided essentially year-round employment of "temporary" workers by repeatedly contracting the same predesignated braceros without having to return them to Mexico. Finally, in shifting responsibility for bracero selection to employers, these administrative inventions contributed substantially to growers' power over the workings of the program, and consequently, to bracero vulnerability. Not only were contract workers by definition captive to their employers—a status carefully guarded by Border Patrol apprehensions of deserters— but in order to secure future employment they were wholly dependent on their employers' perception that they were not "misfits" or troublemakers.

AGENCY AUTONOMY AND BUREAUCRATIC SELF-INTEREST

Administrative inventions such as those created to rationalize the process of selecting and recruiting braceros illustrate the role of the INS in advancing growers' interests. At the same time, there are numerous indications that it played this role at least in part out of its *own* self-interests. As we will see later, there is even evidence that in those relatively few instances in which grower interests did not dovetail with those of the agency, immigration officials gave priority to their own agenda, standing firm against growers' insistent demands. Close attention to the internal decision-making surrounding the establishment and operation of the procedures discussed above reveals an agency that is not a puppet of individual growers—as the instrumentalist "hired hand" analogy implies. Instead, the paper trail of immigration decision-making suggests that the agency was captive to the contradictory pressures of its *own* bureaucratic mandate to keep the immigration of a cheap, abundant, but illegal, labor supply in check.

Prior to Operation Wetback and the entrenchment of the bracero system, the immigration bureaucracy had been faced with "doing the impossible," had abdicated, and had suffered the consequences. By the early 1950s, critics had even proposed dismantling the ineffective Border Patrol and replacing it with an army unit. The expansion of the Bracero Program, and Operation Wetback which made it possible, provided a temporary reprieve from the bureaucracy's catch-22 of having to control illegal immigration despite the demand for cheap and plentiful immigrant labor. In the afterglow of victory in the years following Operation Wetback, General Swing shored up his successes by shifting the agency's focal concern from control of the border, to service to growers through a generous Bracero Program, fully aware that it was the latter that made the former possible.

Communication emanating from the INS and its parent agency, the Department of Justice, indicate that border recruitment through the I-100 card system was an integral part of their enforcement agenda following Operation Wetback. Attorney General Brownell told the Senate Appropriations Subcommittee in the summer of 1954 that, immediately after the enforcement drive, "The first thing we tried to do was to get border recruiting established [through the I-100 card]. We believe that that is very important in the enforcement of the border patrol laws."[86] The following year, Commissioner Swing explained the I-100 card system to the Assistant Secretary of State, "The program is designed principally to assist the Service in its enforcement problems."[87] Deputy Attorney General William Rogers fended off complaints about border recontracting under the I-100 card system in a letter to Senator Carl Hayden, "It [the I-100 card] is of inestimable value in monitoring control of the border against the entry of 'wetbacks.' "[88]

The Special Program was similarly intended to be a buffer against the employment of illegal aliens and therefore an important tool in the agency's enforcement kit. Specials were sometimes thought of as a reward to employers who exchanged their illegal workers for braceros. The District Director in San Antonio reported that ranchers in his area "are entering into the bracero program wholeheartedly and are using more braceros all the time. I think it then becomes our responsibility to do whatever we can to assist them in solving one of the difficult problems they find in the program itself, that of 'specials.' "[89] At a meeting with Arizona ranchers, the Border Patrol explained procedures for obtaining "Special" cowboys. It was proclaimed a success: "The meeting ended in a high spirit of friendliness, and it is felt that our enforcement program benefitted from the meeting."[90]

This enforcement function of the Special Program was most clearly revealed during periodic suspensions of the controversial system. When the processing of Specials at Eagle Pass was briefly halted by Mexican officials in 1958, the Border Patrol warned that unless some way was found to admit the Specials on whom Texas sheep and goat ranchers had come to depend, they would have to deal with several hundred illegal entrants.[91] Fortunately, the officials reported, they were able to elicit the cooperation of the Mexican police "to clear the Mexican side of the Rio Grande in that area of any potential illegal entrants" and to encourage them to relocate in Monterrey, Mexico, where the Special system was still operating. The report concluded appreciatively and apparently with no irony intended, "This harassment of potential illegal entrants is being done as a manner [sic] of cooperation with this Service." Commissioner Swing noted approvingly in the margin of the report, "Good idea and cooperation."

Clearly, the INS had an interest in the I-100 and Special systems in large part because of their utility to growers who might otherwise hire illegal workers. Yet, the systems realized other agency-centered interests as well. For example, the I-100 card was seen as a way to reduce the number of braceros who remained in the United States after their contracts ended, since they could pick up their I-100 cards only upon departure.[92] In addition, the I-100 card was promoted by the overextended immigration bureaucracy as a way to reduce inspection time for the steadily increasing number of braceros. For those pre-screened braceros with the coveted card, immigration inspection at the migratory centers was perfunctory, enabling inspectors to process as many as 100 workers per hour.[93] With the number of braceros increasing every year and INS enforcement successes dependent on the ready availability of this work force to growers, immigration officials approached the inspection process as if it were an assembly line and with a sense of urgency not unlike that which motivated Taylor's time-and-motion studies. In some cases, efficiency studies were implemented to determine the fastest way of processing the most workers effectively, for example replacing officials' written signatures with rubber stamps.[94] Balancing quantity and quality like plant managers, immigration inspectors at the center in Chihuahua, Mexico, calculated that the I-100 card "will permit a longer interview of new recruits without lowering the overall rate of production," which averaged 600 braceros per day and in some cases exceeded 2000.[95] Officials estimated that processing I-100 card holders was almost twice as fast as processing those without the cards.

Last but not least, as Commissioner Swing told the House Subcommittee on Appropriations, the I-100 card system was part of a broader Department of Justice interest in "building up a reservoir of competent tested farm laborers *whose freedom from any subversive tendencies has been thoroughly investigated and established.*"[96] Just as one of the triggers for the elimination of illegal entries during Operation Wetback was Cold War fears of communist infiltration, an important motive behind the I-100 card system was to weed out political undesirables. Prior to being issued a laminated I-100 card, each bracero underwent extensive FBI and CIA checks (referred to as "kickbacks") to determine if they were "clean." As a result, Swing told the House Committee, "we feel that we will have firm control of this large group of laborers."[97]

That the agency's commitment to the I-100 and Special systems was driven largely by its own bureaucratic imperatives—the most critical of which was its mandate to curtail illegal immigration—is further confirmed by evidence that the Immigration Service itself was the *initiator* of these policies, the advantages of which often had to be aggressively "sold" to growers. Rather than simply reacting to growers' demands, INS officials devoted considerable energy to packaging their agenda so as to convince growers to cooperate with them. When the I-100 card was launched in the summer of 1954, Commissioner Swing sent instructions to his district directors informing them of the details of its operation and the importance of "employer education:"

> It should be impressed on the contractors that *they will have to help protect their own interests* in this matter by making sure that laborers en route to Mexico report at reception centers . . . so that the official endorsements may be placed on the cards. . . . And the contractors must be educated to turn in written lists of . . . those workers who are "special" or "satisfactory."[98]

Fliers were sent to bracero employers delineating their role in the system and reminding them of the advantages of their direct participation in the selection of workers. One such notice concluded, "Your whole-hearted cooperation in this program is earnestly solicited. The success of the program will insure that hereafter from season to season employers will be able to obtain the services of satisfactory workers of their own choice."[99] Immigration officials, concerned about the low rate of employer participation in the early stages of the programs, expressed the need for "further missionary work."[100]

They took the initiative in other areas as well, coaching growers on how to use the Bracero Program to their maximum advantage. At one meeting between Rio Grande Valley bracero users and Immigration and Labor Department representatives in the spring of 1956, growers complained of a "lack of flexibility" in the program because it prohibited them from moving braceros from one employer to another according to weather or harvest conditions. According to a district office report, "The farmers requested some change in procedures be made to permit laborers to pick cotton wherever they were needed regardless of the original contract. For example, it was stated that in one area rains might stop the picking of cotton and the pickers would be idle for a week or more while crops in other areas might be ready to pick and not enough pickers available."[101] San Antonio District Director, Walter Sahli, drawing from his experience with the H-2 program in Miami where 30,000 workers were imported by only two large growers' associations, advised the Texas growers that the solution to their problem was to form "fewer and larger associations, thereby broadening the area in which laborers could work and at the same time be employed by their contractor [in this case the association, not the individual employer]."[102]

The INS launched Operation Wetback in its fight with the "windmill" of illegal immigration, and persuaded growers of the advantages of eliminating illegal workers in shoring up the Bracero Program and enhancing control over their work force. Just as the immigration bureaucracy had taken the lead in replacing illegal workers with braceros, it now took the initiative in protecting that strategy, with administrative inventions like the I-100 card system that maximized the agency's ability to admit braceros unilaterally, minimized Mexico's participation, and reinforced grower satisfaction with the program.

Another indication of the agency's assertive posture in entrenching the Bracero Program and thereby achieving is own enforcement objectives was a shift in enforcement priorities and timing. Prior to Operation Wetback, Border Patrol agents were careful to avoid rounding up illegal aliens during periods of peak labor demand. In the years following the 1954 enforcement campaign, this pattern was *reversed*, as Border Patrol reports carefully charted crop conditions and harvest predictions in order to post a sufficient number of enforcement officials in areas of high labor demand.[103] If the realization of the agency's interest in reducing illegal immigration depended on a generous Bracero Program, the continued viability of that program was contingent on INS vigilance over the use of illegal workers, despite any short-term inconvenience to employers that this might entail. A flexible, grower-oriented Bracero Program, and the Border Patrol focus on drying up the supply of illegal labor during the harvest season, were two sides of the same coin—the replacement of illegal workers with braceros.

Finally and perhaps most importantly, the role of agency-centered interests is revealed on those rare occasions when they were at odds with the demands of bracero employers. For, if the INS generally promoted grower interests, *it did not do so unfailingly or irrespective of its own goals.* This was most apparent during an extended controversy over the Special Program—triggered by Mexican objections to the unilateral recruitment—which culminated at an inter-agency, binational conference in Mexico City in April 1956. While both the I-100 card system and the Special Program were applauded by bracero employers, the Special arrangement which allowed them to recontract the same predesignated workers year after year was more central to employers' operations than was the I-100 card system which was more closely identified with INS inspectional procedures. At the Mexico City conference—attended by concerned growers who were not official participants but who showed up anyway, gathering in the halls and waiting impatiently outside the meeting rooms—a rumor was circulated that the Mexican government would not negotiate on the issue of Specials unless the I-100 card was eliminated.[104] According to INS reports of the meeting, growers were quick to let their priorities be known: "The growers frankly stated that if the representations made to them were true, they would request that the I-100 card be abandoned, notwithstanding their past support of the program."[105] An INS representative at the meeting reported ominously from his informal discussions with growers, "If the [I-100] card blocks the 'Special' program, the farmers would not feel kindly towards the I & N Service."[106]

Despite persistent pleas from growers and ranchers, the INS did not back down. Instead, immigration officials insisted in their informal conversations in the lobby of the conference hotel that the "INS was 100% behind both programs" and that "both programs are necessary."[107] Under the circumstances, what this implied was a greater commitment to their I-100 invention than to the Special Program, which was the pet of bracero employers and which was now jeopardized by the agency's position. Under fire from growers, the Department of Labor, and Mexican officials, immigration agency negotiators maintained a "firm stand on the I-100."[108]

The controversy over Specials was left to percolate, the conference having ended with no formal agreement between the Mexican and U.S. delegations.[109] The record does not make it clear—nor do the INS representatives seem to have been certain—whether the Mexicans had in fact imposed an ultimatum involving an exchange of the I-100 card for Specials, or whether the ultimatum was a politically motivated rumor. What *is* clear is that the INS, despite pleas from growers, was unwilling to forfeit its I-100 system to facilitate negotiations on the Special Program.

This capacity for independent, agency-centered action periodically surfaced when dealing with requests for favors from individual growers as well. One of the clearest illustrations of such agency independence occurred in the winter of 1958, when an interruption in the recruiting of Specials threatened to curtail the supply of Texas ranch hands. Abner Sneed, Immigration's Special Projects Officer in the Southwest region, warned the central office by telephone that the suspension of Specials had alarmed members of the enormous Texas Sheep and Goat Raisers Association. He reported further that the president of the association, T. A. Kincaid, planned to call Commissioner Swing to request that their current Specials not be required to depart at the end of their contracts, since it would now be impossible to recontract them once they stepped across the Mexican border: "He wants INS to just permit them to remain and to direct the Border Patrol not to pick them up even though their contracts have expired. His alternative will be to request that if they are required to depart they be paroled into the United States."[110] Instead of the anticipated telephone call, Kincaid and a fellow rancher, accompanied by Congressman O. C. Fisher of Texas, paid a personal visit to Commissioner Swing to plead their case.[111] Following the meeting, a top immigration official contacted Kincaid and informed him that "any permission to employ the workers beyond the fifteen day grace period would be highly unadvisable, both from our standpoint and perhaps for the welfare of the growers as well. . . ."[112] Swing then called Congressman Fisher to "explain" that "the Service is not in a position to accede to Mr. Kincaid's request."[113] This is not to say that the Service was unsympathetic or that they ignored the ranchers' concerns altogether. In fact, they initiated aggressive lobbying efforts with the Department of Labor and officials in Mexico City on behalf of the Texas ranchers in an effort to have the suspension of the Special Program rescinded.[114] What they were unwilling to do, however, was to violate their own enforcement priorities—and perhaps jeopardize the long-term survival of the program—at the behest of this group of albeit powerful and politically well-connected ranchers.

If the INS sometimes acted like the "hired hand on the farm," the analogy is clearly inappropriate. Capable of periodically fending off pressure from individual growers, and more often taking a proactive rather than a reactive role in policymaking, the agency catered to growers mainly because it had a vested interest in their satisfaction with the contract labor system. As fears mounted in the early 1950s over the fiscal and political costs of increasing illegal migration, criticism of the ineffective agency had escalated, and there were even charges that the Border Patrol should be abolished. Remember that

Commissioner Swing was appointed in 1954 largely on his word that he would regain control of the border. With his political reputation on the line and the very survival of the agency at stake, Swing recognized that his success depended on providing growers and ranchers with an attractive alternative to the illegal labor supply. Faced with having to control the border without drying up an important source of agricultural labor, the Bracero Program gave the beleaguered immigration agency a temporary respite from the stubborn contradictions to which it had been subjected for years. Apprehension statistics in the years following Operation Wetback reveal the efficacy of this solution. From 1956 to 1964, apprehensions of illegal aliens averaged fewer than 80,000 a year, down from approximately 400,000 a year in the eight-year period preceding the enforcement drive (see Appendix A).

STRUCTURAL CONTRADICTIONS AND INDIVIDUAL HASSLES: THE PERSONAL AS POLITICAL

Despite the apparent accomplishments of the INS under the leadership of Commissioner Swing, in the first few years of his reign the retired army general was the target of recurring congressional complaints. In February 1955, members of the House Subcommittee on Appropriations lambasted Swing for his reorganization of the Service, focusing on the location of the new regional headquarters. Representative John Rooney (D-New York), Chair of the influential House Committee, pointed out angrily that putting the Northeast regional office in Burlington, Vermont (where there was not even a train station at the time), and the Southeast office in Richmond, Virginia, left New York City in the Northeast region and Newark, New Jersey, in the Southeast region—two of the busiest offices in the country—hundreds of miles away from their respective regional headquarters.[115]

Three weeks later, the Subcommittee on Legal and Monetary Affairs of the Committee on Government Operations held hearings on the "Reorganization of the Immigration and Naturalization Service," and used the opportunity to interrogate Swing at length on his policy of rotating career officers through different districts, often over the officers' protests.[116] The hearing periodically reverted to an angry chorus of congressional charges that Swing was arrogant and unresponsive, as illustrated by one member's complaint that "[i]t has been impossible to get through a phone call to General Swing, and he has even failed to return my telephone calls when I have asked something that I have thought was of particular importance."[117]

The following year, two full-blown scandals haunted the Commissioner. The first came to be known as the "Mexican Maid Incident." Senate Democratic leader Lyndon Johnson, during appropriation hearings in 1956, abruptly changed the subject from budget allocations to ask Swing, "General, do you have a Mexican maid?" The dialogue continued:

> General Swing: "I certainly do."
> Senator Johnson: "Was she recruited through the Immigration Service?"
> General Swing: ". . . This is a Mexican maid who was serving in a restaurant in Juarez, and while I was on one of my inspection trips down in El Paso, I said to the district director, 'It is hard to get a maid in Washington. I wonder if there is any little Mexican girl over in Juarez who would like to immigrate and come over and go to work for me.' . . . . Is this a public hearing?"
> Senator Johnson: "Yes."
> General Swing: "This is off the record. We do have undercover men in all the other towns across the border. Will that please not be—"
> Senator Johnson: "General, I want to warn you it is pretty difficult to keep it off the record when you have a bunch of newspapermen here."[118]

The *New York Times* printed the exchange verbatim, along with the allegation that Swing and other agency officials had used government funds and personnel to recruit personal maids.[119] But the controversy was soon overshadowed by a more extended investigation of charges of misappropriation of funds within the agency. In the summer of 1956, the Legal and Monetary Affairs Subcommittee held hearings on a series of hunting trips in Mexico by Swing and other Immigration Service employees allegedly on government funds and with INS aircraft and jeeps.[120] The interrogation of Swing lasted two grueling days and was punctuated with charges of deceit and dishonesty. Relations between the subcommittee and the agency deteriorated as the investigation proceeded, with the subcommittee chair, Robert Mollohan of West Virginia, accusing the Service of "stony silence or outright refusal" in response to requests for records and information.[121]

The animosity between influential members of Congress and the new Immigration chief was further reflected in a two-year struggle over the appointment of two former army generals—Maj. Gen. Frank H. Partridge and Brig. Gen. Edwin B. Howard—as aides to Commissioner

Swing. Because the two had been military officers, their appointment to the civilian post required special legislation. House hearings and debates on the appointments reveal widespread and deep hostility toward Swing.[122] Not only was there repeated objection to the "militarization" of the immigration agency, but Swing's integrity was impugned by members of Congress who charged him with "cronyism" in selecting former army buddies for the positions.[123] The Commissioner's "arrogance" and unresponsiveness to Congress were berated by others. Representative Wayne Hays (D-Ohio) was perhaps the most outspoken: "I have met a lot of arrogant people in my time, but what I could say about General Swing and the arrogance that he shows in that position would only be limited by what would be printable in the Congressional Record. . . . He made the statement that if he had to be bothered with talking to a bunch of Congressmen he would be damned if he would not resign the job." Representative Hays opposed the appointments entirely on the grounds that they were Swing's choice: ". . . I am suspicious of the men in question because they were picked by General Swing. . . ."[124] After a two-year battle, the former army generals were finally confirmed, but only after persistent pressure from President Eisenhower, a West Point classmate and personal friend of General Swing.[125]

A paradox begins to take shape here. Swing managed to reverse the long-standing pattern of illegal employment in southwestern agriculture, and did so at least in part as a result of the extensive authority that Congress seemingly so gladly abdicated to him. And yet, despite these accomplishments and the extensive discretion that Congress conceded—at times, even aggressively transferred—to the agency, those responsible for immigration matters in Congress were perpetually disgruntled with the Immigration Commissioner during the early years of his administration. Those who most vociferously attacked Swing were Democrats, and therefore the assaults took on a somewhat partisan cast. But this was not merely another turf war between political parties, as evidenced by the conspicuous absence of rebuttals in defense of President Eisenhower's appointee on the part of Republican members of Congress.

Two possible explanations for Swing's difficulties with Congress come to mind. First, one might argue that the congressional disapproval should not be surprising, precisely because Swing had successfully brought an end to the indiscriminate use of illegal labor—a system that for so many years benefitted the economically and politically powerful growers and ranchers of the Southwest and their representatives in Congress. One former immigration official, who worked his way up the ranks to become a district director during Swing's tenure, explained in a personal letter to the author: "Of course this round-up of all illegals brought on much opposition. . . . I believe that was the main reason Congress wanted him [Swing] out. . . . When there is a general widespread movement to apprehend illegals, there will be opposition from wealthy farmers . . . who are losing their employees. . . . Their Congressmen must take action . . . to voice their opposition and it is the Commissioner who has to answer."[126]

This interpretation, however, is contradicted by the fact that most growers, after initial grumblings from some quarters, *applauded* Swing for the uniformity and efficiency of Operation Wetback and for his exchange of plentiful braceros for illegal aliens, and in fact cooperated with the Commissioner in his efforts. Furthermore, it is noteworthy that, with the exception of Senator Johnson from Texas, the most venomous attacks on Swing did not come from the southwestern states where most illegal aliens had been employed, but from regions of the country where Operation Wetback and the bracero work force were largely irrelevant.

One might argue alternatively that congressional disapproval was merely a straightforward response to the corruption and misappropriation of funds with which Swing and the agency were charged. Perhaps, in other words, the troubles that beset the Commissioner could be explained simply as a product of his own misbehavior. However, this too seems unlikely, given the enthusiasm and energy with which some members of Congress sought to uncover the slightest evidence of misconduct, and the passion with which they accused him. This is not to suggest that Swing's behavior was irreproachable, but that the repeated and aggressive nature of congressional investigations suggest that there was more at issue here than Swing's integrity, or even his personal "arrogance."

Clues to unraveling the paradox surface in an extraordinarily candid oral history of Commissioner Swing, carried out several years after he left office.[127] In this extensive interview, Swing discussed his reorganization of the immigration bureaucracy and the logic behind the location of the new regional headquarters. His official explanation for the establishment of regions and district offices accountable to the regions had always been that it increased bureaucratic efficiency,[128] but the oral history discloses a different rationale. In this interview, from which Swing's heirs unfortunately will not permit direct quotation, Swing gleefully volunteered that he decentralized the INS and *deliberately* placed the new regions in out-of-the-way places in order to make it difficult for immigration lawyers to access them, and to insulate the agency from the input of individual members of Congress. He matter-of-factly told the interviewer that the Northeast region was put in Burlington, Vermont precisely so that it would be hard to get to; that the Southeast region was placed in Richmond, Virginia to get it out of Washington; and that he put the Western regional headquarters in a former women's prison on San Pedro Island in order to isolate it. Previously, Swing explained, some members of Congress had virtual veto power over the activities of local district offices in their state, even determining hirings and promotions of the lowest-level employees. By placing policymaking power in the regional offices, and locating them in remote places, Swing intended to reduce this kind of congressional intervention.[129]

Commissioner Swing attempted to reduce congressional influence in other ways as well. The rotation of personnel to which some members of Congress objected was part of a hiring and promotion system that Swing installed in an effort to limit the effect of congressional patronage on personnel decisions in the bureaucracy. As Swing told his interviewer with characteristic bluntness, he launched the promotion system as a way to keep Congress out of the internal affairs of his agency.[130]

Swing was convinced that these efforts to wrench control away from influential members of Congress underlay the repeated investigations into his conduct. The Commissioner argued that the Mexican hunting trip allegations—the scandal that plagued him the longest and did most to undermine his reputation—were the consequence of a vendetta. He explained that the Speaker of the House, John McCormack, had previously exerted enormous control over the Boston district office, influencing hirings and promotions at all levels. According to Swing's account, when he let it be known that he intended to break McCormack's stronghold on the Boston office, the Speaker of the House set out to get him, encouraging Robert Mollohan, chair of the Legal and Monetary Affairs Subcommittee, to investigate Swing's hunting trips.[131]

Swing undoubtedly had a self-interest in defining the hunting trips scandal as a product of congressional spite rather than his own wrong-doing. It makes sense, however, that Swing's efforts to wrest control from members of Congress who had captured local INS districts would confront resistance and trigger congressional indignation at the new Commissioner's "arrogance." In other words, beyond the issue of the Commissioner's culpability in these scandals, perhaps the passion with which he was indicted and the persistence with which his behavior was probed were related to the fact that he had unceremoniously expelled a number of senior members of Congress from their personal king-doms, and through his reorganization moved decisively to limit inter-ference in the immigration bureaucracy. While members of Congress were more than willing to abdicate general policymaking power to the Immigration Service and maximize agency discretion as a way to dodge the windmill of illegal immigration, they were apparently less keen on relinquishing the reins of the mini-empires that they used to dispense favors and court constituents.

A number of political scientists have observed that the electoral system provides incentives for Congress to delegate authority over substantive, but controversial, policy issues to administrative agencies while retaining jurisdiction over pork barrel projects and other patron-age-building ventures.[132] From this perspective, it makes sense that while Congress intentionally abdicated authority for the no-win politi-cal issue of immigrant labor to the less visible immigration agency, individual members of Congress were outraged by Swing's efforts to limit access to the "patronage-building" potential of the agency.

Just as the bureaucratic dilemmas facing the INS derived from the underlying contradictions surrounding immigration, Swing's personal troubles may have been grounded in the nature of those dilemmas and his response to them. Swing came to power on the pledge that he would end illegal immigration, and staked his reputation on his ability to do so. Reducing illegal immigration with Operation Wetback and the entrenchment and expansion of the Bracero Program was possible only through the exercise of substantial agency initiative and independence. Such agency independence, however, is difficult to contain. As Swing moved to regain control of the border by regaining control of the bureaucracy, he incurred the wrath of those whose political fiefdoms were thereby diminished. His personal struggles thus mirrored the bureaucratic catch-22. Hired with the mandate to check illegal immi-gration, Swing's transformation of the Immigration Service from a crippled bureaucratic backwater to a proactive and independent agency meant violating significant political territories, and in the process pay-ing a stiff personal and political toll.

Swing's account of his subsequent damage-control efforts reveals a tactician not unwilling to court Congress with selective favor trading and personal attentions. He stretched the letter of the law to grant a visa to a child from Greece being adopted by personal friends of Senator James Eastland (D-Mississippi), ranking member of the Senate Immigration Committee, and afterwards received the Senator's uncon-ditional support.[133] Following a complaint by the secretary of Repre-sentative Francis Walter, democratic Chair of the House Immigration

Subcommittee, that he had never been to the White House, Swing invited the representative for cocktails with President Eisenhower. The former Commissioner remembered that Chairman Walter originally had given him a difficult time, but that after the visit to the White House they gradually became close friends. In his oral history, Swing even divulged how he won over his archenemy, House Speaker John McCormack—a devout Catholic—by obtaining the mediation of the Chief of Chaplains in San Francisco where Swing had donated money to rebuild a Catholic chapel some years earlier.[134] In 1958, the Commissioner received a large pay raise from Congress, amidst applause for his accomplishments.[135] By 1961, he had so much support from Congressional immigration leaders that newly elected President John Kennedy was temporarily persuaded not to replace him.[136] The Commissioner was a brilliant strategist, and just as he adroitly navigated the bureaucratic dilemmas confronting his agency by eliciting the cooperation of growers during Operation Wetback, he ultimately won over many of his most vociferous critics in Congress.

THE DOUBLE-EDGED SWORD

By legalizing the supply of workers who otherwise would have entered illegally, the Bracero Program temporarily deflected the contradictions surrounding illegal immigration and thereby relieved the pressure on the INS. But those contradictions by no means disappeared, nor did the conflicts that they gave rise to. As we have just seen, the agency independence carved out by Swing triggered a series of battles with Congress. Beyond these micro-level political feuds, however, more fundamental strains were increasingly apparent. For the bracero solution to the problem of illegal immigration itself contained a dynamic that threatened to exacerbate the problem. Specifically, the liberal bracero policies that increased the scope of the program tended both to intensify the dependence of southwestern agriculture on Mexican labor and to enlarge the pool of potential immigrants. In other words, the very policies that held illegal immigration in check by legalizing and expanding the flow, simultaneously increased the size of the potential illegal immigrant population. This heightened the pressure on the Immigration Service when the Bracero Program came to a close. In the short run, the expanding pool of aspiring braceros attracted north to the border in anticipation of work contracts constituted an ongoing threat to immigration enforcement.

The first indication that immigration officials were aware of the double-edged nature of their generous bracero politics surfaced during an exchange between the Chief of the Border Patrol in 1951, Willard Kelly, and Representative W.R. Poage of Texas, during hearings before the House Committee on Agriculture. The debate centered on a provision in H.R. 3048 (a precursor to the bill that later became PL 78) that would have institutionalized the practice of legalizing workers already in the United States. Section 501 of the bill introduced by Representative Poage discussed the conditions under which braceros would be recruited, with Article 1 specifying that the bracero pool would include "any such workers temporarily in the United States," including, presumably, illegal workers.[137] Section 504 reiterated the intention of transforming illegal workers into braceros: "Workers recruited under this title . . . shall be admitted to the United States subject to the immigration laws (*or if already in, and otherwise eligible for admission to, the United States shall be permitted to remain therein*) for such time and under such conditions as may be specified by the Attorney General. . . ."[138]

Although the INS had for years paroled illegal aliens to employers as braceros and legalized others with a symbolic step across the border, the agency balked at formalizing these practices. First, Kelly argued, it was unnecessary since the Immigration Service already had assumed the authority to legalize the illegal, which, he admitted was a "strained construction" of the law, but nonetheless operative and effective. Second, Kelly worried that formalizing the practice would compound enforcement problems:

> Our concern with this particular language is not with our authority or lack of authority to do this. Our concern with it is that it seems to *require* us to legalize aliens who have entered the United States illegally. . . . Our problem has increased from a few thousand 10 years ago to over a half-million this past year. . . . and this sort of provision will just serve to suck them into the United States in greater numbers. . . . That is our objection to this language. . . . *We are opposed to it, because it will aggravate our problem.*[139]

Immigration officials understood that they walked a fine line between using the legalization procedure as a way to reduce the illegal population without interrupting the labor supply, and triggering an ever increasing stream of illegal migration. Keeping the practice informal, to be used only as necessary, helped them navigate that line.[140]

During the peak years of the Bracero Program, the "potential illegal entrants" referred to in monthly Border Patrol reports were almost without exception aspiring braceros who came to the border in the hopes of securing work contracts:

> Small groups of hopeful braceros are arriving at the Monterrey contracting station in anticipation of early employment. The Mexican Department of the Interior has been advising workers to refrain from congregating at these border points until they have been notified that a need exists. However, they are continuing to arrive in spite of these warnings. . . . These workers if unable to obtain a bracero contract will probably attempt to enter the United States illegally.[141]

> The normal seasonal build-up of potential illegal entrants in adjacent Mexican areas continues. This situation stems principally from bracero aspirants who go to the recruitment centers in hopes of obtaining contracts, but who are either rejected for various reasons or do not have the five hundred pesos reported necessary to pay Mexican officials. . . . Interrogation of apprehended aliens reveals that approximately fifty percent of those who have entered the United States illegally . . . have made some effort to secure contracts as braceros.[142]

> A seasonal build-up of potential illegal entrants in the Juarez Valley area continued into the month of September. This build-up occurred due to information circulated in Mexico that laborers would be contracted locally.[143]

In some instances, oversupplies were the direct product of the INS inventions, discussed earlier, that were designed to enhance grower satisfaction with the program and hence cut *down* on the use of illegal labor. For example, in the summer of 1956 there were reports that a "massing" of braceros with I-100 cards, under the impression that the cards were border crossing permits, "were stranded without jobs in the border towns of San Luis and Mexicali."[144]

The expansion of the Bracero Program and immigration policies that catered to growers provided the agency with a way to circumvent the contradictions that had crippled it for years, as its bureaucratic mission to control the border was pitted against the economic utility of the illegal labor force. At the same time, however, the program stoked the migratory movement, forcing the agency to work ever harder to promote the contract system as a substitute for the illegal flow. As the cycle gathered momentum, the bracero "solution" provided the only conceivable escape from the quagmire, and at the same time deepened it.

When Attorney General Brownell came before Congress to discuss the Immigration Service budget in December 1953, he highlighted the social and political costs of continuing to ignore illegal immigration and the difficulties of controlling it, given its central role in Southwest agriculture. He told the Congressional Subcommittee on Appropriations that the only answer was to shape a contract labor system to fit the needs of growers:

> If we can get them [Mexican workers] in here under a system whereby they will be in here legally, we might not have to increase the border patrol. ... I think the present contract could be changed so that many of these people [illegal aliens] who are needed there for the so-called stoop labor could come in legally. ... There are certain provisions in the contract that seem to make many of the employers ... feel there is no use trying to comply with all of the red tape, and they kind of throw up their hands and say "let them come in anyway!"[145]

The evidence presented here on the INS administration of the Bracero Program in the mid-1950s suggests that the agency actively pursued the strategy Brownell described to Congress, and that it did so in large part to prevent growers from "throw[ing] up their hands" and returning to illegal workers. Furthermore, two things seem clear from the paper trail left by agency decision-makers and the Border Patrol front line. First, the INS played to growers not because it was a lackey of agricultural interests, as in the instrumentalist version of the relationship between the state and capital, nor simply because "the state" must maximize capital accumulation, as Marxist structuralists would have it. Rather, the agency tailored its bracero policies to growers because this advanced its own interests as an administrative agency saddled with an official mission at odds with growers' appetite for illegal workers. Only by providing to growers the optimum quantity and quality of contract labor could the Immigration Service hope to reduce the tide of illegal immigration that had tarnished its reputation and eroded its legitimacy. Of course, to point out that the Service pursued agency-centered interests is not to say that it experienced autonomy in any real sense. Nor is it to deny altogether the partial truths embedded in the instrumentalist and structuralist depictions. For both the dilemma that confronted the agency and the employer-oriented strategies required to resolve it were firmly rooted in the structural contradictions surrounding illegal immigration and the necessity not to interrupt the flow of cheap labor to agriculture.

Second, while Brownell was right that catering to growers in the implementation of the Bracero Program could, in the short run and in most cases, alleviate the problem of illegal immigration, the underlying contradictions were not resolved, but instead resurfaced elsewhere. As we have seen, the expansion of the contract labor system did legalize the previously illegal flow, but in the process it created new pools of potential illegal entrants. As growers became more dependent on Mexican farm labor, and Mexican workers were drawn into the migratory circuit in ever-increasing numbers, the long-term enforcement problems of the immigration agency were compounded. In the short term, aspiring braceros comprised a constant threat of illegal entry, for which the only defense was more of the same.

In addition, as we will see in the next chapter, the INS resolution to its bureaucratic dilemmas triggered a head-on collision with the other federal agency that administered the Bracero Program, namely the Department of Labor. Indeed, the bracero "solution" in some ways transformed what was a bureaucratic dilemma into a conflict between these two federal agencies, both of which had responsibility for the program, and each of which had its own set of official mandates.

CHAPTER 5

"WRANGLING" WITH THE DEPARTMENT OF LABOR

The Immigration Service operated within a network of federal agencies that jointly administered the Bracero Program. In the early years the Department of Agriculture had primary responsibility for the program. Consistent with the emphasis on the agricultural emergency that was declared during the war as a result of dwindling farm labor supplies, Congress put the agriculture agency in charge of coordinating the activities of the federal bureaucracies that implemented the emergency labor system. But, as the war came to a close and with it the wartime labor emergency, statutory authority for the program shifted to the United States Employment Service (USES) and the Department of Labor (DOL). PL 893, passed seven months after Congress had terminated the wartime program, effectively resurrected the system by directing the USES to take over responsibility for "supervising" and "coordinating" the transportation of Mexican contract workers.

The statutory primacy of the DOL was reasserted in PL 78 and its subsequent amendments. Indicative of the self-conscious emphasis on "protecting" domestic labor from the effects of importing hundreds of thousands of foreign workers, the law that served as the blueprint for the program from 1951 until its demise gave central authority to the Secretary of Labor. PL 78 directed the Labor Secretary to recruit workers, operate reception centers, provide transportation, and ensure that employers abided by their contracts. It also established that no braceros could be imported until the Secretary of Labor had certified that domestic labor was unavailable, that employment of the foreign workers would not "adversely affect" domestic workers, and that the employer had made "reasonable efforts" to hire domestic labor at comparable wages.

The role of the INS was ostensibly more limited: "Workers recruited under this title . . . shall be admitted to the United States subject to the immigration laws . . . for such time and under such conditions as may be specified by the Attorney General [and through him, the Immigration Commissioner]." While the DOL technically had a larger role under the statute in determining the contours of the program, in practice the INS—and its parent agency, the Department of Justice—exercised enormous power through its broad control over the conditions of entry and departure. This division of labor, established both in the statute and in the field, required that the two federal agencies coordinate their activities and share power. The partnership was not always a harmonious one.

The I-100 card system was a continual source of conflict. Soon after it was initiated in 1954, DOL officials objected to the employer rating of braceros, a practice they said had "the hallmark of a blacklist."[1] A year later, the Assistant Secretary of Labor explained to Assistant Secretary of State Henry Holland, who was attempting to mediate the ongoing disagreement, that the Labor Department "continues to have serious reservations" about the I-100 card system which, he complained, was "unilaterally put into effect" by the Immigration Service.[2] Officials in the two agencies tried to reconcile their differences through inter-agency meetings, but even planning for these affairs involved the exchange of antagonistic memos, referred to by one exasperated INS official as "all these interminable wrangling letters."[3]

So divided were the agencies on this issue, that immigration officials accused their counterparts at the Labor Department of attempting to sabotage the I-100 card system by encouraging Mexico to oppose it. When Mexican officials temporarily suspended the recontracting of braceros with I-100 cards, immigration agents blamed the Labor Department for being "instrumental in this matter" and for "working very closely with the Mexican officials with the express purpose of influencing them against the program."[4] Antagonism over the I-100 card culminated at the 1956 Mexico City conference discussed in the last chapter. Apparently based on earlier communication with Mexican officials on the evils of the I-100 card system, DOL delegates informed growers that unless the INS agreed to relinquish its I-100 card, Mexico would veto the Special Program. DOL representatives may have fabricated this story of a Mexican ultimatum; whether or not the rumor of an ultimatum was true, the point is that the Labor Department engaged in aggressive behind-the-scenes efforts, with growers as well as with Mexican officials, to undermine the I-100 card.[5] For the duration of the conference, they continued to be unresponsive to the Immigration Service's pleas to support the system. An immigration official in attendance at the meeting described his encounter with Al Misler, Labor Department delegate: "He [Misler] said. . . . that if it must be either the cards or the predesignated workers [Specials], they could only support the latter; that otherwise Labor would 'lose' and INS would 'win'."[6] The controversy finally died down in 1957 when the Western Regional Commissioner instructed his district directors and the Border Patrol to discontinue the employer evaluation procedure, and to withhold I-100 cards only from braceros who had deserted, or were otherwise inadmissible under the immigration laws.[7] Hostilities, however, did not cease.

When Assistant Secretary of Labor Newell Brown extended a formal invitation to Commissioner Swing to send representatives to a conference in Mexico City in 1958 for the purpose of institutionalizing the Special Program, the Commissioner conspicuously declined, pointedly recommending that "representatives of employers of agricultural labor" go instead.[8] Swing's refusal to participate contrasts markedly with his appeal to the Assistant Secretary of State two years earlier to be included in all meetings about the Bracero Program: "I would like to respectfully request that representation of this Service be present at all times during such consultations [with Mexican officials]. I will appreciate it if you will keep me informed concerning the time and place of such meetings."[9] He had dispatched a similar request to Assistant Secretary of Labor Rocco Siciliano, urging that "[i]n any such discussion with the Mexican Government concerning this program . . . it is most important that representatives of this Service attend so that we are timely and fully informed concerning any developments."[10] The Assistant Secretary of Labor speculated that Swing refused to attend the 1958 conference "anticipating failure and not wishing to be associated with it."[11] It is more likely that he was not interested in formalizing a Special Program distinct from the I-100 card system. After all, Swing renamed Specials "predesignated workers" and was attempting to ensure that all braceros with I-100 cards could be recontracted. Any institutionalization of the old Special Program in which predesignated workers must have special skills would have defeated his plan. Whatever Swing's motives for not participating, immigration officials reported with barely restrained pleasure that the Labor Department had "failed to accomplish their objective in each proposal they have made"[12] and had "received the coolest reception" in years from their Mexican counterparts.[13]

In 1960, the DOL reversed its position on Specials, after years of vacillation, and put an end to the program that provided growers and ranchers with workers of their own choosing, often on a year-round basis. Since, under PL 78, no workers could be admitted without certification of a labor need, the DOL refusal to certify Specials brought an abrupt end to the practice that for six years provided an administrative detour around many of the restrictions of the official recruiting system. INS policymakers were predictably outraged, denouncing the decision as an "arbitrary and unilateral action in which this Service had no part."[14]

By the time the Bracero Program wound down in the 1960s, communication between the two agencies had deteriorated substantially. Information about DOL activities that circulated within the Immigration Service increasingly took on an air of enemy intelligence reports. Nowhere was this more evident than in Immigration reports of the Senate hearings on migrant labor in July, 1963, at which both Immigration and Labor testified. Immediately upon his return from the hearings, Assistant Immigration Commissioner Irvin Shrode dashed off a report to the Deputy Associate Commissioner including a full transcript of Labor Department testimony. Under Secretary of Labor Henning had made reference to Public Law 414 (Section H-ii), under which workers from the British West Indies and several other countries are admitted temporarily (primarily to Florida and other East Coast agricultural areas). In the course of his testimony, Henning made unfavorable comparisons between the H-2 program, administered primarily by the INS, and the Bracero Program for which the Department of Labor had more official responsibility. In addition to providing the full transcript of Henning's exchanges with various Senators, a perturbed Shrode offered his summary of the testimony:

> He [Under Secretary Henning] made the following assertions during discussions after completing his formal statement: . . . That the farm labor programs under Public Law 414 (Immigration and Nationality Act) are administered by the Immigration and Naturalization Service and that such programs do not provide the same safeguards as Public Law 78 and that such programs could be used in strike-breaking activities. The last statement mentioned was purely gratuitous. . . . It is my opinion that a statement concerning "strike-breaking" was uncalled for. . . . (Note: Mr. Henning's statements concerning Public Law 414 were made almost in an undertone and I was unable to record them verbatim. However, I am certain the above is what was said in substance. His recorded testimony will be checked when available).[15]

Squabbling and inter-agency jealousy ran far deeper than disagreements over the details of individual bracero policies. Clues about the more fundamental nature of these disagreements periodically surface in the archival record. Of primary importance are voluminous Labor Department records that speak to the continuous pressures the agency experienced, emanating simultaneously from growers and domestic farm workers.

THE DEPARTMENT OF LABOR UNDER SIEGE

Labor Department implementation of the contract labor system in the mid-1950s generally satisfied growers and their representatives in Congress. The decentralized nature of the program's operation was well suited to direct input from the users of bracero labor. Within the DOL, the Bureau of Employment Security (BES) had replaced the old USES as the division that was officially responsible for the Bracero Program. Most important decisions were made in the local branches of the BES, the regional offices of the State Employment Services, and the Farm Placement Services. Ellis Hawley describes the effects of this decentralization in California:

> . . . since the whole farm placement system had once been a part of the Department of Agriculture, the men who ran it continued to think in terms of supplying farm labor, not in terms of protecting or finding jobs for farm workers. Repeatedly, such men showed a disposition to accept employers' own determination of "labor shortages," agree to whatever "prevailing wage" the employer associations were willing to pay, and then to recruit a foreign labor force.[16]

It was not just that these officials were "disposed" to believing employers, or that they tended to "think in terms of supplying labor." More direct factors were involved as well. In some areas there was a revolving door between bracero users and the Labor agencies that implemented the program. As Anderson described it:

> The former chief of the California Farm Placement Service is now manager of the Imperial Valley Farmers Association. The Department of Labor field man for Imperial Valley resigned his job to organize a second association of bracero-users in that area. The former manager of the Coachella Valley Growers' Association now manages the bracero recruiting station at

Empalme, Mexico. The former supervisor of the Farm Placement Service in Ventura County is now managing a bracero-
users' association in that county. And so on. The ties that bind
are reminiscent of those in the industrial-military complex.[17]

The ties were sometimes institutionalized in the form of advisory
committees whose sole purpose was to influence Labor Department
policy. Ernesto Galarza, scholar and farm labor activist, confronted
Labor Secretary Willard Wirtz in 1963 with documentation that the
Western region of the BES in the mid-1950s "submitted improperly to
the domination of a committee of agricultural producers and farm
labor employers of California and Arizona." He claimed that "[t]he
group was organized as the Regional Foreign Labor Operations Advisory Committee. . . . the Director of Region X [the Western region of
the Bureau of Employment Security], Mr. Glenn E. Brockway, formally
obligated himself to be responsible to this committee of private employers . . . and to report to that committee on actions taken by him on
its recommendations."[18] Indicative of the grower orientation of the
Western region of the BES, when Galarza authored an exposé of
employer abuses of the contract labor system,[19] Brockway and his
associates wrote an angry rebuttal, drawing on the input of growers,
and engaging personnel and resources from Farm Placement Service
branches throughout California. The published rebuttal was distributed with Labor Department funds and redistributed by growers' associations.[20] As we have seen, the nature of grower influence on the
Bracero Program was far more complex than Galarza's instrumentalist
characterization of the direct links between local officials and bracero
users suggests. Nonetheless, Hawley and Galarza reveal an important
dimension of the forces impinging on the Labor Department in this
period.

In addition to wielding influence at the local level, some grower
organizations played it safe and appealed directly to the Secretary of
Labor. The San Francisco Chamber of Commerce Agricultural Committee was straightforward in its request to the Secretary for favorable
treatment: ". . . it is foreseen that an exceptionally large supplemental
supply of farm labor will be required during a concentrated period
in order that many of California's valuable specialty crops may be
harvested. . . . Your good efforts toward this objective are appreciated."[21]

Access to the decision-making levers of the Labor Department was
disproportionately concentrated among bracero users in the western
states. However, the department was held closely accountable by grow-

ers and their representatives in other agricultural regions as well, as revealed by one incident involving a Labor official and growers in Tennessee in 1953. Growers in West Tennessee had met with the Farm Placement representative regarding the possibility of importing braceros. The official correctly pointed out that the law required growers to make every effort to hire domestic workers before being certified for braceros. According to a subsequent letter of apology from the Secretary of Labor to Tennessee Senator Kefauver, the growers interpreted this as "an 'unfriendly attitude.' "[22]

Grower pressure was also evident when the Special system needed Labor Department support. When Mexican officials suspended the contracting of Specials in 1958, the Texas Sheep and Goat Raisers Association enlisted the help of Congressman O. C. Fisher, to exhort the DOL either to import Specials unilaterally or to allow the Immigration Service to import them under general provisions of the immigration laws.[23] Although Secretary of Labor Mitchell refused to adopt either strategy,[24] Labor Department representatives quickly convened with growers and ranchers before the Mexico City conference, "reversed" their prior criticisms of the Special Program, and assured the employers that they "intended to represent the interests of the farmer" at the conference.[25] According to Immigration reports, "The Labor Department took this stand at least partly in fear of losing Public Law 78" to the jurisdiction of the INS, if they were unresponsive to growers' needs.[26] Following the Mexico City conference, the Assistant Secretary of Labor reported that Department officials had met with "affected Congressmen" [i.e., those representing growers and ranchers] and, as a result of their "successes" in Mexico City, "received a warm and cordial reception . . . and that the meeting wound up with several speeches of commendation for the Department from some of our severest critics."[27]

In the spring of 1958, the Labor Department began discussing "plans for tightening up" the Bracero Program.[28] The year marked a turning point in agency/grower interactions. Not that growers ceased to exert pressure on the agency; rather, the pressure took on a reactive quality, usually coming in the form of threats and angry complaints—complaints that often enough forced the DOL into a compromise mode. For example, when the Department announced new methods for determining prevailing wages and piece rates in 1958, the reaction from growers was intense and well orchestrated. Labor Department officials touring agricultural areas in the Southwest to discuss the new methods, found "stiff-necked resistance . . . which promises loud and steady static from growers and the Congress."[29] The promised "static" came from a variety of powerful quarters, as described in an article by Milton Plumb in the *AFL-CIO News*. According to the union report, the Labor Department moves:

> have brought down upon Labor Sec. James P. Mitchell and department officials the biggest storm of corporate farm employer protests and drummed up pressure they have been subjected to in many years. . . . It is known that the powerful Southwest farm employer lobby has sent as its errand boys to call on the Secretary and other officials in person a major portion of the members of Congress from the states of California, Texas and Arizona, where most of the Mexican workers are used. Even some Senators from those states have been represented. A considerable number have put direct pressure on the department to retract its new policies.[30]

Even more controversial was the Labor Department proposal to establish a new minimum wage for piece rate. In an effort to ensure that braceros did not depress wages, the DOL proposed that braceros who were paid by piece rate be guaranteed at least 50 cents an hour. This proposal had its greatest potential effect on cotton growers. Predictably, cotton growers called the proposal "prohibitive"[31] and claimed that any minimum wage for cotton picking "would encourage laziness and reward slow workers."[32] The Governors of Arizona, Texas, and New Mexico joined members of Congress from bracero states in protest.[33] An angry Texas businessman and grower sent a no-holds-barred letter to Secretary of Labor Mitchell, with copies to the National Chairman of the Republican Party and Chairmen of the Republican Party in each bracero state. The letter is worth quoting at some length:

> Yesterday I attended a meeting in San Antonio, Texas, of ranchers, farmers, bankers, merchants, implement dealers and other business representatives affected by agriculture's economy. This meeting was called in protest to your Department's recent regulations establishing minimum wages on piece work done by Mexican braceros, such as harvesting cotton. This was the maddest bunch of people I have ever seen. . . . You heard rumblings that even the Democrats did not treat them that rough. . . . You may feel the Republicans can win without the West, Southwest, and Midwest states, or you may not even care whether the Republicans win again or not, however, if this is your attitude, you are a worse political liability to the Republican party than Mr. Sherman Adams.[34]

The pressure paid off. Meetings between growers and Labor officials in July 1958 resulted in a compromise agreement.[35] Instead of a guaranteed minimum wage, a "90–10 formula" was devised, allowing growers to set piece rates so that 90% of their crew averaged at least 50 cents an hour. According to one report, "The Labor Department expressed hopes of improved relations with farmers who use imported Mexican farm labor as the result of the compromise agreement."[36] The anticipated "improved relations" never materialized, however, as growers continued to complain loudly about the compromise measure.[37] The pattern was repeated whenever the Labor Department attempted to implement the provisions of PL 78 designed to protect domestic workers against adverse effects of the Bracero Program. When it raised the prevailing wage for picking cotton in Arkansas from 40 cents an hour to 60 cents in 1960, hundreds of irate cotton farmers crowded into a local armory to listen to their Congressman, E. C. Gathings—himself a grower and a bracero user—denounce the increase. Once again, the DOL ceded to the pressure, reducing the proposed increase by half.[38]

Growers were not adverse to using intimidation to elicit decisions more to their liking. When the San Joaquin Farm Produce Association was prohibited from hiring braceros to pick the tomato crop during a strike, the Regional Director of the BES received a 40-minute phone call from the president of the association, followed by a threatening telegram. According to the association president's telegram, ". . . my secretary monitored and took notes of the entire [telephone] conversation." The grower called the BES official "morally unfit to hold public office," and concluded, "[c]opies of this telegram are being sent to the Secretary of Labor, California newspapers, the California Senators and Congressmen. Petition for restraining order will be filed tomorrow."[39] The threats worked, or as Deputy Under-Secretary of Labor put it discreetly, "the matter" was "amicably disposed of."[40]

Despite such concessions, growers continued to charge the Labor Department with "fear and harassment" and "wage-fixing."[41] Their congressional allies lobbied the Department with angry denunciations of its lack of "help and sympathy . . . in the constant struggle our producers in the Southwest are having in trying to find workers to enable them to stay in business and pay their taxes."[42] Some claimed that the Secretary of Labor had "been duped by organized labor . . . and 'do-gooder' groups."[43] The besieged Department was even accused of "socialism" and "governmental interference."[44] By 1960, growers were so incensed over DOL restrictions that they proposed that all Department decisions relating to the Bracero Program be subject to

Department of Agriculture review and veto power.[45] They reluctantly dropped the proposal when the Secretary of Agriculture declined to endorse it, but they continued to campaign for restrictions on the Labor Secretary's power.[46]

At the same time that the Labor Department was subjected to a steady barrage of grower pressure, it was the target of organized labor's campaign to restrict the contract system, and ultimately to eliminate it. Farm workers had long struggled with the daunting obstacles confronting their efforts at unionization, and could count only sporadic and momentary victories. The IWW made periodic efforts to organize farm workers earlier in the century; the Southern Tenant Farmers Union was active in the Delta during the desperate years of the great depression; and the National Farm Labor Union (NFLU) faced off against growers in the late 1940s, before they were roundly defeated by the DiGiorgio Fruit Corporation, a 4600-acre enterprise in California's rich Central Valley. It was this DiGiorgio defeat, made possible by the importation of braceros who were sent through the NFLU's 20-mile picket line, that set the pace for farm labor organizing in the 1950s.[47] The effectively crippled farm labor movement possessed little real power and was only loosely organized through the mid-1950s when bracero recruitment was at its peak. Hawley, noting the weak support of urban labor for western agricultural workers and the relative lack of electoral power among this largely migrant work force, observed that domestic farm workers had little chance of influencing national policy. "When it came to getting action," he said, "conscience was often a poor substitute for power."[48]

In 1959, muscle was added to that conscience when the AFL-CIO formed the Agricultural Workers Organizing Committee (AWOC) and contributed $500,000 to help organize farm workers in California.[49] Over the next six years, the AFL-CIO put another $1 million into the organizing efforts of AWOC.[50] Although AWOC was not always successful against powerful California agribusiness, the support of the AFL-CIO injected new life into the farm labor movement, culminating in the strike and boycott successes of the United Farm Workers union in the late 1960s and 1970.[51] It was within this context that organized labor, at first tentatively and later with more force, approached the Labor Department.

Ernesto Galarza's description of the struggles of the National Agricultural Workers Union (NAWU, formerly the National Farm Labor Union, or NFLU) in California in the 1950s, and its efforts to influence Labor Department decision-making on the Bracero Program provides useful documentation both of the difficulties faced by farm labor organizers in that period and the slow but steady progress they made in their attempts to be heard.[52] According to Galarza, domestic farm workers were forced to "retreat" North in the summer of 1953, away from the border and the influx of braceros.[53] The long-standing difficulties of organizing an impoverished migrant work force, spread over vast territories and unprotected by federal labor standards, were compounded by the arrival of hundreds of thousands of foreign laborers who by law were denied the right to negotiate with their employers. The NAWU, confronted with such disheartening odds, focused their energies less on keeping the union in the fields despite the bracero system, and more on eliminating the system altogether. In this struggle, the Labor Department was their prime target.

Initially, the union concentrated on accessing detailed records from the Department, so that they could document the effects of the Bracero Program on wages and working conditions, the illegal use of braceros as strikebreakers, and the importation of braceros despite an abundance of domestic workers. For two years, the union unsuccessfully requested DOL records of "Authorizations to Contract," with which they planned to confirm that braceros were certified even in areas where domestic labor was available. Finally, in 1956, the Department instructed state employment agencies to make public "the number of workers which will be necessary" and "prevailing wages." Four months later, it began releasing Authorizations to Contract as well, a move that Galarza attributes to the fact that a number of powerful unions, including the Brotherhood of Maintenance of Way Employees, had pledged their support to the NAWU.[54]

By the early 1960s, organized labor moved more aggressively, demanding that bracero regulations, regarding such things as labor shortages and the use of braceros during strikes, be upheld. In 1963, the Emergency Committee to Aid Farm Workers compiled a list of nine major farm worker strikes since the infamous DiGiorgio strike in the late 1940s, the role of braceros in breaking those strikes, and the largely passive posture of the Labor Department.[55] When AWOC entered the fray, it did so with no illusions, and fully prepared for battle. The Director of AWOC, C. Al Green, made it his job to oversee DOL enforcement, focusing on the illegal use of braceros as strikebreakers. Green doggedly pursued his goals with a series of letters (copies of which were sent to George Meany, President of the AFL-CIO) to the Under Secretary of Labor, John F. Henning—whom he addressed familiarly as "Jack"—telephone calls, and personal visits. In one set of letters, Green complained that California growers had developed a strategy to circumvent the prohibition against importing braceros when domestic workers were available. They apparently deliberately hired a labor contractor, Thomas Garcia, with whom AWOC had a labor dispute, to recruit their domestic workers. As Green explained the strategy:

> They knew, in the first place that with a labor dispute Tom Garcia would be unable to recruit domestic workers to fill the orders the growers would request. It would make it very easy for the California Department of Employment to issue those 3401's [certification of labor shortage].[56]

Green's letters prompted concern at the Labor Department, as he requested information that the department was reluctant to supply. The Deputy Under Secretary advised his boss to withhold answers to some of Green's questions: "My reason for this is that you will find that the answers to the questions he raised are not ones which Mr. Green will appreciate. Under these circumstances, no answer at all to these points would be preferable."[57] The Department in fact did not supply Green with all the information he requested, and he complained that he was "tired of being shuffled back and forth between the U.S. Department of Labor and the California Department of Employment."[58] Nonetheless, the pressure paid one small dividend, forcing DOL officials to admit that "[t]here seems to be a loophole in our compliance machinery" and to launch an investigation into the employer abuses.[59]

The role of organized labor was not confined to that of critic or overseer of bracero operations. By the late 1950s, as the Labor Department began to tighten regulations and was under increasing assault from growers, labor became an important ally. When wage scales were changed in 1958, prompting a flurry of angry letters from growers and emergency visits from Senators, House Representatives, and Governors, Labor Department officials were consoled that at least organized labor supported the action. The Assistant Secretary of Labor reported to Secretary Mitchell, "The recent moves to tighten up on the importation of Mexican workers appear to have made us at least one grudging friend [referring to the article by Milton Plumb in the *AFL-CIO News* quoted above]—a friend, however, who carries considerable weight in the labor movement."[60]

When the Department finally abandoned its support for the Bracero Program in the early 1960s, it carefully tracked the interest of organized labor on the subject.[61] It even used labor leaders as a buffer for the virulent criticism from growers' powerful congressional allies. When Under Secretary of Labor Henning testified before Congress on the evils of the contract labor system in 1963, he was sent letters of congratulations from organized labor, with copies pointedly forwarded to the most antagonistic members of Congress.[62]

The DOL was in a no-win situation. Pressed on one side by growers and their representatives to provide a plentiful and cheap bracero work force, and on the other by domestic labor to curtail the contract labor system that crippled their organizing efforts, the agency waffled, rhetorically espousing neutrality.[63] Whatever the official posture, however, there was no escaping what a weary Secretary of Labor referred to in a candid moment as "the bracero headache."[62]

As early as 1951, the President's Commission on Migratory Labor noted the deleterious effects of the bracero system on domestic farm labor. On this premise, they pointed out the conflict inherent in a program that required State Department negotiators to obtain foreign workers under the most favorable conditions possible for U.S. employers:

> The inherent conflicts in this situation are quite apparent. If the Department of State negotiates with respect to the general interests of the Nation . . . it can scarcely be expected that the private interests of farm employers will, at the same time, be fully satisfied. Conversely, if the State Department . . . were to represent farm employer interests exclusively, the general interests of the Nation . . . might well be neglected or jeopardized.[65]

A similar conflict racked the Department of Labor. As political scientist Richard Craig points out, the DOL was given "the incompatible functions of recruiting Mexican labor while simultaneously protecting domestic farmworkers from any ill effects stemming from bracero contracting."[66] Activist and scholar Henry Anderson described the resulting dilemma, noting that DOL officials:

> are asked to represent the worker against his employer, and the employer against his workers, simultaneously . . . This is an impossible assignment. The administrator, expected to balance himself on the cutting edge of a razor, must fall off that razor in one direction or the other, or else be cut to death.[67]

Implicit in these observations is a recognition of the contradiction between capital and labor and the role of the Bracero Program in the playing out of that contradiction. While all of the state agencies involved in administering the contract labor system (State, Justice, Labor, and in the early years, Agriculture), inevitably dealt with this contradiction, the Labor Department experienced it most directly. After all, it is the mandate of the Labor Department to oversee labor-management relations, and to provide an institutional arena in which the interests of American workers can at least be voiced, if not always realized. When the Department of Labor was first established in 1913, Samuel Gompers, President of the American Federation of Labor, proclaimed it "Labor's Voice in the Cabinet."[68] If government agencies can be distinguished according to their "clientele groups,"[69] organized labor might well be considered the primary clientele of the Labor Department, much as the Department of Agriculture represents agricultural interests. This by no means implies that the DOL uniformly favors labor in its decision-making (we have seen that this was not the case), merely that it can not consistently appear to ignore the needs of its most "attentive public."[70]

The primary mission or official mandate of the DOL—overseeing labor-management relations—within the context of its constituent relationship with organized labor, subjects the agency to the full weight of the capital/labor contradiction. One could even argue that it is the institutional function of the Labor Department to grapple with the ramifications of this contradiction and to contain its damage. The unrelenting pressure brought to bear on the agency both from the ranks of growers and from domestic workers was the visible embodiment of this class conflict and the role of the Labor Department as its principal navigator.

Secretary of Labor Mitchell revealed in a 1959 interview that Labor officials considered the Bracero Program "just kind of a left-handed adjunct to the department" and of less importance than the Department's other activities.[71] Despite the fact that the DOL had greater statutory authority for the Bracero Program, it was far more central to the operations of the immigration agency. For the Labor Department, the program was at best "a left-handed adjunct," at worst "a headache" that exacerbated the capital/labor conflict with which it had to deal. For the INS, it was a central ingredient in the agency's ability to dodge its bureaucratic dilemmas, at least temporarily.

BUREAUCRATIC DILEMMAS AND INTER-AGENCY CONFLICT

Just as the INS was confronted directly with the contradictions surrounding immigration, given its institutional mandate to control the border, the DOL was faced with the task of juggling the class contradiction, given *its* particular location in the state apparatus. The way these respective institutional imperatives played themselves out in the Bracero Program set the two agencies on a collision course. INS policies that ensured plentiful, cheap bracero labor resolved its catch-22 regarding illegal immigration, yet brought into vivid focus the class nature of the foreign labor program and intensified conflict for the Labor Department. By the same token, DOL efforts to protect domestic labor by "tightening up" the program jeopardized the INS solution, as disgruntled growers threatened to return to using illegal aliens. In other words, not only do the contradictions inherent in the larger political economy penetrate these state agencies as distinct bureaucratic dilemmas, but as the agencies work to resolve their own particular dilemmas, they are reproduced as inter-agency conflict.

A closer look at the nature of these skirmishes confirms this interpretation. One point of friction between the two agencies centered on DOL restrictions concerning labor shortage certifications, wage rates and other work standards. Equally contentious was the problem of jurisdictional boundaries between these two agencies that shared responsibility for the Bracero Program. The details of these two primary points of contention, the battles that they precipitated, and the reactions they elicited from growers, workers, and Congress highlight the importance of the agencies' differing bureaucratic mandates as a fundamental component of the ongoing tension.

The DOL began tentatively to impose more rigorous restrictions on the Bracero Program through the regulatory process, becoming steadily more assertive as the program evolved. In December 1956, it established stringent housing regulations,[72] and it quickly became clear that it intended to enforce the new guidelines. Six months after the regulations were put into effect, the Labor Department had closed 10% of the camps in California and Arizona for violations.[73] In 1958, the Department imposed two controversial regulations concerning wage rates. The first specified that in order to reduce the adverse effect of braceros on domestic wages, the prevailing wage for a given area would be calculated as the hourly wage that at least 40% of the domestic workers in that area earned. The second stipulation was the "90–10" formula that applied to piece work, designed to guarantee most braceros an effective wage of at least 50 cents an hour.[74] The following year, Secretary of Labor Mitchell appointed a group of consultants to study adverse effects on domestic workers resulting from the Bracero Program. The consultants' report was devastating, documenting not only adverse effects, but deliberate grower abuses and violations, and provided a legitimating base from which the DOL pursued more rigorous regulations and enforcement in the final years of the program.[75]

When Congress passed a two-year extension of PL 78 in 1961, they attached a number of amendments, some of which were based on the consultants' recommendations. The amended version prohibited *de facto* year-round employment through recontracting, and precluded using braceros to operate power-driven farm machinery or for processing, packing, and canning work.[76] On signing the legislation, President Kennedy urged the Secretary of Labor to use all of his authority to enforce the provisions rigorously, and to protect farm workers' wages and working conditions.[77] A year later, Secretary of Labor Goldberg set "adverse-effect wage rates" for the twenty-four bracero states. Replacing the local prevailing wages that had been based on the 40% formula, the new policy meant that growers had to offer at least the minimum wage stipulated by the Secretary of Labor for their state. The effect was to raise bracero wages substantially, at least in some areas.[78]

The INS objected strenuously to the changes, charging that the new policies would trigger a return to the use of illegal workers. They blasted the DOL for tampering with the prevailing wage formula, which they said would "cause a spiraling upward of wages,"[79] and "a lessening of cooperation on the part of some farmers and ranchers who feel that their successful operation depends on use of minimum wage labor."[80] When adverse-effect rates were imposed in 1962, immigration officials in Texas alerted the central office: "Growers are quite outspoken in their opposition to the current minimum wage rate (70 cents per hour) and its application to piece rate. Several of the larger Valley growers have [said] that they have just about reached the point where they will not use Braceros any longer but will hire anyone coming up the road."[81]

When it became clear that the DOL meant to enforce the amendment prohibiting the use of braceros for the operation of power-driven machinery, immigration field personnel predicted a rapid increase in their enforcement problems. A Texas official called the Labor Department's refusal to allow growers "to continue to use braceros as they have been used in the past" an "adverse ruling," and anticipated that growers' reactions would include "locked gates and open hostility to patrolmen."[82] Similar protests accompanied the Labor Department's increasing reluctance to certify labor shortages. When DOL officials hesitated to allow the huge Yuma Producers Cooperative Association to import braceros in the spring of 1960, local Border Patrol agents charged angrily, "It goes without saying that a shortage of 600 workers during the harvest of the cantaloupe crop would open job opportunities for illegal entrants."[83] As Labor Department opposition to the Bracero Program crystallized, the INS was increasingly wary of the Department's ability to sabotage the system by denying certifications for braceros. Thus, when the DOL transferred authority for the certification process to the local level, Assistant Immigration Commissioner Irvin Shrode dashed off a handwritten memo plotting strategy: "I can see no objection on our part to the proposed delegation. . . . If it doesn't work—i.e. if the state employment service should get stuffy about certifying—we can always reject the procedure and require national level certification."[84]

Immigration officials reserved their most intense criticism for the Labor Department's handling of the Special Program, and it is here that their underlying motive was most transparent. Beginning in 1958, the Border Patrol warned that "[t]he slowdown in the 'Specials' contracting program continues to create a situation that could result in a group of [bracero] aspirants becoming . . . illegal entrants. . . ."[85] When the DOL terminated the Special Program in 1960, these fears escalated, as reports from the field anticipated that growers and ranchers would turn to illegal aliens en masse to fill the gap. In Texas, where ranchers depended on a plentiful supply of year-round Specials, the reports were particularly ominous, with immigration officials predicting that "many [livestock ranchers] will revert to the use of illegal entrants."[86] Immigration's Special Projects Officer, J. G. Frye, whose job it was to keep the central office informed of any developments affecting INS operations, issued a similar alarm. "It is quite possible," he warned, "that elimination of the predesignated worker program will result in the growers' inclination to use illegal entrant workers on ranches in West Texas and *therefore increase our enforcement problem.*"[87] The District Director in San Antonio added his voice of concern, highlighting the magnitude of the problem that the immigration bureaucracy could face as a result of the DOL decision to put an end to Specials contracting:

> About ten thousand specials are contracted in this district annually, roughly half of them going to ranches and combination farm-ranch operations. . . . There is among them [the ranchers] a feeling of consternation over the situation they are facing, that is, losing their specials. We can cope with a threat from one solitary rancher to lock his gates and go back to wets. Within the next year, however, unless some means is found to avoid it, this situation will be multiplied a thousand-

fold. *I can not over-emphasize my concern over the possibility of our losing ground in the control of illegal aliens.*[88]

The steady stream of central office memos and reports from the field left little doubt that the INS placed priority on ensuring a generous supply of low-wage braceros, that this supply was considered integral to resolving their "enforcement problem," and that the DOL was perceived as their antagonist in this endeavor.

Jurisdictional disputes compounded the tensions. Ever since its inception, the Bracero Program had triggered territorial jealousies, with each agency accusing the other of trying to " 'move in' on the operation of the legal program."[89] In 1960, the DOL drafted a bill that attempted to specify the adverse effect principle and authorized the Secretary of Labor to issue rules and regulations to implement the measure.[90] Every immigration official who reviewed the bill as it was routed around the central office opposed it, on the grounds that "it could possibly encroach upon the authority vested in the Attorney General," that it was "a further attempt by the Department of Labor to gain complete control of this and ultimately of all foreign worker programs;" and that it would give the Secretary of Labor "even greater authority."[91] Adding insult to injury, the DOL had left Immigration Service review of its draft legislation until the last minute, eliciting heavy sarcasm from immigration officials: "Service got about 2 days to consider it."[92] The DOL was equally sensitive to any perceived encroachments on its authority, for examples resisting the I-100 card system on the grounds that "[i]t ignores the statutory authority of the Secretary [of Labor]" and "will completely circumvent the local . . . employment office."[93]

These inter-departmental battles were not just about turf. Both their intensity and their predictable pattern suggest that they were fought to preserve more than territory. Immigration officials' resistance to the 1960 adverse-effect legislation was at least in part based on their fear that the Secretary of Labor would use his newly acquired authority "to the detriment of a good labor program . . . arbitrarily eliminating a supply of workers."[94] Frank Partridge, one of the two army generals Commissioner Swing hired over congressional protest in the mid-1950s, put it most bluntly. By restricting the contracting of braceros, he said, the adverse-effect bill:

> would bring about a demand for workers to replace them and it can be safely predicted that many employers would be unable or disinclined to hire domestic workers and would seek to again utilize illegal aliens. . . . *Any legislation unduly restrictive*

to bracero contracting would adversely affect enforcement and should be opposed.[95]

Just as immigration officials did not trust the Labor Department to preserve the generous supply of workers with which to feed the insatiable appetite of growers, the Labor Department was unwilling to relinquish any of its authority to an agency with a track record of "circumventing" the statutory requirement "to give preference for employment opportunities to our own workers."[96] No doubt some of the jurisdictional wrangling was over bureaucratic turf, pure and simple. But it was their respective bureaucratic dilemmas that accounted for the sense of urgency in this tug of war. If the INS was to maintain the fragile control of the border that it had so painstakingly achieved through the contract labor system, it had to maximize its authority over that system. Just as the Immigration Service stretched its authority in the interpretation of law—and on more than one occasion took "a walk around the statute"—in order to dodge the contradictions that confronted it, it was willing to fight for position, crowding the territory of other agencies if necessary, to preserve that solution.

TAKING SIDES

Not surprisingly, bracero employers lined up behind the INS in its rivalry with the DOL. When growers complained about the red tape or restrictions involved in the Bracero Program, they were careful to distinguish between the Immigration and Labor Departments, reserving their criticism for the latter. According to the INS public opinion survey conducted in 1957, Texas growers reported that relations with the "Border Patrol today were much better than they were during the wetback days;" that "the Labor Department is making the program so rigid that the farmers cannot comply with the restrictions;" and that "the criticism was not directed at the Immigration Service, but all the criticism . . . was directed at the Labor and State Departments."[97]

Indicative of their special relationship with the INS, growers even used officials in the immigration agency as mediators in their attempts to be heard by the DOL. When a cattle rancher and lawyer for cattle interests covering 300,000 acres in Southern California was denied certifications for several hundred braceros in 1956, he appealed to Commissioner Swing because "he knew the Department of Labor would do nothing about the situation" and "he knew the Immigration Service has done everything in its power to have a workable program."[98] The rancher was assured by senior immigration officials who met with him personally that the I-100 card system was designed to allow him "to obtain the workers he desired at the time he desired them," and that "pressure" was being applied to the Bureau of Employment Security "to force [it] to go along."[99]

Bracero employers went out of their way to deal with the immigration agency rather than the less accommodating Labor Department. Furlough procedures worked out informally between growers and local immigration agents are illustrative of this preference to bypass the DOL whenever possible. According to the international agreement with Mexico, all bracero furloughs of fifteen days or more had to be approved by the BES in the Department of Labor and the Mexican Consul. A furlough letter countersigned by the employer, the BES, and the Mexican Consul, was to be given to the bracero by his employer. This letter was then to be left with immigration inspectors at the port of departure and retrieved by the bracero when he was readmitted. The policy was designed to protect braceros from extended involuntary "furloughs" due to lack of work.

In the summer of 1957, violations of this furlough rule came to light—violations in which both the INS and bracero employers were implicated, and in which circumvention of the DOL was a primary motive. On August 7, 1957, the Regional Director of the BES wrote the Manager of the Yuma Cooperative Association,

> It has been brought to our attention that many Mexican Nationals employed by you cross the border on a furlough basis. This office has no record of participating in such furlough arrangements. . . . It is possible that some informal arrangement may exist between you and an Immigration Officer at San Luis, the Arizona Port of Entry, to permit a type of furlough system to operate without the participation of this agency. . . .[100]

The manager confirmed that the producers' association did "have good cooperation with the Immigration Service on our system."[101]

As it turned out, the arrangement was not confined to Arizona. The Acting Regional Immigration Commissioner explained matter-of-factly to BES officials, "In May 1956 this Service abandoned the procedure of requiring the lifting of furlough letters from all Braceros departing from the United States on furloughs."[102] In fact, the INS had stopped enforcing the furlough regulation long before May 1956. In December 1955, a memo from the Southwest region explained to the central office that the Service's own Operating Instructions with regard to furloughs were being violated in the interest of removing any hurdles in the employment of braceros. The memo elaborated:

> Departure control is no longer in effect, making enforcement of the requirement that departing workers surrender . . . [furlough] letters, physically impossible at most ports. . . . To stop this flow [of workers on furlough] would not only create an enormous workload but . . . it would also bring many complaints from employers in whose education to the use of legally-contracted workers the Service has a considerable investment. . . . All in all, it appears highly undesirable and impractical to attempt to enforce the Operations Instructions literally.[103]

The practice was to readmit all braceros with valid I-100 cards, and "not examine the bracero to determine whether he has stayed longer than 15 days."[104] The effect of this arrangement was to avoid having to obtain DOL authorization for furloughs, a requirement that immigration officials said was too "cumbersome" and "expensive."[105]

The grower/INS alliance often translated into mutual lobbying efforts. As we have seen, the immigration agency was frequently asked by growers to intervene on their behalf with the Labor Department. Perhaps more unusual, the INS was not adverse to encouraging growers to reciprocate the favor by using their considerable clout to bring the DOL into line with the Service position. When the DOL denied braceros to one of the largest ranching interests in California, the Immigration Service used the occasion to lobby for its I-100 card system. Promising the ranchers that the I-100 card system would solve their problems, immigration officials pointed out that the DOL had to be coaxed into accepting the procedure. To this end, the officials said, the ranchers "could do us a good turn if [they] could put a little heat on."[106]

Growers supported every effort to increase the official responsibility of the immigration agency for the Bracero Program, relative to that of the Labor Department. They even spearheaded an unsuccessful attempt to remove the Special Program altogether from the jurisdiction of the Labor Department. Subsequent to the suspension of Specials contracting in 1958, Texas ranchers proposed to Congress that "all future processing of specials . . . be handled by the Immigration and Naturalization Service," so that the DOL "would be relieved of what seems to be quite a headache to that agency."[107] The House Agriculture Committee agreed, raising their own objections to the way the DOL had handled the Special Program. Representative Poage of Texas, Vice

Chair of the Agriculture Committee, and a staunch ally of bracero users, interrogated DOL officials, "You have had very little success [furnishing Specials]. . . . Now would you object to trying to turn that over to somebody else. . . . Would you object to turning that over to the Immigration Service? . . . You have made a failure for a good many years."[108]

When the Labor Department terminated the Special Program in 1960, it unleashed an onslaught of criticism and another round of proposals to place the program under the "exclusive jurisdiction" of the INS.[109] Growers' advocates in Congress joined in the call to hand the Special Program over to the immigration agency. Representative O. C. Fisher of Texas, angry at the testimony of the Assistant Secretary of Labor that there was no real shortage of farm labor, told the Labor Department official, "You do not know what you are talking about," and urged that Specials be admitted under the H-2 program administered by the INS.[110]

It was not the first time that proponents of the Bracero Program had suggested using the H-2 program as an alternative route for securing Mexican farm workers, and as a way to bypass the inconvenient restrictions of the DOL. Because the H-2 program was authorized by the Immigration and Nationality Act, the INS had primary responsibility for its implementation, with the Labor Department cast in a secondary role. Like the Bracero Program, the H-2 program allowed foreign workers to be admitted on a temporary basis; however, for the duration of the Bracero Program, Mexican farm workers were not eligible to participate in the H-2 program. When the Labor Department revamped the prevailing wage formula and piece rates in 1958, Representative Fisher, complaining of the "cost of the Bracero Program" and the "difficulties that have arisen," questioned Commissioner Swing's Executive Assistant on the possibility of admitting Mexican farm workers through the H-2 program.[111] The same year, growers swamped the central office of the INS with letters inquiring about importing their braceros through the H-2 program, "due to . . . ever-increasing regulations by the Labor Department."[112]

Organized labor, of course, vehemently opposed any transfer of authority to the INS. Citing as an example the importation of several thousand Japanese farm workers under the H-2 program, the Treasurer of the Joint U.S.-Mexico Trade Union Committee told Congress that protection of the rights of workers depended on continued DOL involvement in the Bracero program. "We have already seen the kind of labor program that we could expect," he said, if the contracting of Mexican labor were to be placed in the hands of the Immigration and Naturalization Service . . . for the present Japanese labor program, set up with the approval and support of the present Immigration Commissioner produced conditions of work and a contract so far inferior to the Mexican labor contract that organized labor has been forced to condemn the Japanese program as amounting to little more than peonage.[113]

No official redistribution of power was ever agreed to by Congress (although, as we have seen, the INS stretched its own authority to its limits), nor was the H-2 program ever used for Mexican braceros. Nonetheless, these repeated attempts to shift authority away from the DOL to the INS serve as one more manifestation of the schism between these two agencies and their differing orientations towards growers' interest in an abundant foreign labor supply.

This is not to say that the DOL was unresponsive to growers' demands. The historical record is replete with illustrations of the ability of growers to win concessions from the Labor Department. But the contradictions and related bureaucratic dilemmas faced by the two agencies were distinct, and this distinction shaped their different orientations. On one hand, the INS confronted the contradictions of illegal immigration and saw the Bracero Program as a unique opportunity to realize its bureaucratic mandate to control the border despite these contradictions. On the other hand, the DOL saw the contract labor system as a "headache" that compounded, or at least brought into high relief, the class contradiction with which it was forced to grapple. The agencies' differential exposure to contradictions embedded in the larger political economy not only guaranteed that the INS would be more generous with growers, but also spawned the inevitable tension between them. In other words, the conflict between the INS and the DOL was symptomatic of their respective locations within the state— locations that situated them differently *vis à vis* the contradictions within which the Bracero Program was inserted.

The president of the Rio Grande Valley Farm Bureau, Frank Schuster, angry at what he claimed was DOL "wage-fixing," depicted metaphorically the relationships among growers, the Labor Department, and the immigration agency. As told by the *Brownsville Herald*,[114]

> Schuster recalled that approximately seven years ago . . . Immigration Department officials had given Valley farmers "a solemn promise" that if they would cooperate with the Border

Patrol by using braceros instead of "Wetbacks," the Department would help in making the new program work. "This arrangement worked," Schuster said, "until the Secretary of Labor stepped up and began acting like a mother-in-law, meddling in the affairs of newlyweds."

The Texas rancher was right. The immigration agency and growers *were* newlyweds of a sort, united by their mutual interest in an abundant supply of braceros. And the Labor Department did "meddle," although not out of idle curiosity or the tendency to interfere in the affairs of others that the stereotypical mother-in-law metaphor implies. Rather, the DOL had its own statutory responsibility for the program, and its own set of dilemmas that guaranteed friction with the newly betrothed immigration agency. The historical record bristles with the tension, as sparks fly back and forth in memos, letters, and reports of all kinds. But this picture of discord and dissension would be incomplete without reference to the ties that ultimately bound these two federal agencies. For better or for worse, they too were wed.

A UNITED FRONT

Having located the sources of tension between the Labor and Immigration agencies, it is important not to lose sight of the fact that they were required to work through their differences. For the INS and the DOL were bound together by a number of common structural and political forces. First, as we have seen, neither could altogether ignore the economic utility of an immigrant labor supply, nor turn a deaf ear to the considerable pressure that Southwest growers brought to bear. For the INS, the issue was straightforward and unidimensional, as satisfying growers' demand for legal braceros helped fill its own bureaucratic needs. The DOL confronted growers on more complex terrain. While it is true that the Labor agency increasingly tempered its policies with consideration for their effect on domestic labor, nonetheless the Bracero Program was at base a device used by growers to stabilize wages and more generally neutralize the power of labor by suspending the law of supply and demand in the labor market. With primary statutory responsibility for operating this program, the Labor Department was not only a major participant in this process, but was vulnerable to the persistent demands of growers to facilitate their use of this powerful weapon. It was the job of the Labor Department to oversee labor-management relations and to navigate the class contradiction. While this required them to affirm periodically their concern for the interests of labor, it simultaneously required that they assist growers in the procurement of alternative supplies of labor, and opened them up to the power of agribusiness as it attempted to secure favorable administrative decisions. Thus, while it was the respective contradictions faced by the DOL and the INS that generated tension between them, it was at the same time the nature of those contradictions that supplied the least common denominator, that is, the economic utility of bracero labor.

Beyond this larger structural context, there is extensive evidence that both agencies were aware that they needed to compromise or, where this was not possible, at least to present a "united front" in public. Small concessions were regularly made in the interest of harmony. For example, when the DOL objected to the dominance of growers in the selection of braceros through the I-100 card system, the INS deleted the message in Spanish from its I-100 cards: "If your boss recommends you as a satisfactory worker the Service of Immigration will deliver to you a plastic card."[115] An immigration official explained that the message implied that growers unilaterally determined which workers would be admitted as braceros, and thus provoked conflict with the Labor Department: "In view of our recent talks with the Department of Labor I think we should eliminate this."[116]

On less cosmetic and more difficult to resolve issues, the two agencies were concerned at least to present a uniform position in public. This was particularly true when negotiations with Mexico were involved. Commissioner Swing wrote the Assistant Secretary of Labor in 1955, as he was putting the finishing touches on his controversial I-100 card system:

> Undoubtedly, in the near future there will be need for conferences with the Mexican officials concerning the extension of the Mexican Agreement. I think it would be advisable if you and I and Mr. Murphy [Deputy Under Secretary of State] could have a further discussion in relation to this subject . . . *in order to make sure that . . . the presentation by this Government of its position . . . be uniform in every respect.*[117]

Even at moments of the most intense friction, uniformity was nurtured, at least at the level of rhetoric. At the 1956 Mexico City conference on the Special Program, despite allegations that the Labor Department was sabotaging the I-100 card system behind the scenes, the DOL delegate assured Immigration representatives that "we would continue to present a united front at all meetings."[118]

The State Department was often the mediator, a role that it came to naturally and had a vested interest in since, as the negotiator with Mexico, its task would be compounded by public dissension between the feuding agencies. In some cases, State Department mediation was initiated at the request of Immigration or Labor officials. For example, Commissioner Swing, concerned for the survival of his I-100 card system, in the summer of 1955 asked the Deputy Under Secretary of State to set up meetings with the Department of Labor, "anxious as I am in establishing a united position so far as this government is concerned before discussions are had with the Mexican Government."[119] Before the Mexico City conference the following year, the Assistant Secretary of Labor requested that his counterpart at the State Department arrange a meeting for the purpose of reconciling the INS and DOL positions:

> I feel . . . that it is extremely important that prior to our conference with the Mexican Government a uniform position be arrived at among the interested agencies. . . . I am sure that you will agree that it would be exceedingly unfortunate for the United States to attempt to resolve internal differing views at the conference.[120]

After the conference, the Secretary of State asked the two agencies for their respective interpretations of the agreements reached with the Mexican delegates. Anticipating a difference of opinion from the agencies that had spent their time at the conference in internecine quarreling, the Secretary of State's memo concluded with a warning:

> It is, of course, essential that the views of the Department of Labor and of the Immigration and Naturalization Service be coordinated before they are forwarded to the Department in order that they might be transmitted to the Mexican Government as representing an authoritative United States position.[121]

Even encounters with other branches of government called for coordinating efforts in the interest of presenting a consistent position. Before officials of the two agencies testified to Congress in 1963, a conference was convened to discuss strategy. Fearful of the political fallout of presenting conflicting views, Deputy Under Secretary of Labor, Millard Cass, "emphasized the extreme importance of each government agency being fully aware of the Administration's policy and the necessity for the agencies involved putting forth a united front."[122]

Despite their differences, the INS and the DOL were thus "united." They were united at one level by structural forces related to the very contradictions that underlay their frictions. But they were bound by political forces as well. The political imperative to present a "united front" was most obvious when negotiations with Mexico were involved, where internal dissension would be taken as an indication of weakness and could be exploited to enhance Mexico's bargaining position. But coordination was important in the domestic political arena too, where the agencies were called on to represent the position of the executive branch, and where lack of uniformity would be interpreted as indecisiveness.

The conflicts described here highlight the inadequacy of any theory that depicts the state as a monolithic whole. However, if these federal agencies were not simply interchangeable parts of a monolithic state, neither were they discreet and independent domains. Instead, they were tied together in an uneasy balance of conflicting interests and interdependent agendas, political necessity and structural imperatives. Much as Anderson[123] described the DOL as balanced on the edge of a razor between capital and labor, these agencies of the state were involved in another balancing act as they walked the fine line between their disparate and common domains.

It has been argued that the INS operation of the Bracero Program, in particular its accommodating relationship to bracero users, derived from the contradiction underlying immigration and the dilemmas that this contradiction posed for the immigration bureaucracy. If this interpretation is correct, then we would expect the Department of Labor— with its own bureaucratic mandates and corresponding dilemmas—to have a somewhat different policy agenda. The historical record of INS/DOL interactions is consistent with this interpretation. Not only did the two agencies have distinct agendas, but they periodically clashed in pursuit of those agendas. Furthermore, the paper trail left by these confrontations suggests that they were grounded in the agencies' distinct mandates, and the nature of the contradictions to which they were differentially exposed as a result of those mandates. In a 1980 summary of the Bracero Program, the Congressional Research Service notes: "History appears to indicate that the bracero program only served to reduce illegal migration when it was combined with both a massive law enforcement effort ('Operation Wetback') and an expansion of the farm labor program to the point where it almost certainly had an adverse impact on the wages and working conditions of domestic workers."[124] For the two agencies responsible for checking illegal migration and protecting domestic workers, respectively, confrontations was inevitable, and mirrored the underlying logic of the program itself.

As the Bracero Program wound down in the early 1960s, the INS faced the unraveling of the system that for over twenty years provided growers with a cheap, captive, and legal labor supply, and gave the immigration agency a temporary reprieve from its institutional dilemma. The next chapter traces the INS reaction to the collapse of its carefully crafted bracero solution.

CHAPTER 6

LOSS OF CONTROL

The Bracero Program flourished throughout the 1950s, in large part as a result of the diligent efforts of the INS to promote grower satisfaction. The number of braceros rose steadily, reaching more than 445,000 in 1956, and exceeding 400,000 a year for the rest of the decade (see Appendix B). The average number entering annually between 1951 and 1959 was *ten times* higher than the number admitted during the wartime program of 1942–1947, when a labor emergency had been declared. In 1959, nearly 50,000 farms employed braceros, with the vast majority concentrated in Texas, California, Arkansas, Arizona, and New Mexico.[1]

As the domestic work force was forced to flee the effects of the foreign supply, Texas was both the largest importer and the largest exporter of migrant labor.[2] Citing the erosion of farm wages in cotton, sugar beets, and "heavily dominated" fruits and vegetables in bracero states, the Department of Labor consultants' report concluded that adverse effects on domestic workers were a virtually inevitable consequence of the bracero system.[3] One observer, noting the logical fallacy of the adverse effect protection in the Bracero Program, drew a tongue-in-cheek analogy:

> [A]ll housewives would get together and decide how much they could pay for groceries. If they cannot find enough food at the prices they have decided to pay, the housewives' association notifies the Secretary of Agriculture that there is a food shortage. He then imports cheaper foreign food. But this is to have no adverse effect on the neighborhood stores.[4]

With braceros plentiful and cheap, the number of illegal aliens apprehended continued to decline, as growers gratefully accepted the advantageous exchange that Commissioner Swing offered them.

But by 1960 the tides began to turn, as opposition to the contract labor system grew in both numbers and influence. One indication of this shift was the series of regulations issued by the Department of

Labor beginning in the late 1950s. Another was the increasing reluctance of Congress to rubber-stamp extensions of the program. The Bracero Program was extended three times in the 1950s with only minor controversy and without significant amendment. In contrast, the extension proceedings of 1960 were a political crossfire of accusations and recriminations.

In retrospect, this Congressional battle was a watershed, as bracero users were put decisively on the defensive, where they stayed for the duration of the program. Introducing amendments to give the Secretary of Agriculture veto power over DOL policies and to bar the Secretary of Labor from setting minimum wages and working conditions for domestic farm workers,[5] growers' allies in Congress attempted to have the program extended in this amended form for two years. They failed on all counts; the amendments were defeated and the program was extended for a mere six months. While opponents of the Bracero Program were unsuccessful at making changes in the program based on the recommendations of the DOL consultants' report, they had nonetheless won their first round, dealing a resounding defeat to growers and their Congressional advocates.[6]

The following year, Congress passed the amendment prohibiting the use of braceros on power-driven machinery and for canning or packing activities, and confining them to temporary employment. For the seasoned Congressional proponents of the contract labor system—many of whom were themselves bracero users—the two-year extension they obtained this time must have seemed a bittersweet accomplishment, as they chafed at the increasing restrictions.[7] On December 4, 1963, the program was extended for one more year. Not only were grower-sponsored amendments to curtail the power of the Labor Department rejected, but growers' advocates, anxious to secure at least this one-year extension, promised that it would be the last.[8] As promised, the controversial program was allowed to die in December, 1964.

Most observers agree that the program's demise was the product of a number of related factors, the most commonly cited of which is political-ideological. It is pointed out, for example, that "welfare groups and the powerful AFL–CIO were gaining in strength and congressional representation,"[9] and that the Kennedy Administration was far less sympathetic to growers than the Eisenhower Administration had been.[10] According to this interpretation, "The new concern with migrant labor was a part of the broad changes that produced the New Frontier and the Great Society. . . . [I]n a climate that produced the Civil Rights Act and the War on Poverty, the perpetuation of PL 78 became a moral issue and urban support became much harder to secure."[11] The moral position of the program's opponents was but-tressed in late 1960s by the widely acclaimed CBS documentary, "Harvest of Shame," which graphically depicted the poverty and despair of migrant farm workers, and "touched off a reaction of astonishing proportions," swamping both the television network and members of Congress with mail from an outraged and conscience-stricken public.[12]

While these ideological factors undoubtedly contributed to the program's termination, they did not act alone. Rather, they were an integral part of the larger political and economic context—a context that was undergoing rapid and substantial transformation. One critical ingredient was the increasingly strict set of regulations imposed by the Labor Department. Political scientist Richard Craig maintains that the Secretary of Labor deliberately strangled the Bracero Program, "While he was himself unable to bring about an end to large-scale bracero recruitment, the Secretary of Labor was able to render the procurement of braceros so inconvenient that their employment became all but prohibitive."[13] Whether or not the DOL had a pre-conceived plan to sabotage the Bracero Program through regulations, its policies had that effect. By 1962, fewer than 200,000 braceros were imported, the smallest number since Operation Wetback, and by 1964 the number of braceros was lower than at any time since the institutionalization of the program in 1951 (see Appendix B). As organized labor grew in numbers and influence, and with the AFL–CIO lending political and financial support to farm workers—most notably in the Agricultural Workers Organizing Committee—pressure on the Labor Department appeared to have paid off. An Immigration Service report from Texas in 1962 blamed the Department's stricter regulations for "farmer resistance to the Bracero Program":

> The U.S. Department of Labor announced that all Braceros contracted for work in the State of Texas would, by regulation, be paid 70 cents per hour instead of the former 50 cents per hour. . . . A large percentage of Texas farmers immediately stopped contracting Braceros. Texas contracting is now 10 to 12 thousand below the normal for the reporting period.[14]

Stiffer regulations and the reduction of braceros were accompanied by an increasing reliance on the "iron men of machinery." Some have even argued that the mechanization of bracero crops, most notably cotton, and the changing labor demands resulting from these production changes, were largely responsible for the termination of the contract labor system.[15] In 1951, 8% of the cotton produced in the United States was harvested by machine. By 1964, the production of cotton had undergone a radical transformation, with 78% being mechanically harvested.[16] As cotton was mechanized, the pattern of bracero contracting was dramatically altered. In 1961, growers in Texas—where the major bracero crop was cotton—employed 40% of all braceros, and California contracted 34%; one year later, the percentages had shifted to 15% and 60%, respectively.[17] By 1964, braceros were largely confined to California specialty crops where mechanization still proved elusive.[18] The result was not only a decreased demand for braceros overall, but shifting regional alliances as California growers were increasingly isolated in their dependence on the contract labor supply. With braceros rendered more expensive by Labor Department regulations and more expendable by increased mechanization, organized labor's refrain that the peonage of foreign contract labor was unacceptable in a liberal democratic society—a message they had been sending for almost two decades—was finally heard.

The demise of the Bracero Program over the protests of powerful California agribusiness reveals the inadequacies of monolithic instrumentalist and structuralist models of the state, and highlights the importance of the *modus vivendi* hammered out between the state and capital, noted by Fred Block. Eschewing both instrumentalism and the reification of much structuralist theorizing, Block explains the "rationality of the capitalist order" and the nature of the *modus vivendi* which requires compromises from both state managers and capital, as "a consequence of the three-sided conflicts among capitalists, state managers, and the working class."[19] By the early 1960s, working class political gains, related DOL regulations, and the increased mechanization of agriculture, contributed to the dismantling of the Bracero Program. While bracero users complained loudly as the program was phased out, its demise was part of a *modus vivendi* that was perhaps harder on the INS than it was on growers who returned to using illegal labor.

SWIMMING AGAINST THE TIDE

Raymond F. Farrell, a career civil servant, replaced General Swing as Immigration Commissioner in January, 1962. Farrell is described by those who worked with him as a "caretaker commissioner" who, in his personal connections with members of Congress and his "don't-rock-the-boat" style, contrasted markedly with the assertive and independent General Swing.[20] But despite the vast differences in the Commissioners' personal styles, agency policies related to the Bracero Program were relatively unaffected by the transition. From the first decline in the number of braceros admitted in 1960, until the last braceros departed in 1965, the immigration agency struggled to accommodate growers' continued demand for Mexican workers, just as it had for more than a decade.

As the Bracero Program wound down, immigration officials toed the Administration line in public, refraining from openly criticizing DOL regulations and volunteering no explicit opinions on the program's impending termination during their repeated congressional appearances. In private, the INS and its parent agency the Department of Justice, were less circumspect, warning that tightening the system would cause a rapid increase in illegal immigration, farm worker wage increases, and higher food prices.[21] Their position had little impact on the formation of Administration policy or on the fashioning of DOL regulations. Faced with Labor Department restrictions which threatened to undermine the utility of braceros to growers, immigration officials designed agency strategies to offset the effects of those policies.

Remember that the Immigration Service had for years limited collective action by braceros, by apprehending and deporting those suspected of "subversive" activity. Having convinced growers of the advantages of a controlled legal work force with no bargaining power, the agency strove to preserve that subordinate status. But, if one advantage of the contract system is control, another is predictability. As the DOL began to enforce the prohibition against the use of braceros to break strikes, and with the number of strikes steadily increasing, the system's predictability—long touted as one of the system's chief virtues—diminished. A former Deputy General Counsel summarized bluntly the attitude of immigration officials toward farm worker unions, "The INS doesn't care about what labor unions think. By and large, it's a conservative organization."[22] Memos and internal reports from the early 1960s show a reluctance to ascribe legitimacy to " 'labor disputes' " and the " 'Union' " (both consistently referred to in quotes, presumably signifying skepticism of labor's motives), as well as a grower's orientation toward the size and value of the crops threatened by striking workers.[23] The INS reaction to unions was not confined to semantics. As the DOL removed braceros from struck farms, the immigration agency worked to secure their re-entry. One reported strategy was to allow truckloads of Mexican workers, headed for the struck farms and ranches from which many of them had been removed, to cross the border with 72-hour visitor permits. In one such episode, AFL–CIO officials telegrammed the Secretary of Labor, "In deliberate contempt of your order removing braceros from 15 struck ranches in Imperial Valley, growers are importing . . . Mexican Nationals into the United States with the aid and connivance of the U.S. Immigration Service."[24]

In their efforts to prop up the deteriorating system, immigration officials even reversed policies that they themselves had set during the program's heyday in the 1950s. In 1956, "as another step in furthering our enforcement program," INS Operating Instructions made Mexicans who had entered the U.S. illegally in the year prior to their bracero stint, ineligible for bracero status. Braceros later found ineligible according to this provision, were to be deported.[25] In 1961, this provision was rescinded. With the DOL certifying fewer and fewer braceros, an INS directive stated:

> Contract laborers reported illegally in the United States by reception centers on the basis of information developed subsequent to their admission are not to be apprehended unless there is an extremely serious record—for example, subversiveness.[26]

The rationale was that "the employer . . . is not at fault in the admission of the alien and therefore should not be penalized." In addition, braceros who had been arrested "for minor infractions and committed to jail" would not be apprehended "if their employer is willing to take them back."[27]

Reconsideration was even given to issuing immigrant visas to Mexican farm workers, despite the agreement some years earlier among the State, Labor, and Justice Departments, that potential braceros should be barred from receiving permanent immigrant status. The DOL continued to oppose granting permanent visa "green cards" to Mexican farm workers on the grounds that it might adversely affect the labor market. The Director of the Bureau of Employment Security explained:

> Historically, the extreme heat conditions under which agricultural laborers are required to work . . . have resulted in extremely high labor turnover. The departure of workers at will, which is possible under the permanent entry proposal, could result in serious job competition with domestic workers in other areas.[28]

However, immigration officials shared the concern of growers and ranchers that with the suspension of the Special Program in 1960, employers would no longer have access to their "key workers."[29] As a result, the INS and the State Department relaxed their ban on permanent visas, allowing a number of former employers of Specials to bring their braceros in through regular immigration channels. This practice contributed to a gradual increase in the number of Mexican visas granted in the early 1960s (see Appendix C).

That the Immigration Service and the State Department, the two agencies responsible for granting visas, suspended the ban on Mexican farm workers at least in part because of the increasing difficulty of obtaining braceros, was implicit in State Department testimony before Congress in 1963. Allen B. Moreland, Director of the Visa Office in the State Department, explained to Congress that the increase in Mexican visas coincided with the termination of the Special Program in 1960 and the 1961 statutory restrictions on bracero hiring. "With the cumulative effect of these two restrictions on the operation of the bracero program," he said, "more and more users of farm labor in the southern tier of states have been resorting to the immigrant visa process as a means of getting people in to work in the States of California, New Mexico, Texas, and Arizona."[30]

In addition to cushioning the impact of the DOL's decision to end the Special Program, permanent immigrants were seen by growers as a weapon in the escalating class war in the fields—a use to which the INS gave its tacit approval. An INS Special Projects Officer in California kept in regular telephone contact with the central office to report on strike developments in Imperial Valley.[31] Having cautioned growers on the drawbacks of a free immigrant work force, he reported, "The farmers are aware of prior experience on laborers brought in as [permanent] immigrants but feel that this is the only way in which they can combat efforts to unionize farm laborers in the valley."[32] Prohibited from hiring braceros during a strike, growers were increasingly willing to take their chances with a less captive, permanent immigrant work force.

A change in DOL regulations in 1963 made it more difficult for farmers and ranchers to use this channel for accessing legal immigrant labor. Before 1963, if an employer sponsored fewer than twenty-five workers for permanent visas, the DOL was not required to issue a labor certification, making it relatively easy for growers to circumvent the DOL by sponsoring green-card workers in groups of twenty-four. To obtain a larger number of permanent immigrants, some growers enlisted the help of local used car salesmen or other businessmen who requested groups of twenty-four Mexican workers and then passed them on to the farmers—a viable strategy since once these green-card immigrants entered, they were not bound to any particular employer.[33] In 1963, Labor changed its regulations to require that for every worker sponsored by an employer as a permanent immigrant, a certification had to be issued that no qualified domestic worker was available.[34]

The Labor Department was not generous with these certifications, especially for unskilled agricultural labor. Between July 1, 1963 and December 1, 1965, it received 23,010 applications for permanent visas from Mexican farm workers; of these, only 10% were certified.[35] Almost overnight, the number of Mexican visas returned to its earlier low level.

NO ALL-OUT EFFORT

Growers and their allies in Congress had for years harbored the hope that any interruption in the Bracero Program would be offset by the importation of Mexican farm workers through the H–2 program.[36] The Immigration and Nationality Act of 1952[37] provided for the admission of temporary alien labor in case of a certified labor shortage, and thousands of such H–2 workers entered the U.S. annually, primarily to cut sugar cane in Florida and to pick apples and harvest vegetables on the east coast. While the Bracero Program was in effect, the H–2 program excluded Mexican workers by executive agreement. As the Bracero Program expired, however, growers and their supporters explored the possibility of importing former braceros as H–2 workers. California Governor Edmund Brown even urged Secretary of Labor Willard Wirtz to phase out the Bracero Program gradually over a 5–year period during which Mexican H–2 workers could be imported to take the place of braceros.[38]

Secretary Wirtz opposed this *de facto* extension of the Bracero Program. In late 1964, he held a series of public hearings on the issue of H–2 workers and their potential effect on local economies.[39] Less than three weeks later, he issued new regulations requiring employers to offer domestic workers substantially higher wages than specified under the old "prevailing wage" formulas, before H–2 workers could be certified; extended the housing, transportation, and other benefits that had applied to the Bracero Program to the H–2 program; and limited H–2 certifications to 120 days. The Secretary's intentions were clear. In announcing the new regulations, he wrote, "It is expected that such use [of H–2's] will be very greatly reduced, and, hopefully, eliminated."[40]

On rare occasions, the DOL certified large groups of Mexican workers to harvest crops, as when 8,000 Mexican farm workers were provided to nine California growers' associations to harvest tomatoes in 1965.[41] But, by and large, Labor regulations and certification procedures proved to be prohibitive. With growers increasingly discouraged by the red tape, and the Secretary of Labor determined to end the foreign labor system, the INS saw the writing on the wall. Assistant Commissioner for Enforcement, Donald Coppock, wrote to the Deputy Associate Commissioner in January, 1965, "Recent developments in the farm labor situation make it imperative at this time for us to review the entire matter as it relates to our Mexican border operation." He continued,

> Secretary of Labor W. Willard Wirtz, in hearings before the Senate Agriculture Committee, testified that sufficient domestic labor is available, and that to reinstitute the bracero program . . . would be morally, economically, and legally wrong. . . . Additionally . . . it appears that as long as domestic labor is available, certifications by the Department of Labor will not be made for the importation of laborers under Section 101(a)(15)(H)(ii) of PL 414. With such being the case, *a new light is shed upon our planned operations in the Southwest Region.*[42]

Coppock went on to explain,

> The situation will be different from that which we faced in 1954 and 1955, in the era of the "wetback." During that period, legally imported braceros were available but were not being used by the farm groups, as they resorted to the use of "wetbacks". . . . Now, imported labor will not be available either through the enactment of legislation . . . or through the provisions of PL 414 under Section 101(a)(15)(H))(ii). It has also been indicated that tighter control of immigrants from Mexico will be exercised by the Department of Labor through certifying against such visa applicants. . . . *It appears that the Service will be expected to exert every effort to stop illegal aliens from gaining entry. . . . The Service can ill afford to allow the situation to revert back to the conditions existing during the so-called "wetback" era.*[43]

The Assistant Commissioner was right. A "new light" *was* shed on INS enforcement. The immigration agency was once again expected to control the border without providing employers with any alternative sources of foreign labor.

In 1960, the number of illegal aliens apprehended in the United States increased for the first time since Operation Wetback, and by 1962, apprehensions were double what they had been just three years earlier (see Appendix A). The immigration agency, chronically short of funds and facing the renewed influx of illegal aliens, resorted to "periodic 'Show-Of-Force' operations" designed "to present to prospective employers of potential illegal entrants . . . the *impression* of a substantial increase of officer personnel."[44] Predictably, this smoke-and-mirrors approach was inadequate to quell the demand for foreign labor. The year after the Bracero Program was terminated, illegal alien apprehensions exceeded 100,000 for the first time in a decade.

Immigration officials had long understood that growers' cooperation with them was contingent on a plentiful supply of legal foreign labor. With that supply now cut off, the agency once again came face-to-face with the contradiction it had managed to elude briefly at the height of the Bracero Program. On one hand, as Assistant Commissioner Coppock[45] warned, "large numbers of aliens . . . if allowed to build up, would create additional unnecessary socio-economic burdens . . . as were created during those ['wetback'] years," and subsequent political demands for their exclusion. On the other hand, immigrant labor was an integral part of the Southwest economy, with access to Mexican labor considered by Southwest growers to be a natural right attached to their propitious border location.[46] The immigration agency was caught squarely in the middle.

Teetering on the edge of this particular razor, the agency alternated between short-lived but visible enforcement campaigns, and what one former immigration official called "benign neglect."[47] As the Bracero Program came to a close, worried agency managers caucused. An internal memorandum describing their telephone conference documents the approach decided upon:

> A telephone call was made to Mr. Fargione, Southwest Regional Office, at which time Messrs. Noto, Robinson, Hardin, and myself spoke to him with regard to the action to be taken by the Service with the expiration of Public Law 78, particularly in light of the regulations which are being issued by the Department of Labor. Mr. Fargione was informed [of] the Service position with respect to those "braceros" who are in the United States when the Act and the grace period (January 5, 1965) expired. . . . *Neither an all-out effort nor a de-emphasized effort is to be made to effect the removal of these aliens.* Good judgment should prevail. . . .[48]

Five months later, Deputy Associate Commissioner James Greene introduced "A Plan to Bolster the Border Patrol on the Mexican Border." He explained, "With the expiration of this act [PL 78], a marked increase in the number of Mexican nationals who will attempt to enter the United States surreptitiously may be expected," but clung to the hope that H–2 workers might still be available. "If recruitment is permitted under this provision [H–2] and the number of laborers admitted meets the demand for labor," he wrote, "then little change from the present problem is anticipated. . . . [But] if the foreign labor supply is cut off, then the attempted entry of illegal aliens may possibly create a serious enforcement problem."[49] Despite the anticipated "serious enforcement problem," the plan relied on reshuffling personnel, and the report concluded that no budget increases should be requested.

A memo from Greene to the Southwest Regional Commissioner in January 1965, hints at the rationale behind the on-again, off-again commitment to enforcement in the post-bracero period. Greene placed his comments within the context of "1) expiration of PL 78; 2) public statements by Secretary of Labor Wirtz concerning future importation of H–2 labor; 3) enforcement problems caused by Mexicans who illegally seek employment opportunities heretofore available to braceros." Given this bleak scenario, Greene advised, it would be necessary to gear up for increased enforcement activities: "The continuing emphasis on apprehension of illegal agricultural workers will be necessary to prevent circumvention of national policy and *to avoid the development of any embarrassing pockets of illegal workers.*"[50] Caught between the economic utility of immigrant workers, and its own official mandate to control the border, the immigration agency saw illegal migration as an "embarrassment." As the former general counsel for California Rural Legal Assistance, a farm worker advocacy organization, put it in 1969, "It is not pure fantasy to conclude that the policy of the Justice Department on illegal entry is to do just enough to avoid wholesale criticism, without arousing the serious anger of antiunion employers who favor an abundance of cheap labor."[51]

Apprehensions of illegal aliens continued to climb, more than tripling between 1965 and 1970. An INS report entitled "Effect of Termination of Bracero Program on Enforcement Problems on Mexican Border," shows apprehensions of adult male Mexicans employed in agriculture increasing 600% in this period.[52] The contract labor system had further entrenched the interdependence of southwest growers and Mexican labor, exacerbating in the long-run the dilemma that in the short-run it helped resolve. Summarizing the effects of the 22–year program, the Congressional Research Service concludes, "The bracero program appears to have been simultaneously a major cause of as well as a significant cure for the illegal alien problem. . . ."[53]

AFTER THE BRACERO

A senior immigration official during the Carter Administration commented on the agency's liberal use of administrative discretion, "The Service has had to be very creative. . . . The subject matter is boiling up all over the place. The Service has to be creative to make it work."[54] The agency certainly had been "creative" during the Bracero Program, taking an active role in shaping the system to fit the needs of growers, and in the process sometimes circumventing statutory formalities. In the aftermath of the program, as illegal immigration soared—stoked by the 22–year experience with Mexican contract labor—the Service once again turned to "creative" interpretations of the law and its own authority. Nowhere was this more evident than in the case of "commuter aliens."

Commuter aliens, also known as "green-card commuters," are migrants who at one time received immigrant visas entitling them to permanent residence in the U.S., but who live in Mexico (with a much smaller number residing in Canada) and commute to the U.S. to work on a daily or seasonal basis. A permanent visa allows resident aliens temporary absences from the U.S. of up to one year without forfeiting their green card, and it is on this basis that the INS permits the daily or seasonal re-entry of green-card commuters. While immigrants who are sponsored by an employer must receive labor certifications from the DOL, those receiving their visas through the family preference system established by the Immigration and Nationality Act Amendments of 1965, are exempt from this bureaucratic hurdle.[55] After 1965, the large number of border inhabitants with immediate relatives in the United States could qualify for the green-card commuter status independent of labor certification.

These migrants are similar to permanent resident aliens in that, unlike the bracero or H–2 worker, they are not tied to any one employer or sector of the economy, and certification of domestic labor unavailability, where applicable at all, is required only for the initial admission. However, like the bracero and H–2 worker, these border-crossers come and go, putting down relatively few ties in the communities in which they work and carrying few social or economic costs for those communities. Indeed, green-card commuters are in some ways an even more ideal labor source than braceros, since the costs of renewal (housing, food, clothing, medical care, etc.) are paid on the Mexican side of the border. These Mexican commuters, in other words, constitute a labor supply stripped of most of its human needs.

The green-card commuter has been called by former INS General

Counsel, Charles Gordon, an "amiable fiction" and "a device of convenience."[56] Gordon explains, "Although the commuter status has never . . . been authorized by statute, it has been sanctioned by administrative interpretation and practice. . . ."[57] The practice was introduced in 1927 in response to a Supreme Court ruling that nonimmigrant aliens were prohibited from accepting employment in the United States.[58] Rather than applying this ruling to the thousands of border-crossers from Mexico who commuted daily to work in the U.S., and who until then had been defined as "nonimmigrants" who entered for a temporary stay, the INS issued an administrative regulation proclaiming the commuters "immigrants," ostensibly admitted for permanent residence.[59] As if by magic, a new immigrant status was born: the non-resident immigrant. When the Immigration and Nationality Act of 1952 specifically defined an "immigrant" as one who has been admitted for *permanent residence* to the U.S., the Board of Immigration Appeals concluded that the practice of admitting commuters with permanent visas as immigrants—despite the fact that they clearly did not reside in the U.S.—need not be interrupted. The Board argued that immigrant visas extended to their recipient the *privilege* of residing in the U.S., rather than requiring it.[60]

As the Bracero Program came to a close, commuter aliens were seen as a critical substitute for the contract labor supply. George Pickering, President of the Yuma Producers Cooperative Association, told the Select Commission on Western Hemisphere Immigration in 1968, that while in previous years members of his association had relied on bracero labor, they now depended on commuter labor:

> The commuters are a vital part of our farm labor force . . . the green carders almost exclusively take care of this ["stoop labor"] work. . . . Any curtailment in the use of green carders would drastically curtail the production of lettuce and melons. Just the cost of bringing these two crops to harvest is more than $10 million, and would certainly have an adverse effect on the economy of this area [*sic*].[61]

Other growers repeated the message. The Executive Vice President of the Texas Citrus and Vegetable Growers and Shippers provided a concise history of growers' dependence on Mexican labor and its various sources:

> Any action, legislative or administrative, that would disrupt or curtail the present supply of green card workers would have disastrous effect upon our industry and upon the entire

economy of the border area. Mexican citizens have always made up a large share of the work force on our fruit and vegetable farms. For many years they entered the United States illegally as wetbacks, then in 1954 [*sic*] the bracero program was instituted under Public Law 78 . . . which program was discontinued in 1964. Since 1964 there has been an increasing dependence upon the green card workers.[62]

Although the INS did not keep an official count of commuters, in-house surveys suggest that the number increased significantly between 1961 and 1967. A one-day spot check by the Service in 1961 recorded fewer than 20,000 commuters; a similar survey in 1969 put the number at over 47,000.[63] While these studies were fraught with methodological deficiencies, and undoubtedly undercounted commuters in both periods, agency officials and immigration scholars generally agree that the numbers reflected a real and dramatic increase.[64] In fact, the increase was probably larger than suggested by these data, as the proportion of commuters in seasonal agricultural work—who by virtue of their *seasonal* commute are less likely to be captured in daily spot-checks—increased with the end of the Bracero Program.[65] By 1969, it was estimated that commuters constituted a large percentage of the agricultural work force on the Southwest border, and that as much as 85% of the farm labor in California's Imperial Valley were green-card commuters.[66]

Commuters not only refurbished the supply of legal farm workers that was depleted with the end of the Bracero Program, but they also provided a ready supply of labor with which to break the farm labor strikes that gathered momentum in the early 1960s as the contract system wound down. In 1960, a suit was brought by the Amalgamated Meatcutters Union as a result of INS practices during a strike at an El Paso packing company. The Secretary of Labor had certified that a strike was in progress and that the entry of commuters to break the strike would adversely affect domestic labor. The INS determined that the ban on commuters was not applicable to green-card immigrants and refused to bar green-card commuters from the struck plant. The court confirmed the contention of the Amalgamated Meatcutters Union that these commuters were in fact *nonresidents* entering to perform temporary labor, and thus were subject to all the certification procedures and restrictions of other nonimmigrants, such as H–2 workers.[67] To conclude otherwise, the court noted, would "make a shambles" of the immigration law. The finding had potentially devastating consequences for the amiable fiction of the "nonresident resident," but the

INS chose to restrict the ruling to the specific strike, which by then was long over. When the AFL–CIO tried again in 1964, the court ruled that it lacked standing to challenge Immigration Service enforcement practices.[68]

Largely cosmetic changes were made by the Service in 1967 when it issued a regulation barring use of the green card as a border-crossing card in cases where the commuters intended to work at the site of a strike.[69] The regulation did little to curtail the use of commuters as strikebreakers, primarily because it applied only to those who had been hired *after* a labor dispute was certified. Senator Kennedy called it "a rather empty regulation and ruling," since

> [i]f the strike started today, there would be nothing in the regulation that would prohibit that farmer . . . going across the border and bringing in all the green cards he wanted until the Secretary of Labor certified that there was a strike. . . . So, in effect, the grower says: "These fellows are going to strike. I am going to go down there and fill up that truck and bring them on through. . . ."[70]

Enforcement practices further undermined the effectiveness of the narrow regulation. Cesar Chavez described INS enforcement to the Senate Subcommittee on Immigration and Naturalization, pointing out that as the aliens cross the border, they are asked by an Immigration inspector where they intend to work, ". . . and, of course so far no one has stated that it is their intention to go to Delano or to Texas to break the strike. It is a farce really. . . ."[71] The Executive Assistant to the Immigration Commissioner admitted, "I have to acknowledge that the job . . . to determine which of the possibly 5,000 agricultural places of employment . . . this particular alien is going to is well nigh impossible."[72] The Secretary of Labor observed in 1967 that to his knowledge, no commuters had been barred as a result of the regulation.[73] While the Border Patrol investigated struck farms to determine if any of the workers were commuters illegally admitted as strikebreakers, Commissioner Farrell reported that even under that procedure, "we are not finding many."[74] It should not be surprising, since the INS kept no record of when commuters last entered, and therefore had no way to determine if it was before or after the strike was certified.[75]

It was widely recognized that the use of green-card commuters as strikebreakers was unaffected by the 1967 regulation. Secretary of Labor Wirtz said unequivocally, "The green carders, living in Mexico and working in the United States, are strikebreakers . . . it is just that simple."[76] Organized labor documented the extensive use of commut-

ers as strikebreakers, who were often driven from the border to the
struck fields by company trucks, in some of the most hotly contested
labor disputes of the period.[77] In one case, the United Farm Workers
Organizing Committee reported that when over 900 farm workers
went out on strike against Giumerra Vineyards outside of Delano,
California, the grower quickly replaced the work force with commuters
whom he bused from the border and housed in company camps.[78]

The INS had originally established the commuter status by administrative fiat, and perpetuated the practice despite a number of legislative
attempts to end it. Amendments made to the Immigration and Nationality Act in 1965 (8 U.S.C. Section 1181[b]) appeared to restrict the use
of the green card as an entry permit to "returning resident immigrants,"
defined by Section 1101(a)(27)(B) as "an immigrant lawfully admitted
for permanent residence, who is returning from a temporary visit
abroad." The definition of "residence" was "principal, actual dwelling
place in fact." As the General Counsel of the California Rural Legal
Assistance described this change, "No distortion of the English language could result in a finding that the commuter was entering the
United States after a temporary visit abroad to return to his principal,
actual dwelling place."[79] The Immigration Service ignored the statutory
change. When challenged by members of the House Judiciary Committee several years later, INS General Counsel Charles Gordon explained
matter-of-factly, "These people [commuters] all obtained lawful admission for permanent residence, but they don't reside here."[80]

Those who had fought to close down the bracero system now focused their attention on this administrative substitute. Senator Harrison Williams of New Jersey, longtime opponent of the Bracero Program, was harshly critical of the commuter practice and questioned
INS motives. Permanent visas, he said, were intended for permanent
residents of the U.S., and were not meant to be border-crossing cards.
Noting the absence of any statutory basis for the commuter practice,
he complained, "It seems to me we were moving in the right direction
here in Congress when we . . . let Public Law 78 reach its extended
conclusion. But we speak about loopholes a lot around here. Evidently
in practice a loophole has developed with the green card situation."[81]
Senator Walter Mondale added, "*This is less of a loophole than a truck
hole.*"[82] Others condemned the system as "a creature of administrative
ingenuity, without statutory base," "the trick," "the magic," and "an
extraordinary anomaly."[83]

Congressional critics charged that the INS did everything in its
power—and beyond—to keep open the "truck hole" despite their
periodic attempts to close it. Senator Edward Kennedy had "reason to

believe that such a practice is an abuse of the intent and purpose of the Immigration and Nationality Act."[84] Senate Immigration Subcommittee Chair Senator Ralph Yarborough of Texas agreed, "This represents an executive suspension of the immigration laws. . . . This green card is something outside the law."[85] It was pointed out repeatedly that the law relating to green-card immigrants assumed that immigrants would reside in the U.S. with only brief, temporary visits abroad. Senator Kennedy confronted INS General Counsel Gordon, "It [the law] says [immigrants] are residing permanently in the United States, they [commuters] are not residing permanently in the United States."[86] Senator Yarborough made the same simple point, "You say he is a resident alien when he is not a resident alien."[87]

The courts confirmed the fictitious nature of the commuter status, but generally upheld the INS practice. In 1968, when two California farm workers attempted to prohibit the admission of green-card commuters in *Gooch v. Clark,* the district court granted the Service motion for summary judgment. The court recognized that there were no statutory grounds for the commuter practice, and that the Immigration and Nationality Act might require the "exclusion of the commuter who is not a permanent resident of the United States." Nonetheless, it upheld "the long practice of the Immigration and Naturalization Service in treating the commuter as a special immigrant," maintaining that there was no explicit reference to the commuter status in the final Senate report or the conference report of the Immigration and Nationality Act amendments of 1965, and thus the Congressional intent was arguably still unclear.[88] One observer noted sardonically,

> When analyzed, the rule of the district court in the *Gooch* case, presents a role-reversal, in which the public agency makes the law, and Congress, sitting as a sort of judicial board of review, has the obligation to nullify it—not by enactment of law itself, but by interpretive commentary appended to the law. In fact, even an unambiguous statement of purpose in an act of Congress . . . is not sufficient in the eyes of the court to offset the informal interpretation of the public agency.[89]

In 1968, the Select Commission on Western Hemisphere Immigration recommended that the commuter practice be eliminated.[90] Congress did not act, however, preferring to delegate any further treatment of this controversial issue to the executive branch. Even the system's most vociferous congressional opponents favored dealing with the issue administratively rather than tackling it in the political arena of Congress. During hearings on the commuter practice in 1967, Senators

Yarborough and Kennedy quizzed the Secretary of Labor and the INS General Counsel on how it could be restricted or terminated without recourse to legislation.[91] Despite the proddings of critics of the system, and the recommendations of the Select Commission, the Immigration Service did not relent. According to the testimony of a representative of the League of United Latin American Citizens (LULAC), the Deputy Assistant Immigration Commissioner told him, "It is our ruling that these people are lawful residents of the United States although not domiciled." The LULAC representative was impressed by the linguistic ingenuity, if not the logic: "Isn't this statement the epitome of illogic; a resident who does not reside, an immigrant who does not immigrate?"[92]

No doubt the agency's reluctance to end the 40–year commuter status was in part related to the perceived costs of requiring commuters to reside on the U.S. side of the border. The low cost of labor force renewal was recognized as a major virtue of this system in which low-wage labor worked in the U.S., but lived in Mexico. Immigration policymakers of the 19th century who wrestled with the problems of admitting a supply of impoverished immigrant workers would have been impressed by the solution of their 20th century counterparts. Not only were commuters a "gift" to be "gladly received," but entering the United States on a daily basis only to work, they exacted no fiscal cost on the host society. Time and time again, growers, congressional proponents of the system, and immigration officials warned of the inability of U.S. border communities to absorb the cost of the low-income housing, public school facilities, and health care that would accompany the transfer of poor Mexican workers and their families to the United States.[93]

In part, the INS retained the amiable fiction to avoid "the wrath of growers" or even the impression that they were "harassing" growers by restricting the commuter flow.[94] The agency was the target of intense pressure from border employers, as growers and their representatives insisted that the agricultural economy would be devastated without access to the commuters.[95] A former INS General Counsel explained the agency response to this pressure, "It was a practice that was helpful to business; [Commissioner] Farrell was not going to antagonize business by changing the practice."[96]

At least as important, with the termination of the Bracero Program and the DOL restrictions on H–2 workers, commuter labor was the only alternative to the illegal source. David North, a consultant to the Department of Labor, in 1970 observed that "the commuter is this generation's bracero."[97] Not only were many commuters "graduates of the bracero program," but in the late 1960s the commuter took the bracero's place as the legal work force of choice for border growers. It makes sense that the immigration agency, which was now required to check illegal immigration without the substitute bracero supply, would exercise its substantial administrative power to provide growers with the "truck hole" of green-card commuters. The General Counsel quoted above reflected on the 1960s green-card commuter decisions, "There was a source of labor in Mexico and getting it into the U.S. was the problem."[98] Just as the INS had for over a decade used its policymaking powers to maximize grower access to braceros in order to solve its enforcement dilemma, it tried once again to "walk around the statute."

This time the walk was destined to fail. Despite the agency's conspicuous administrative ingenuity, and one might say unyielding illogic, the commuter practice was inadequate as a substitute for the vast contract labor system. As illegal immigrants, many of whom were former braceros, poured across the border in increasing numbers, the INS was once more faced with doing the impossible. Accepting defeat, it withdrew from battle.

DEFEAT AND RETREAT

When Raymond Farrell replaced General Swing as Immigration Commissioner in 1962, he inherited an agency on the verge of a new era. With the Bracero Program closing down and DOL restrictions limiting other temporary worker entries, it was inevitable that the immigration agency would succumb to the impossibility of its assignment. A vast literature has developed in recent years on regulatory agencies that do not regulate.[99] One tradition within this literature focuses on the economic-structural constraints on certain kinds of federal regulatory agencies. A number of studies of the Occupational Safety and Health Administration, for example, document the bind of that Labor agency whose job it is to protect the health and safety of American workers without, however, interfering with profits.[100] Similarly, environmental protection agencies have the unenviable task of preserving the environment from industrial pollutants without exacting substantial sacrifices from the polluting industries.[101]

A comparable bind now faced the INS, as it was charged with controlling illegal immigration but precluded from doing so by the significant economic utility of a porous border. Commissioner Swing, facing congressional animosity for bolstering agency autonomy at the expense of certain influential members of Congress, had used a public relations campaign and well-calculated personal favors to repair the damage. As the INS confronted certain failure in fulfilling its mandate to control the border in the aftermath of the Bracero Program, Commissioner Farrell turned this micro-level politics and favor-trading into the informal function of the bureaucracy. Unable to realize the agency's formal mandate, Farrell redefined the agenda.

When the *New York Times* reported President Kennedy's appointment of Raymond Farrell, it noted that the new Commissioner had "both political and bureaucratic support. Representative John J. Rooney, Brooklyn Democrat, head of the House Appropriations subcommittee on State and Justice Department and judiciary appropriations, has been a backer and friend of Mr. Farrell."[102] In the ensuing years, that friendship and others with key congressional actors became an integral component of the new bureaucratic agenda. Officials in the agency and Congressional aides during the Farrell Administration are convinced that the personal connection with Rep. Rooney—which reportedly included trips together to consulates around the world and grouse-shooting expeditions in INS vehicles—was central to the agency's ability to avoid aggressive oversight by the House appropriations committee.[103] As one former Immigration official put it, referring to Rooney's reputation for tough questioning of bureaucratic expenditures, "Rooney, who was a real "watchdog," pestered the State Department, but wouldn't knock the [Immigration] Agency."[104]

Other connections further enhanced the cozy relationship with Congress. Most important was the personal and political relationship between Farrell's Associate Commissioner, Ed Loughran, and Senator James Eastland of Mississippi, longtime chair of the Subcommittee on Immigration of the Senate Judiciary Committee. So close was the bond between Senator Eastland and the agency that there was said to be a "revolving door" between the INS and Eastland's staff—the most notable illustration of which was the transfer of Loughran from the upper echelons of the Immigration Service to become Senator Eastland's Chief of Staff.[105] It has been noted that during the Farrell Administration, there was on the part of the Senate Judiciary, "shockingly inadequate oversight of the Immigration and Naturalization Service, one of the Justice Department's most troubled agencies."[106] In fact, between 1968 and 1978, Eastland's committee held *no* immigration hearings. The year 1972 was typical. That year, not only were there no oversight hearings, but no hearings were held on any of the 17 bills assigned to the Senate immigration committee, and not a single bill was reported out.[107]

This insulation from the public eye did not come free, nor was it based solely on personal friendships. Rather, the INS was in many respects placed under the direct control of Senator Eastland and Rep. Rooney. Pulitzer Prize winner John Crewdson explains, "Together Eastland and Rooney controlled the agency's top appointments, in return for protecting the INS from meddlers, reformers, and other outside interference."[108] The Immigration Service in this period seems to have operated as a kind of political slush fund for influential members of Congress. According to officials in the agency at the time, positions up and down the INS hierarchy were filled entirely on recommendations from Eastland, and to a somewhat lesser extent, Rooney.[109] Even part-time summer employees were recruited from among Eastland's constituents in Mississippi.[110] A career official with the INS for thirty-four years wrote to the Select Commission on Immigration and Refugee Policy in 1980 that Farrell made the agency "100% political, even down to the lowest clerical position."[111] Two others recalled how it worked, "Service personnel who wanted to be promoted into particular vacancies simply contacted Eastland and asked for that particular job, and then Congress [sic] called Farrell and said 'that's who I want.' "[112] Reflecting on the grouse-hunting trips, control over the INS promotions roster, and a variety of other factors that the agency provided individual members of Congress, these two officials noted ruefully, "Immigration *Service*'—Yea, we were a 'Service' agency all right—we served the *Hill* [Congress]."[113]

Another central component of Commissioner Farrell's new agenda, and related to this "politicalization," was a commitment to bureaucratic obscurity. Farrell himself maintained a low profile, some have said virtually handing the reins of the agency over to Loughran, who was described by a former colleague as the " 'gray eminence' who ran things."[114] But Commissioner Farrell charted the course of least resistance for the agency too. More than one former associate has referred to him as the "don't-rock-the-boat Commissioner" who avoided controversy at all costs.[115] A former senior official described it this way: "He [Farrell] wouldn't stick his neck out about anything. His motto was, 'Don't be visible, someone might take a shot at you. If someone in Congress is interested in something, get it done for them. Otherwise, lay low.' "[116]

It was a defensive posture that suited well an agency in defeat. With illegal immigration continuing to swell, Farrell surrendered to the contradiction that Swing had managed temporarily to dodge. As illegal immigrants now provided the cheap and vulnerable labor force that braceros once supplied southwest growers, the caretaker commissioner avoided controversy by accepting defeat, and relying on the good will of Congress not to dwell on that defeat or to question the surrender.

Senator Eastland was unlikely to complain. Eastland himself was a Mississippi planter, and, according to a staff member for the Senate Subcommittee on Immigration, "All he cared about was being able to keep his illegals."[117] A former head of the Border Patrol put it more equivocally. "Eastland had a growers' interest in immigration," he said. "And heaven forbid, if you were the Border Patrol, you should go into Mississippi." And then, after a pause, "There were no Border Patrol [agents] in Mississippi. . . . It's a good thing there were no illegals in Mississippi [sic]."[118]

Defying the conventional wisdom that bureaucracies have a self-interest in budgetary increases and expansion, Commissioner Farrell conspicuously resisted such increases. Between 1963 and 1969, apprehensions of illegal aliens more than tripled, yet the INS budget increased by less than one-third—not even enough to keep up with inflation—and the number of permanent staff positions actually *declined*.[119] Despite the spiraling workload, Farrell steadfastly insisted no new funds were necessary.[120] An investigative reporter with the *New York Times*, in a scathing exposé of the agency, contended that Farrell "did not provide the funds for the agency that middle-level immigration officials deemed crucial."[121] Not only did Farrell resist requesting funds commensurate with the rapid increase in illegal immigration, but he ordered his subordinates in the underfunded agency to suffer in silence. As one of these subordinates recalled, "Under the Farrell Administration, we were told to say everything's fine with the budget."[122] Others expanded, "We were not allowed to tell the truth. Even though there was no gas in the cars, we weren't allowed to say so."[123] An INS Investigator, testifying before Congress in 1971, hesitated to respond to a question about how much the Immigration budget would have to be increased "to do the job." He told Congress, "I made that [recommendation] once when I was in charge of the Dallas office and I almost got charged with treason."[124]

As Rourke points out, "The most embarrassing kind of jurisdiction an agency can acquire is control over an activity that is anathema to its own constituency."[125] As we have seen, the INS falls in this category of agencies with an "embarrassing" jurisdiction. Agricultural employers have historically provided the Service with a major base of support, and growers' advocates in Congress have been among its staunchest and most powerful allies, who during the Farrell–Eastland Administration provided a virtual shield against oversight. The situation, however, is even more "embarrassing" than this essentially pluralist account suggests. For underlying this political catch–22 was the more fundamental and intransigent structural one, in which the economic role of immigrants as a cheap labor force collides with the social and political costs of that economic strategy. To the extent that the immigrant work force is *illegal,* the primary burden of reconciling the irreconcilable falls on the immigration agency. Commissioner Farrell's response was to accept the inevitable defeat, and to court influential members of Congress who protected the agency from some of the political fallout of his agency's glaring inadequacies. At one level, the strategy worked well. Despite the undeniable failures of his agency, Farrell retained his position for over eleven years, longer than any other Immigration Commissioner in history.

Self-imposed budget restrictions were an integral part of his strategy. Unable to realize the agency's border control mandate, Commissioner Farrell preferred to avoid the scrutiny that accompanies requests for budget increases. Furthermore, he apparently used the budget issue as a way both to solidify his alliances in Congress and to present the agency as "efficient," if not effective. A former senior Immigration official alleged that Farrell struck an agreement with Senator Eastland that if the Commissioner "did not rock the boat, his agency would be let alone—no increases in the budget, but no decreases either."[126] In the House, there was reportedly a "tacit agreement between Farrell and Rooney on what to ask for in the budget."[127] According to a former senior Border Patrol official, Farrell and Rooney—who he said were "Irish drinking buddies"—"cut the budget deal under the table and then staged it at the hearing. In part, Farrell probably said he didn't need more money because he wanted to look good. You know, 'we can do the job without increases . . . we're a lean operation.' "[128] One General Counsel, reflecting on the "chaos" and severe underfunding of the Immigration Service, claimed that the agency suffered "self-inflicted wounds."[129] Those wounds were not the product of bureaucratic masochism or mindless self-destruction. Nor were they due simply to corruption, incompetence, or indifference. Rather, they were symptoms of a structural—and ultimately a political—bind that required choosing between mutually exclusive prerequisites of bureaucratic power.

An impaired reputation as an effective agency, and deep demoralization within the ranks, followed. In 1972, Representative Peter Rodino held a lengthy series of hearings on the issue of illegal aliens. Representative Jack McDonald began his comments with an across-the-board indictment of the Immigration Service, calling it "a shambles of a once

proud and effective branch of the Federal Government" which suffered
from "a schizophrenic, paranoid type of management."[130] Representative Elizabeth Holtzman was less caustic, but no less to the point: "It
is disappointing to think that the Federal agency charged with the
administration of our laws could perform as inefficiently and ineffec-
tively as the Immigration and Naturalization Service."[131] To the recom-
mendation that the INS look to the Bureau of Prisons for advice on
setting up a reform task force, she scoffed, "That is like asking the
lame to lead the blind."[132] Senator Dennis DeConcini, speaking at
authorization hearings the following year, used the occasion to express
his concern:

> I am very frustrated. . . . It is just such a discouraging operation
> to sit on these authorization hearings and see a good arm of
> the Department of Justice go down hill like a roller coaster.
> . . . It is the most discouraging thing I have had to deal with
> on the Judiciary Committee. Year after year I see the border
> patrol and INS not able to get a grasp of the problem.[133]

Representative Joshua Eilberg, Democrat of Pennsylvania and Chair
of the House Subcommittee on Immigration, was straightforward:
"The INS at the present time is totally incapable of administering and
enforcing provisions of the Immigration and Nationality Act."[134] The
General Accounting Office drew the same conclusion in its study entitled "Prospects Dim for Effectively Enforcing Immigration Laws."[135]

The media assault began in 1980. *Foreign Affairs Magazine* called
the INS the "whipping boy and the laughing stock of the executive
branch."[136] An article in the *Los Angeles Times* proclaimed it "the
most tangled bureaucracy in government."[137] The *U.S. News and
World Report* began its cover story on "The Great American Immigration Nightmare": "The Immigration and Naturalization Service,
guardian of the nation's borders, is like a huge animal neck-deep
in quicksand. The harder it struggles, the deeper it sinks."[138] John
Crewdson, winner of the Pulitzer Prize in journalism, called the Immigration Service "the worst-managed, least effective federal agency in
Washington."[139]

Not surprisingly, INS field personnel were frustrated and demoral-
ized. A senior bureaucrat in the Washington office described a conversation he had with a Border Patrol agent in San Ysidro, California:
"The agent told me, 'You know we're down here playing a game. They
[in Washington] don't want us to do our job. Illegal aliens come in and
feed the economy and we're not allowed to do our job. It's a game.' You
know, they're [the agents] not dumb."[140] In 1980, Michael Harpold,

President of the National INS Council—the union representing INS employees—testified before Congress,

> I would say that the employees working for the Department of Justice that we represent are the most frustrated. . . . They are charged by law with locating, detaining and processing illegal aliens in this country. . . . Yet, they find policies and procedures and programs . . . that on every hand seem to frustrate their ability to do that job. . . . On the one hand, they must comply with the agency policy, or they are in violation and they lose their job, and on the other hand, if the procedures of the agency don't allow them to do it, then that also can be used against them. *So they find themselves damned if they do and damned if they don't.* The frustration levels are very high . . . [there is] a very severe . . . morale crisis within the INS work force.[141]

"Damned if they do and damned if they don't." The frustration expressed by INS personnel in the post-bracero period was the micro-level embodiment of the structural dilemma confronting the agency. For one brief decade following Operation Wetback, the Immigration Service managed to elude that dilemma through the Bracero Program and its considerable administrative ingenuity in the program's operation. A senior Border Patrol officer under the Swing and Farrell Administrations, reminiscing about "the good old days" of the Bracero Program and the changes he had seen in the Service following its demise, reflected simply, "Most Border Patrol people felt it was a real shame to end it. It made enforcement so much easier."[142]

Traditional structural depictions of Operation Wetback and the Bracero Program, focusing on capital accumulation and legitimation needs, are useful in placing these state activities in a broader political–economic context.[143] However, their tendency to portray the state as monolithic, reacting directly and uniformly to the structures of civil society, is clearly at odds with the evidence of internal dissension and conflict presented here. Furthermore, the ability of such structural accounts to explain *shifts* in policy—for example, the demise of the Bracero Program, or the crackdown on illegal aliens in 1954 versus the "benign neglect" exercised subsequent to 1964—is limited by the high level of abstraction to which these models are confined. In the absence of empirical data tracing the historical contingencies, working-class victories, and compromises between state managers and various

contingents of capital (what Fred Block calls a *"modus vivendi"* between the state and capital) that often precede such shifts, structural
explanations risk tautologically affirming the omnipotence of the state.
Finally, the decision-making process itself, through which structural
imperatives are actually translated into policy, and which inevitably
involves real people with a variety of institutional interests, career
concerns, and political persuasions, is left out of most structural explanations altogether. The result—ironically, given the ambitious intent—
is a truncated analysis with only limited explanatory power. Where in
such a model is there a place for the feuding between the Immigration
and Labor agencies? The old-boy networks of influence among Eastland, Loughran, Rooney, and Farrell? The aggressive, independent
style of General Swing as he pushed his agency to the limits of its
autonomy? Or the favor-trading that salvaged Swing's relationship
with Congress and, perhaps, the viability of his crusade against illegal
aliens?

If we want to account fully for the policymaking process, we clearly
must bring the policymakers back in. However, it is at least as important not to get trapped at the microlevel. If Commissioner Farrell's
low-profile style and old-boy connections with Congress contributed
to the withdrawal of the Immigration Service from pursuit of its official
mandate, these were merely facilitating factors, easing the decline and
cushioning senior bureaucrats from the repercussions of their inevitable
failure. From the time of Commissioner Farrell's retirement in 1973 to
the present, there have been seven different Immigration Commissioners (including two interim Acting Commissioners), each with his own
personal style and political agenda. The agency has been piloted by the
retired military general Leonard Chapman—much in the tradition of
General Swing—whose tough, no-nonsense style was epitomized by
the "standing desk" he had built for his office so he could conduct
business standing up, and the humanistic, immigrant-service oriented
Leonel Castillo, appointed by President Carter. But, the agency that is
referred to in Washington as the "step child" of the Department of
Justice[144] has remained a bureaucratic backwater, paralyzed by the
contradictions that permeate it and ridiculed for its impotence.

CHAPTER 7
CONCLUSION

"America must regain control of its borders" went the battle cry of immigration reformers in the 1980s.[1] In 1986, twenty years after the last braceros left the fields, apprehensions of illegal immigrants reached over 1.5 million.[2] With the bracero solution to illegal immigration dismantled, not only did employers return to using illegal labor, but the flow was redoubled. The contract labor system had strengthened the historical dependence of western growers on Mexican labor. And so the dialectical sequence of contradictions and conflicts plays on, as the solution of one period prepares the way for the conflicts of the next.

Some immigration scholars maintain that the increase in illegal immigration has been actively tolerated, if not encouraged, by U.S. policies.[3] Citing the lack of funding to the INS, and an attitude of benign neglect both in Congress and in the agency itself, they argue that the economic advantages of illegal immigration encourage a hands-off stance. There is no doubt that illegal immigrants provide a substitute for the bracero of the past, not only for agricultural employers but increasingly for urban sectors of the economy as well. More captive and vulnerable than U.S. citizens or permanent residents, undocumented immigrants "work scared and hard," as Secretary of Labor Ray Marshall put it in 1978.[4] One 1980 study of undocumented Mexican women working in the Los Angeles garment industry indicated the depths of these immigrants' fears and their resulting vulnerability, reporting that 41% of the women received less than the legal minimum wage.[5] The Human Rights' Commission in San Francisco discovered one garment sweatshop in which undocumented workers had not been paid for eight months and had lodged no complaint.[6] So valuable is this cheap labor that the Chambers of Commerce of U.S. border cities advertised its availability throughout the 1970s in an attempt to lure industry to the area.[7]

But the drawbacks of the illegal labor source remain what they were prior to Operation Wetback. Undocumented workers, like braceros, in theory can be drawn into the labor market and expelled as the demand requires, reducing the political and fiscal costs associated with a more permanent immigrant work force. However, unlike braceros, the supply can not be turned on and off at will. By the 1980s, the perception was widespread that millions of illegal immigrants had made a permanent home in the United States, and that the numbers were increasing as the border spun out of control. While this perception almost certainly exaggerated the numbers crossing the border with the intention of remaining in the United States,[8] nonetheless the uncontrolled nature of this shadow work force, and the political backlash that it provoked, were its primary drawbacks. This contradiction between the political and fiscal costs of an illegal labor supply versus the economic benefits of that very illegality—and the curious dilemmas that this contradiction generates—were summed up by the ingenuous remark of one bewildered citizen confronting the pros and cons of illegal immigration. "Well then," she said, "how about putting a quota on the number of illegals to be admitted each year?"[9]

In 1986, Congress passed the Immigration Reform and Control Act (IRCA, Public Law No. 99–603). Its provisions not only echo the debates of the past, but in their internal inconsistencies reflect the broader contradictions permeating immigration. The new law officially recognizes the economic utility of immigrant labor. Most notably, it includes a Special Agricultural Worker (SAW) provision—described in the *Washington Post*[10] as a "cave-in" to agricultural interests—that legalized undocumented workers who had worked in U.S. agriculture for at least 90 days between May 1985 and May 1986.[11] The SAW legalization program was accompanied by a Replenishment Agricultural Worker (RAW) measure providing for the import of additional Mexican farm workers should labor shortages develop as a result of newly legalized SAWs deserting agricultural work for urban employment. At the same time, however, the law was touted as a *restrictive* measure designed to reduce the costs associated with uncontrolled illegal immigration. Indeed, the political engine in IRCA was the employer sanctions provision, making it illegal to knowingly employ unauthorized workers. Reminiscent of the unsuccessful bills introduced by Senator Paul Douglas and others in the early 1950s, the employer sanctions measure was hailed by its restrictionist advocates (who in this round, in contrast to the earlier period, tended to be conservative and moderate Republicans), as a way to regain control over the border by closing job opportunities to undocumented workers. Employer sanctions were enormously popular politically, with polls showing the American public overwhelmingly in favor of such an approach.[12]

However, the provision was doomed from the beginning. An "affirmative defense" clause protects employers from prosecution as long as they request documentation from workers, regardless of the validity of the documents presented. Senator Alan Simpson (R-Wyoming), the principal sponsor of the law, was clear about the motivation behind this clause, warning his colleagues that it was important not to make sanctions "an onerous burden" on employers.[13] By 1985, the U.S. Chamber of Commerce, which was adamantly opposed to employer sanctions before the addition of the affirmative defense protection, officially *endorsed* the measure. Agricultural lobbyists largely ignored the employer sanctions provision, devoting their full attention to securing the generous SAW and RAW programs.[14]

Enforcement policies compound the effects of the affirmative defense loophole, stretching it wide enough and deep enough for all but the most ill-informed employers. The Deputy Commissioner of Immigration assured Congress that the agency would make it "pragmatically easy" for employers to comply with the letter, if not the spirit, of the law.[15] The Service was true to its word. An agency regulation requires inspectors to give employers a three-day warning before inspections of their hiring records, ample time to prepare the forms that constitute an affirmative defense against prosecution. Admitting that the warning allows employers to "clean up shop" before the INS arrives, a senior immigration official in Washington explained that the purpose of the regulation was to avoid "harassing" employers or interrupting business.[16] A district director in the Southwest explained the concern not to "harass" employers in practical terms: "Our lawyers want to avoid court injunctions."[17]

Finally, and more fundamentally, employer sanctions were doomed by the mere strength of the push-pull economic forces that trigger immigration in the first place—forces that are far too compelling to be repressed by legislative fiat. A General Accounting Office study reveals that even in countries with counterfeit-proof identification cards, employer sanctions do not stem illegal immigration.[18] Employers, attracted by the substantial economic advantages of an illegal work force, use a number of strategies to elude the law (such as extensive subcontracting), and immigrants from Third World countries continue to be drawn to the possibility of eking out a living on the margins of the First World. The observation of one immigrant-dependent employer in Southern California underlines the resilience of such economic forces. Questioned about his apparent lack of concern for the impact of the recently passed employer sanctions law on his firm, the employer shrugged, "Employers will find some way of finding cheap labor, that's what capitalism is all about."[19] Apprehension statistics since IRCA was enacted suggest that illegal immigrants continue to provide this cheap labor. After an initial decline, steep increases in apprehension rates have been recorded since mid-1989,[20] leaving little doubt that the "windmill" of illegal immigration still turns, flattening this latest attempt to grapple with it.

This story of the INS and the Bracero Program focuses on one 22-year period in the ongoing saga that began with the influx of unskilled European immigrants to the United States in the last century. Grounded in a dialectical-structural model of law and the state, the study documents the linkages between the broad structural contradictions that have historically plagued immigration policymakers, and the day-to-day decisions of real-life political actors. Thirty years ago, C. Wright Mills urged social scientists to develop a "sociological imagination."[21] Adequate sociological analysis, Mills insisted, requires linking history and biography, social structure and individual action. While some have answered his call—mostly in the area of social psychology, and often favoring the psychological over the social structural—scholars interested in understanding law and the state have largely ignored Mills' challenge. The following section addresses this and other issues in the development of state theory and concludes with a discussion of how this analysis of the Bracero Program may contribute to bridging the gap between macro- and micro-level explanations of political outcomes.

BRINGING PEOPLE BACK IN: THEORIES OF THE STATE REVISITED

Theories of the state can be distinguished at the most general level according to how they view the relationship between the state and civil society. It has recently become fashionable to draw a dichotomy along these lines, between "society-centered" theorists who posit the causal primacy and political dominance of forces in civil society, and "state-centered" theorists who claim that the state is capable of substantial autonomy, has its own set of interests, and plays an independent role in shaping the structure and social relations of civil society.[22] This dichotomy, which I will argue later is largely arbitrary and counterproductive to the theory-building enterprise, provides a useful categorical device, particularly since state theorists have generally come to identify themselves with one side or the other of this paradigmatic divide.

Society-centered approaches have dominated state theorizing for most of this century. Until the late 1960s, one variety of society-centered theory—pluralism—enjoyed a virtual monopoly of the field.[23] Pluralism, best exemplified by Robert Dahl's (1961) classic study of community power in New Haven, Connecticut, and the "multiple-influence" approach of Arnold Rose (1967), views American society as an amalgam of special interest groups operating within the context of a fundamental value consensus. According to this depiction, interest groups compete in the neutral arena of the state, the ground rules and structure of which are set by the underlying value consensus. The laws and policies resulting from this competition represent a compromise among participating interest groups. Furthermore, while on any given issue the compromise is likely to favor the most organized, persistent, and/or resourceful interest group, no one group regularly gets its way. Not only is the state itself neutral, but there is no elite in civil society that is consistently successful at maneuvering in the state arena.

The long-standing dominance of the pluralist model is undoubtedly attributable to a combination of its ostensible empirical merits and its political appeal. The political process in a capitalist democracy at one level *does* resemble a pluralist tug of war between competing interest groups, and the outcome is unfailingly presented by participants in that process as a compromise. In the bracero context, for example, congressional legislation as well as the international accords were without exception characterized as products of negotiation among interested parties, including in this instance the Mexican government.[24] Beyond this apparent empirical confirmation of the pluralist model, it has ideological appeal in a society that defines itself as the archetypical political democracy.

In the late 1960s, as overt social conflict and a shifting ideological climate simultaneously eroded both pluralists' ability to explain policy outcomes and their ideological edge, alternative models of social power and policymaking effectively challenged the comfortable pluralist view. Most notably, a neo-Marxist tradition developed around the work of William Domhoff and others who argued that the state in capitalist society is not, and can not be, neutral.[25] Rather, the state consistently operates in the interests of the economic elite who effectively use their resources to shape both the rules of the game and policy outcomes. The mechanisms through which the economic elite exert this influence are direct (the state elite are themselves drawn from the ranks of the economic elite) and indirect (in the form of campaign contributions and ownership and control of the mass media and other vehicles of idea-formation). Ellis Hawley, adopting an essentially instrumentalist position to explain the dominance of growers in defining "labor short-ages" and "prevailing wages" in the bracero era, argues that the local branches of the Farm Placement Service in California were puppets of grower associations.[26] Henry Anderson was more specific, describing details of the economic and personal connections between the largest bracero users in the state and the California Farm Placement Service.[27]

The virtue of this instrumentalist model lies in its concrete documentation of both the specific vehicles of economic elite dominance, and, in the case of Domhoff's work, the actual individuals, and their corporations and financial institutions, that comprise the economic elite in the United States. In fact, the instrumentalist school offers extensive empirical data to refute the pluralist notions of a neutral state and diffuse social power. But its main weakness is likewise empirical, for it is unable to account for a significant number of cases in which the state not only acts independently of any apparent efforts on the part of the elite, but actually *contradicts* the desires of the business community. For example, when Congress passed the Emergency Quota Law of 1921—which for the first time imposed quotas on the number of immigrants to the U.S.—leading industrialists and financiers almost uniformly opposed the measure, warning Congress that the proposed restrictions on the immigrant labor supply would amount to economic suicide. Congress, influenced by pseudo-scientific theories of southern Europeans' "racial inferiority" and concerned about the potential threats that the influx of low-wage, increasingly unionized, immigrants posed to the established order, not only passed the restrictions over the protests of the most influential capitalists of the period, but further tightened them in the Quota Law of 1924.[28]

The instrumentalist model is similarly incompatible with the data presented in Chapter 4. As these data suggest, while the Immigration Service catered to growers on a wide range of bracero issues, the bureaucracy had its own set of interests which were not always parallel to those of bracero employers, and upon which it was capable of acting. Perhaps the best example of such independent action—which temporarily set the Service in opposition to some of the most powerful growers and ranchers in the Southwest—was its refusal in 1956 to entertain the possibility of an exchange of its I-100 program for the ranchers' preferred Special system. Despite concerted lobbying by bracero users, and Mexican officials' rumored ultimatum that either the Special Program or the I-100 system must be terminated, the INS maintained a "firm stand on the I-100."

In addition to such empirical deficiencies, the instrumentalist approach is sometimes little more than an empirical generalization lacking in any real theoretical base, in that there is nothing in the analysis to suggest the theoretical *necessity* of capitalist influence on the state.[29]

In this respect, instrumentalists do not stray far from the pluralist view that state power is accessible to those who have the resources to acquire it. In marked contrast to this atheoretical quality of instrumentalism, structuralists like Althusser[30] and Poulantzas[31] posit an "objective relation"[32] between the state and capital that guarantees that the capitalist state will operate in the long-term interests of capitalists *independent* of their participation in the policymaking process. This objective relation hinges on the complementarity of interests between a state in any particular social formation and the dominant class in that formation.[33] According to this structuralist view, the state has "relative autonomy," in that it is relatively free from the manipulation of individual capitalists; at the same time, it is not autonomous from the structural requirements of the political economy within which it operates and which it must work to preserve.[34]

Max Pfeffer employs this structural model in tracing the state response to the labor needs of "corporate agriculture" in the form of bracero labor, and later undocumented workers and commuters.[35] Having specified the nature of the agricultural production process and the advantages of a captive, controlled farm work force, Pfeffer spells out the ideological considerations behind the termination of the Bracero Program. Within the political context of the early 1960s, he says, ". . . officials of both Congress and the Executive were leary of . . . creating the possibility of domestic dissent."[36] Similarly, Robert Bach highlights "the processes of capital accumulation and various manifestations of class struggle" to explain U.S. policies on Mexican immigration in general, and the Bracero Program in particular.[37]

If instrumentalists overemphasize the influence of the individual actor and rarely go beyond empirical generalization, structuralist analyses often lack empirical data, and reify structure. This lack of data and the reification of structure go hand in hand. For once social structures themselves have been imbued with the ability to act, detailed empirical study of flesh and blood actors seems both unnecessary and, in any case, difficult to link to the theory; looked at the other way around, without the human actors that inhabit the world of empirical data, it must be the structures that by default do the "acting."[38] The analyses of Pfeffer and Bach are good examples. While Pfeffer and Bach make important contributions toward understanding the economic imperatives of corporate agriculture and the role of foreign labor in that context, their inattention to the way these structural imperatives are actually translated into state policies leaves a pronounced gap in their causal logic. The state is also oversimplified in this structural model. In the absence of empirical data about the workings of specific state agencies such as that provided here, the state becomes monolithic and operates from a singular motive—the preservation of the political and economic status quo.

Finally, structuralists often exaggerate the rationality of the state and its ability to preserve the social order. Not only are very real divisions within the capitalist class and inherent contradictions in the economy downplayed, but the ability of grass-roots social movements to affect policy (as when organized labor successfully pressed the Labor Department to enforce restrictions on the use of braceros in the early 1960s) is either ignored or explained tautologically as an illustration of the state's "social harmony" function. Ironically, while the character of the state and state policy are dependent on the structure of civil society in this model, the state takes on an aura of omnipotence as it simultaneously accommodates capital and defuses social conflict.

"Dialectical-structuralists," while building on an essentially structuralist base, avoid this implication of omnipotence by centering their analyses around the concept of conflicts and contradictions that inhere in the political economy of capitalism. From this perspective, law and policy constitute the state's attempts to resolve the conflicts stemming from underlying contradictions.[39] Since policy outcomes are the products of social contradictions and struggle, whether or not these policies benefit the capitalist class in any given case is an empirical question. Allen Whitt applies the model to conflicts surrounding the construction of BART (Bay Area Rapid Transit) in San Francisco, demonstrating that contradictions in the urban economy produced conflicts, the attempted solutions to which reproduced conflict. Having unleashed urban sprawl and devastated the inner city, Whitt explains, the capitalist class reaped what it had sown.[40] Whitt's study is not explicitly an analysis of the state. However, in his recognition of the centrality of contradictions in limiting the effectiveness of capitalists' actions as well as state policy, his dialectical analysis of class power makes an important contribution to state theory.

By placing social conflict and struggle at the center of analysis, dialectical-structuralists at least implicitly put human beings back into human history and replace the deterministic quality of Althusserian structuralism with an emphasis on historical contingency. But the nod to human agency often remains an abstraction; in practice, contradictions and conflicts themselves take on causal primacy. More importantly, the state remains reified, retaining its anthropomorphic ability to "act"—this time in the form of devising resolutions to the contradictions that confront it. Having taken social contradictions as the unit of analysis, dialectical-structuralists often depict the state as a monolithic reactor to those contradictions. Not only do divisions within the state and potential conflicts among the institutions of the state generally remain unexplored, but the model—in distilling those divisions out of the analysis—implicitly negates their causal importance.[41] But anyone who examines empirically the creation of social policy by focusing attention on the agencies and political actors that shape those policies, discovers the obvious—that the state not only is not monolithic but is beset with continual, sometimes intense, internal strife. As we have seen in the case of the Bracero Program, the nature of that strife and its influence on policy outcomes must be central ingredients in any theory that purports to explain the connections between society, law, and the state.

In both structuralism and its dialectical variant, the state is presented at one level as an entity of impressive faculties, empowered not only by its status as an actor, but by its uniformity of purpose and extensive mechanisms of repression and persuasion. At another level, however, the state is little more than a lackey, shackled to the forces that inhere in civil society. With no distinct state agenda and no incentives independent of those imposed by the dynamics and structures of civil society, the reified state is less of an actor than a reactor.

Theda Skocpol, criticizing society-centered theorists for their "unwillingness . . . to grant true autonomy to states," argues that an "intellectual sea change is under way" that "involves a fundamental rethinking of the role of states in relation to economies and societies."[42] What Skocpol calls "state-centered" theorists focus their efforts not on calculating the influence of particular individuals or structures on state policy, but on establishing the independent power of the state itself.[43] Indeed, much of this research represents an effort to document "state autonomy," defined as the ability of state actors to successfully pursue their own agendas.[44]

A major strength of this approach is that it unpacks "the state" by focusing on specific state agencies, institutions, or cadres of state managers. Skocpol and Finegold, for example, document the active participation of the U.S. Department of Agriculture (USDA) in the early 1930s in shaping New Deal agricultural policies, and contrast the successes of the USDA to the failures of the National Recovery Administration.[45] Tracing empirically the policy agenda of the department and its ability to implement that agenda despite opposition from the agricultural lobby, they build a middle-range account of New Deal policy that explicitly recognizes the diversity of the state and the institutions that make it up. Not only are those institutions variable in terms of their autonomy (the USDA in the early 1930s is referred to as "an island of state strength in an ocean of weakness"[46]), but agency-specific agendas may vary as well.

The problem in these state-centered theories is that, while the state is no longer granted anthropomorphic power, its political power, autonomy, and causal primacy are often exaggerated. Most recent literature in the state-centered tradition recognizes the danger of adhering to a crude Weberian model in which state autonomy is automatically assumed. Gregory Hooks, in an article analyzing the U.S. Department of Agriculture in three historical periods, thus writes: "The state-centered theory I defend rests on the argument that the state *may* be autonomous. . . ."[47] Similarly, Skocpol argues that forces in civil society may be important in understanding policy outcomes. In her article comparing neo-Marxist explanations of the New Deal, she concludes her point about the relative strength of the USDA as compared to less effective federal agencies in the industrial arena: "Capitalists, industrial workers, and farmers certainly helped to shape and limit the New Deal, as did the contours of the massive economic crisis itself."[48] Nonetheless, probably because this approach developed largely in response to the limitations of society-centered models, the tendency is to focus empirical research on state institutions that are noteworthy for their autonomy, to study the processes and dynamics that contribute to that autonomy, and to neglect or relegate to a footnote, the social forces that *limit* state power.

While the distinction between society-centered and state-centered theories may be a useful categorical device, it is arguably counterproductive to the theoretical endeavor. Once the paradigmatic line has been drawn, the tendency is to take sides, defend one's position, and discourage traffic. The relationship between the state and society is an interactive one, and to deny the importance of this interaction—or to downplay the significance of one side or the other of this interactive equation—in the interest of paradigmatic purity, is to preclude theoretical development.

Fred Block is one of the few state theorists to cross this paradigmatic divide, offering a synthetic model that combines the insights of both traditions.[49] Starting from the premise that "state and society are interdependent and interpenetrate in a multitude of different ways," Block maintains that the state/society debate is a waste of intellectual energy.[50] Like Skocpol, he assumes that "state managers collectively are self-interested maximizers, interested in maximizing their power, prestige, and wealth."[51] These state actors enjoy some autonomy, and are capable of restricting the activities of even the dominant classes. This is so not only because, as Max Weber argued, the state has a monopoly on legitimate violence, but because the dominant classes are dependent on the state for a variety of essential services, not the least of which is checking the excesses intrinsic to the capitalist mode of production. Thus, state managers and the propertied classes work out a *"modus vivendi,"* in which *both* sides must make concessions.[52] While state managers have their own interests as well as substantial power to impose their agendas on the dominant classes in civil society, precisely what those interests are, how they are realized, and indeed *whether* they are realized, depends in large part on "the capitalist context."[53] In describing this context, Block notes the structural dependence of the state on economic growth, the economic elite's ability to buy influence over policymakers and control the media, and the limitations imposed by inherent contradictions in the political economy, thereby integrating instrumentalist, structuralist, and dialectical-structuralist approaches. In addition, he argues that the international environment and the "competitive state system" provide an important component of the capitalist context within which the state operates.[54]

Block makes a unique contribution to state theory by emphasizing the importance of the agendas of state managers and by linking those agendas to the "capitalist context." Equally important, human agency, in the form of state managers acting on their career and institutional interests, is added between the structure of capitalism and policy outcomes, providing the missing causal link in the essentially teleological argument of structuralists, and breaking down the reification of the state. However, if the state is no longer reified in Block's rendition, it remains implicitly monolithic. Nowhere does Block address divisions and conflicts within the state. Instead, he refers to "state managers" collectively, the implication being that they are a cohesive group with shared interests—interests that are shaped and limited by the capitalist context, but internally consistent. As we have seen in the case of the INS and the DOL, however, state actors have specific sets of interests and face differential constraints depending on their location in the state apparatus and their particular exposure to the various ingredients of the "capitalist context." What those interests and limitations are at particular historical junctures, how they are connected to the contradictions of the political economy, and how they interact with the interests of state managers in other locations—these are among the primary research questions asked in this study of bracero policymaking.

An extensive literature in political science focuses on the nature of federal administrative agencies and the dynamics of administrative policymaking. While scholars in this tradition are less interested in advancing a general theory of the state than in deciphering the forces that impinge on, and in turn are affected by, government bureaucracies, they nonetheless speak directly to the question of what motivates state actors and thereby drives the state machinery. Despite the theoretical limitations of much of this research, it highlights dynamics within and between institutions of the state that are central to understanding the policymaking process. For instance, one group of studies focuses on the ties between executive agencies and Congress, and the relative power of each to affect policy. Several of these studies document the increasing role of the federal bureaucracy in *de facto* lawmaking, and link this encroachment into the legislative realm to congressional political incentives. David Rosenbloom argues that the increased legislative role of the administrative agency is the consequence of congressional abdication. Congress, he says, delegates its authority to the federal bureaucracy in the interest of efficiency, since administrative agencies have more "fluid rule-making procedures," unencumbered as they are by electoral politics and the tedious process of consensus-building.[55]

Congressional oversight is often limited, further increasing the administrative role in policymaking and enhancing the discretion of public administrators. While formal and informal mechanisms for oversight are well established, in practice a number of disincentives discourage congressional intervention in administrative policymaking. James Davis argues that Congress has neither the time nor the resources to engage in effective oversight.[56] Scher[57] and Aberbach[58] maintain that vigorous oversight is politically unrewarding compared to other congressional activities and thus not worth the substantial time commitment. Finally, Ripley and Franklin address the protection accorded administrative agencies through their alliance with powerful congressional committee members. Although such alliances submit the agency to the will of its congressional allies, they can insulate it from more general oversight, as members of Congress play "a reverse form of backscratching—'you don't investigate my program and I won't investigate yours.' "[59] These alliances between federal bureaucracies and individual members of Congress are likely to be particularly useful to potentially controversial or ineffective agencies, acting as a shield against public exposure. As we have seen, such congressional protection was a top priority of Commissioner Farrell in the years following the Bracero Program, as the Immigration Service in effect retreated from its border control function.

While administrative agencies are increasingly empowered with *de facto* legislative authority, this literature suggests that their autonomy may be limited by their relationship to a variety of special interest groups. Emmette Redford maintains that special interests are courted by administrative agencies as a base of power from which to resist budget cuts or other hostile intervention in their programs.[60] Aaron Wildavsky describes the advantages of this system for agencies whose formal functions are compatible with the needs of influential interest groups: "For an agency that has a large and strategically placed clientele, the most effective strategy is service to those who are in a position to help them."[61] But, according to Wildavsky, the functions of some agencies are such that they have no natural constituency or their constituencies are relatively powerless. He notes, for example, that "men and women incarcerated in federal prisons . . . are hardly an ideal clientele" for the Bureau of Prisons and hence it must take "extraordinary measures" to develop alternative interest group support.[62] Finally, as Francis Rourke explains, some agencies' functions actually *contradict* the interests of important clienteles, in which case the official goals of the agency may be sacrificed to retain its base of support.[63]

This analysis of the Bracero Program is grounded in a dialectical-structural model of the state. At the same time, it is driven by the conviction that adequate explanations of state action must trace empirically and theoretically the links between structural factors and human agency. In my effort to bring people back in, I borrow from state-centered theorists like Skocpol, Finegold, Hook, and others who insist that the state, and the institutions that make it up, have their own interests and periodically enjoy substantial autonomy; from Block who recognizes the central role of state managers with distinct state agendas; and from the literature on federal agencies that describes the complex interactions among state institutions and between those institutions and their "clienteles." The analysis is broadly synthetic, attempting to incorporate insights from these camps without succumbing to their own distinctive sets of blinders.

The book began by describing the contradictions of immigration in a democratic capitalist society. Confronted on one hand by the economic utility of immigrants as cheap labor and on the other by the political and fiscal costs of nurturing a surplus labor supply, lawmakers have historically attempted to resolve the ensuing conflicts through symbolic laws addressing the demands of organized labor (as in the Anti-Alien Contract Labor Law of 1885) or tampering with restrictive measures designed to reduce the costs associated with a destitute immigrant population (as in the public charge provisions of the 1880s, and employer sanctions in the 1980s). The underlying contradictions are not resolved, however, the stop-gap measures at best work only temporarily, and the dialectical sequence is reproduced as each new generation of policymakers copes with a historically specific set of immigration dilemmas.

Within this context, Mexican immigration is seen as a uniquely elastic supply of labor. Since early in this century, policymakers have appreciated Mexican immigrants as a source of cheap labor stripped of many of the human costs associated with the more permanent immigrant supply. In 1911, the Dillingham Immigration Commission noted the special advantages of Mexican immigration:

> Because of their strong attachment to their native land . . . and the possibility of their residence here being discontinued, few become citizens of the United States. The Mexican migrants are providing a fairly adequate supply of labor. . . . While they are not easily assimilated, this is of no very great importance as long as most of them return to their native land. In the case of the Mexican, he is less desirable as a citizen than as a laborer.[64]

The Bracero Program was an attempt to institutionalize these advantages, to render the supply of Mexican workers more predictable, and to routinize it. The bracero solution fit well with the needs of southwestern agriculture for a readily available captive work force with which to offset the unpredictability of agricultural production and to minimize worker resistance to arduous working conditions and barely subsistence wages. Despite its pronounced economic advantages, the program was fraught with political hazards. While a temporary foreign worker program may reduce the fiscal costs associated with a permanent immigrant work force, the resulting reduction of wages and erosion of the power of workers highlight the class nature of that solution. As the Bracero Program evolved, and evidence mounted that it exacted a heavy toll on domestic farm workers, it was increasingly mired in controversy. Following the logic of the literature on the rise of the administrative state, it makes sense that congressional actors—buffeted by domestic political pressures and the no-win quality of immigration conflicts—would attempt to resolve their dilemmas by passing them on to the far less visible administrative agencies that ran the Bracero Program.

The Immigration Service used liberally the power it was granted, fashioning policies to maximize the utility of the contract labor system to growers. The agency was not a lackey of growers, however, nor was it merely a "bearer" of the structure of capitalism. Rather, immigration officials and bracero employers worked out a *modus vivendi,* the nature of which was contingent on the mandate of the immigration bureaucracy to control the border. Just as the contradictions surrounding immigration penetrated the congressional arena in the form of political/electoral dilemmas, resulting in the delegation of powers to the INS, the way the Immigration Service used those powers depended on its own institutional exposure to those contradictions.

While the immigration agency crafted policies designed to satisfy growers in order to ensure their cooperation in curtailing illegal immigration, it frequently had to contend with the Department of Labor in the process. If the Bracero Program gave the Immigration Service a respite from the bureaucratic dilemmas associated with immigration control, for the Labor Department the program was primarily a "headache," as the Secretary of Labor had called it. The Bracero Program, by providing growers with an almost unlimited supply of cheap captive labor, temporarily solved for the INS the illegal immigration problem; but, the grower-oriented nature of this solution, and its adverse effects on domestic labor made the foreign labor system a headache for the Labor Department, whose chief clientele is organized labor and whose function it is to mediate the conflict between labor and capital. Officials of the two agencies, motivated by their respective organizational and career interests—interests that were decisively shaped by their institutional locations in the state—clashed and negotiated in letters, in memos, on the telephone, and in person. Piecing together the paper trail of these confrontations and the effect they had on bracero policies, it is impossible to discount such conflicts as simply micro-level clutter in some broader grand theory of "the state." Rather, this inter-agency conflict was a central component of the state policymaking process.

If the state is not monolithic, neither is it a composite of "disconnected collections of competing agencies."[65] The conflicts between the Immigration and Labor Departments were intense precisely because their policies had to be coordinated. Occasionally, particularly in the early years, this coordination was achieved with relative ease. After all, both agencies operated within the same capitalist context, and thus the distinctive dilemmas of each shared at least this common denominator. But, as domestic labor exerted increasing pressure on the Labor Department, and the conflicts between the agencies intensified, the coordination increasingly had to be imposed, either through extensive inter-agency "wrangling," or through the mediation of the State Department.

State Department mediation was particularly important given the international nature of the bracero system. As Evans *et al.* remind us, ". . . states are intrinsically Janus-faced, standing at the intersections of transnational and domestic processes. . . ."[66] Nowhere was this more apparent than in the Bracero Program, which by nature was essentially a domestic economic policy hammered out in collaboration with a foreign government. While the State Department negotiated on behalf of growers, Mexican representatives attempted to secure an agreement as advantageous to the braceros as possible given the circumstances. Periodically, Mexican negotiators were able to wrench concessions from the U.S. regarding such things as wage standards, working conditions, and recruitment policies. As we have seen, administrative discretion was often used to recoup some of these concessions. The point here is that the international quality of the Bracero Program, and the related need for a uniform U.S. bargaining position, made State Department mediation between the Immigration Service and the Labor Department all the more critical.

By the 1960s, the bracero solution that the Service had worked so hard to construct began to unravel, and with it the agency's reputation as an effective bureaucracy. As Galarza observes, "The ['wetback'] traffic was suppressed only when it became possible to assure farm employers, substantially on their terms, that they could have as many contract laborers as they might demand."[67] When this supply was no longer available, the INS faced inevitable defeat, to which it soon surrendered. Commissioner Farrell, remembered by his subordinates as the "caretaker" commissioner, shifted the agenda from immigration control, which was an impossible enterprise, to forging alliances with those who might help shield the agency from the repercussions of its failures. Theda Skocpol, addressing the historical variation in state autonomy, notes, "State officials are most likely to try to do things that seem feasible with the means at hand."[68] Gregory Hooks, in his analysis of the U.S. Department of Agriculture and the rise and decline in its autonomy, points out, "It is . . . possible for a state [and, presumably, state agencies] that is dependent and reactive at one time to subsequently play a proactive role."[69]

This examination of the INS confirms the historical variability in what it is "feasible" to achieve "with the means at hand," and reveals the agency's capacity to take an active rather than simply a defensive posture in the formulation of policy. My aim throughout has been to follow Mills' advice, connecting history, biography, and structure. It is hoped that this study will contribute to a more integrated approach to the state, or at least will provoke others to explore further the potential for such an approach. One thing is certain. Structures don't act, people do. If we are to progress beyond the current impasse in state theory, we must bridge the methodological and analytical divides that have limited our theoretical vision, and incorporate in our analyses both social structure and the political actors who are situated within those structures.

NOTES

Notes to Chapter I

1. Halsell, 1978, pp. 8–9.
2. Althusser, 1971.
3. Poulantzas, 1969; 1973.
4. Bach, 1978; see also Burawoy, 1976.
5. See, for example, Anderson, 1963; Galarza, 1977; García, 1980.
6. Hamilton, 1791, p. 123.
7. Carnegie, 1886, pp. 34–35.
8. *New York Journal of Commerce*, December 13, 1892, p. 2.
9. Ware, 1931; Montgomery, 1972.
10. *Congressional Record*, 1884, p. 5364; and 1885, p. 1786. See Calavita, 1984, for an analysis of this law.
11. See, for example, *Congressional Record*, 1882, pp. 5106–5108.
12. Quoted in Markovits and Kazarinov, 1978, p. 373.
13. Castles and Kosack, 1973; Miller, 1981; Miller and Martin, 1982; Garth, 1986.
14. U.S. Congress. House Committee on Immigration and Naturalization, 1919, pp. 24–25.
15. See Calavita, 1984, pp. 68–71.
16. McWilliams, 1968.
17. See Calavita, 1984, p. 136.
18. U.S. Congress. House Committee on Immigration and Naturalization, 1919, pp. 24–25; U.S. Congress. Senate Committee on Immigration, 1921, p. 87.
19. U.S. Congress. Senate Committee on the Judiciary. Subcommittee on Immigration and Refugee Policy, 1981, p. 86.
20. *Congressional Record*, 1986, pp. 10589–90.
21. *Ibid.*, p. 10588.
22. *Ibid.*, p. 16892.
23. See Calavita, 1989; 1990.
24. Chambliss, 1979.
25. For additional discussion of these models, see Chapter 7.
26. Like the Bracero Program, the H–2 Program (created by Section 101[a][15][H][ii] of the Immigration and Nationality Act of 1952) allowed for the admission of a small number of foreign contract workers on a temporary

basis; however, for the duration of the Bracero Program, the H–2 program was deemed inapplicable to Mexico.

27. See C. Wright Mills' (1959, pp. 50–75) critique of "abstracted empiricism."

28. Skocpol, 1985, p. 28.

29. Evans *et al.*, 1985, p. 360.

30. Not only are there few INS documents from the later period available at the National Archives, but after William Preston's book, *Aliens and Dissenters: Federal Suppression of Radicals, 1903–1933*, was published in 1963 using information from INS records, the INS withdrew the records used by Preston from the National Archives. Thus, not only is the INS not depositing materials for public access on a regular basis, but researchers are in effect *losing* ground.

31. PL 89–487; 80 *Stat.* 250 as amended by PL 93–502; 88 *Stat.* 1562; 5 U.S.C. 552.

32. Wasserman, 1976, p. 325.

33. American Library Association, 1984; see also Landau in the *Washington Post*, November 28, 1981, p. A23.

34. *Iowa Law Review*, 1970.

35. *Ibid.*, pp. 141–142.

36. *Ibid.*, p. 148.

37. Select Commission on Immigration and Refugee Policy. Letter from the INS representative on the Select Committee on Immigration and Refugee Policy, to INS Commissioner David Crosland, April 17, 1980. Files of the Select Commission on Immigration and Refugee Policy.

38. Although some of the material from the accessed boxes was "sanitized" in this way, primarily to conceal the personal identities of non-government actors, none of these sanitized materials were among the documents used in this study.

Notes to Chapter 2

1. Rasmussen, 1951, p. 200.

2. President's Commission on Migratory Labor, 1951, p. 50; hereafter cited as President's Commission. President Truman established the President's Commission on Migratory Labor in June 1950, in response to the National Farm Labor Union's pleas for an investigation into the problems of migrant farm workers. For a discussion of the makeup of the Commission, its hearings, and its final recommendations, see Kirstein, 1973, pp. 173–209.

3. U.S. Department of State, 1943.

4. The USES was located in the Federal Security Agency until it was returned to the Department of Labor in 1949.

5. U.S. Congress. House Committee on Appropriations, 1943, pp. 49–51.

6. Gamboa, 1990, p. 51.

7. President's Commission, 1951, pp. 38–40.

8. McWilliams, quoted in Anderson, 1963, p. 10.

9. President's Commission, 1951, p. 16.

10. *Ibid.*, p. 20.

11. The *New York Journal of Commerce*, 1892, p. 2.

12. Fisher, 1953, p. 124.
13. Scruggs, 1988, p. 240.
14. Quoted in Craig, 1971, p. 47. The Farm Security Administration had been established in 1937 to administer programs aimed at improving the conditions of poverty-stricken farm families.
15. American Farm Bureau Federation, 1942.
16. Letter from a grower to the FSA Administrator, quoted in Scruggs, 1988, p. 198.
17. Scruggs, 1988, pp. 238–240.
18. 57 *Stat.* 70–73. Extensions, modifications, and additional appropriations were enacted in December 1943 (57 *Stat.* 643); February 1944 (58 *Stat.* 11); December 1944 (58 *Stat.* 853); July 1945 (59 *Stat.* 361); December 1945 (59 *Stat.* 645); and April 1947 (61 *Stat.* 55).
19. 57 *Stat.* pp. 70–73, Section 4[a], Section 4[n].
20. Scruggs, 1988, p. 226.
21. Fisher, 1953, p. 108.
22. President's Commission, 1951, p. 59.
23. Kirstein, 1973, p. 44.
24. 39 *Stat.* 875. It was from this same provision that the INS Commissioner had derived the authority to exempt Mexicans from the literacy test in the years following World War I.
25. 57 *Stat.* pp. 70–73, Section 5[g].
26. *Federal Register*, May 11, 1943, p. 6013.
27. Kirstein, 1973, p. 45; Scruggs, 1988, p. 249.
28. According to Scruggs (1988, p. 252), the Secretary of State put pressure on the INS to rescind its liberal interpretation of the law, which permitted it to admit braceros unilaterally at the border, primarily because of the implications for relations with Mexico, and potentially damaging consequences for the international agreements.
29. Memo quoted in Scruggs, 1988, p. 252.
30. Rasmussen, 1951, pp. 231–233.
31. Craig, 1971, p. 47.
32. U.S. Congress. House Committee on Appropriations, 1945, pp. 106–117; 802–852.
33. A similar program, importing over 130,000 Mexican workers to work on U.S. railroads during the war, was terminated soon after hostilities ceased. For a discussion of this program, see Jones (1945).
34. 61 *Stat.* 55, emphasis added.
35. Kirstein, 1973, p. 131.
36. *Congressional Record*, 1947, pp. 3202–3214.
37. *Ibid.*, pp. 3203–3206.
38. *Ibid.*, p. 3206.
39. *Ibid.*, p. 3206.
40. *Ibid.*, p. 3210.
41. U.S. Congress. House Committee on Agriculture, 1947.
42. *Ibid.*, p. 30.
43. *Ibid.*, p. 30.
44. *Ibid.*, p. 30.
45. *Ibid.*, p. 32.

46. *Ibid.*, p. 32.
47. *Ibid.*, p. 35.
48. U.S. Immigration and Naturalization Service, *I and N Reporter*, July 1956, p. 5.
49. *New York Times*, March 28, 1951, p. 34.
50. President's Commission, 1951, p. 65.
51. *Ibid.*, p. 65; emphasis in the original. "Wetback" is the term widely used in this period to refer to an illegal alien from Mexico. Translated from the Spanish "espaldas mojadas," the term originally referred to Mexicans who crossed the Rio Grande River to gain entrance to the United States. The English term quickly took on racist overtones, and has since been replaced by "illegal alien" or "undocumented worker," both of which are themselves laden with negative connotations. "Wetback" is used here only when it is a direct quote; otherwise—in the absence of a more value-free label—the conventional terms "illegal alien" or "undocumented worker" are used.
52. President's Commission, 1951, p. 53.
53. Galarza, 1964, p. 63.
54. President's Commission, 1951, p. 65.
55. Paraphrased by Kirstein, 1973, pp. 159–160.
56. Quoted in the President's Commission, 1951, p. 45.
57. Copp, 1963, p. 189.
58. Kirstein, 1973, pp. 142–146; Scruggs, 1988, pp. 404–407.
59. Kirstein, 1973, p. 144.
60. *Ibid.*, p. 144.
61. Quoted in *Ibid.*, p. 147.
62. President's Commission, 1951, pp. 58–59.
63. *Ibid.*, p. 60.
64. *Ibid.*, pp. 13–14.
65. *Ibid.*, p. 8.
66. For critics' views of this use of the Bracero Program, see the *New York Times*, August 13, 1950, p. 63, and March 3, 1951, p. 6; U.S. Congress. Senate Committee on Agriculture and Forestry, 1951, pp. 13–16 and 123–135.
67. U.S. Immigration and Naturalization Service, *Annual Report*, 1959, p. 54; *Farm Labor Developments*, 1968, p. 14; Congressional Research Service, 1980a, p. 65.
68. Hadley, 1956, p. 336.
69. For a discussion of these difficulties, see U.S. General Accounting Office, 1982b, pp. 17–18.
70. Hadley, 1956, pp. 343–344.
71. In order to be chosen as a bracero candidate by local Mexican officials, it was often necessary to pay a "mordida," or bribe, of as much as $36 (*Hispanic American Report*, 1957, p. 520; Anderson, 1963, p. 18).
72. Letter cited in Rasmussen, 1951, p. 221.
73. Quoted in President's Commission, 1951, p. 76.
74. Cited in Kirstein, 1973, p. 195.
75. American G.I. Forum and Texas State Federation of Labor, 1976, p. 42.
76. Quoted in Scruggs, 1988, p. 308.
77. *Congressional Record*, 1949, Appendix, p. A2283.

78. Quoted in García, 1980, p. 112.
79. U.S. Congress. House Committee on Agriculture, 1951, p. 88.
80. U.S. Congress. House Subcommittee on Legal and Monetary Affairs of the Committee on Governmental Operations, 1955, p. 13.
81. Personal interview with a former senior official of the INS, 18 November 1988.
82. Aleinikoff and Martin, 1985, p. 83; Crewdson, 1983, p. 114; Teitelbaum, 1980, pp. 54–55; U.S. General Accounting Office, 1980, pp. 24–26.
83. U.S. Immigration and Naturalization Service, *Annual Report*, 1959, p. 54; U.S. Congress. Senate Committee on Labor and Public Welfare. Subcommittee on Labor and Labor-Management Relations, 1952, p. 133.
84. *Newsweek*, March 11, 1946, p. 71.
85. U.S. Congress. House Committee on Agriculture, 1947, p. 36.
86. Quoted in Scruggs, 1988, pp. 306–307.
87. Quoted in *ibid.*, 1988, p. 307.
88. Scruggs, 1988, p. 424.
89. Quoted in *Ibid.*, p. 424.
90. *New York Times*, March 28, 1951, p. 31.
91. Quoted in *Ibid.*, p. 31.
92. *Ibid.*, p. 31.
93. Cited in Scruggs, 1988, p. 425.
94. U.S. Congress. House Committee on Agriculture, 1951, pp. 89–90.
95. U.S. Congress. Senate Subcommittee of the Committee on Appropriations, 1953, pp. 245–246.
96. *Congressional Record*, 1952, p. 2200.
97. Hadley, 1956, p. 39.
98. *The Washington Post*, April 14, 1952, p. 6.
99. U.S. Congress. Senate Subcommittee on Labor and Labor-Management Relations, 1952, p. 130.
100. *Ibid.*, p. 743.
101. *Ibid.*, p. 743.
102. Quoted in the *New York Times*, March 28, 1951, p. 34.
103. U.S. Congress. House Committee on Agriculture, 1947, p. 36.
104. U.S. Congress. Senate Committee on Agriculture and Forestry, 1953, pp. 24, 26.
105. Quoted in the *New York Times*, March 28, 1951, p. 31.
106. Scruggs, 1988. pp. 439–440.
107. President's Commission, 1951, pp. 78–80.
108. See, for example, the *New York Times* five-part series on illegal immigrants, March 25–29, 1951.
109. The *New York Times*, March 29, 1951, p. 29.
110. U.S. Congress. Senate Subcommittee on Labor and Labor-Management Relations, 1952, pp. 129–130.
111. Mosher, 1968; Lorch, 1969; Rosenbloom, 1983.
112. Fiorina, 1977; Rosenbloom, 1983.
113. Rourke, 1969, p. 85.
114. The *New York Times*, March 28, 1951, p. 34.
115. President's Commission, 1951, p. 53.
116. Quoted in the *New York Times*, March 28, 1951, p. 34.

Notes to Chapter 3

1. Craig, 1971, p. 55.
2. American Consul at Reynosa, Mexico, in a memo to the Department of State, quoted in Scruggs, 1988, p. 427.
3. Braceros in the Northwestern states of Washington, Idaho, and Oregon during the wartime program were unusual in this regard, as they regularly "stood up to their employers" through strikes and other protest activities (Gamboa, 1990: xiii). Unlike their counterparts in the Southwest who could easily be replaced with both legal and illegal Mexican labor, Northwest braceros, remote from the border and supported by Mexican Consuls in the region, periodically were able to exact concessions from employers, or at least bring them into compliance with the terms of their contracts. This balance of power, predicated in large part on distance from the Mexican border, was at least partially responsible for the demise of bracero contracting in the Pacific Northwest by the late 1940s (*Ibid.*).
4. Anderson, 1963; Galarza, 1964.
5. U.S. Congress. Senate, 1951. *Senate Report* No. 214, p. 2.
6. President's Commission, 1951, p. 46.
7. Craig, 1971, p. 68.
8. Growers' association representatives met in Washington, DC, in January 1951, to discuss the effect of the war on labor needs. They estimated that 300,000 to 400,000 Mexicans would be required to meet crop demands; cotton growers meeting in Mississippi announced a need for at least 500,000 foreign workers to produce a projected 16,000,000 bales of cotton (*New York Times*, January 27, 1951, p. 3).
9. Scruggs, 1988, p. 430.
10. 65 *Stat.* 119.
11. See U.S. Congress. Senate Committee on Agriculture and Forestry, 1951, pp. 72–77, 123–135, and 155–159.
12. *Ibid.*, p. 57. Among farm organizations, only the National Farmers Union, whose members were primarily owners of self-operated farms, opposed the measure, which they argued amounted to a "federal subsidization of the factory farm at the expense of the family farm" (*Ibid.*, p. 68).
13. *Ibid.*, 1951, pp. 40–42 and 111–112; *Congressional Record*, 1951, pp. 4420 and 7521.
14. Anderson, 1963, p. 12; Lyon, 1954, pp. 259, 318–319.
15. *Ibid.*, p. 260.
16. State Department letter cited in *Ibid.*, p. 260.
17. U.S. Congress. Subcommittee on Labor and Labor-Management Relations of the Senate Committee on Labor and Public Welfare, 1952, p. 350; U.S. Congress. House Committee on Agriculture, 1954, p. 79; 1960, p. 214.
18. *New York Times*, July 13, 1951, p. 24.
19. Quoted in Lyon, 1954, p. 274.
20. Quoted in *Ibid.*, p. 275.
21. Quoted in *Ibid.*, p. 275; emphasis added.
22. Runsten, 1981, p. 51.
23. President's Commission, 1951, p. 69.
24. *Ibid.*, pp. 87–88.

25. *Ibid.*, p. 80.
26. *Ibid.*, p. 84.
27. Hawley, 1966, pp. 159–160.
28. *New York Times*, March 25–29, 1951.
29. See for example, *Life*, May 21, 1951, pp. 30–37; *Time*, April 9, 1951, p. 24; *Business Week*, October 24, 1953, p. 66.
30. *New York Times* Service broadcast, May 9, 1953, quoted in Myers, 1971, pp. 79–80.
31. Todd, 1953, p. 164.
32. Roy Rubottom, to the Subcommittee on Labor and Labor-Management Relations of the Senate Committee on Labor and Public Welfare, 1952, pp. 129–130.
33. Eckels, 1954, p. 28.
34. U.S. Immigration and Naturalization Service, *I and N Reporter*, 1954, p. 37.
35. Quoted in the *New York Times*, August 16, 1953, p. 1; *New York Times*, August 17, 1953, p. 11.
36. Quoted in the *San Francisco Examiner*, August 17, 1953, p. 20.
37. *Ibid.*, p. 20.
38. President's Commission, 1951, p. 83.
39. Quoted in U.S. Congress. Senate Subcommittee on Immigration and Naturalization of the Committee on the Judiciary, 1954, p. 4.
40. *Ibid.*, p. 37.
41. U.S. Immigration and Naturalization Service, *I and N Reporter*, 1954, p. 38.
42. Rep. Edward Gossett, Press Release, December 20, 1949, p. 2. Department of Labor Files. National Archives. Record Group 174, Box 54. All subsequent citations of National Archives data refer to these Department of Labor Files.
43. *New York Times*, August 21, 1951, p. 11.
44. U.S. Immigration and Naturalization Service, *Annual Report*, 1951, p. 39.
45. *Ibid.*, p. 3.
46. Quoted in *Congressional Record*, 1954, p. 2564.
47. *Ibid.*, p. 2559.
48. *Ibid.*, p. 2558.
49. Quoted in *Ibid.*, p. 2560.
50. Quoted in the *New York Times*, May 3, 1954, p. 12.
51. Quoted in U.S. Congress. Senate Subcommittee on Immigration and Naturalization of the Committee on the Judiciary, 1954, p. 4.
52. *New York Times*, August 18, 1953, p. 16.
53. *Congressional Record*, 1954, p. 15174.
54. U.S. Congress. House Subcommittee of the Committee on Government Operations, 1956, p. 38.
55. *Ibid.*, p. 40; see also Oral History Interview with INS Commissioner Joseph Swing, Eisenhower Administration Project, Columbia University Library.
56. U.S. Congress. Senate Subcommittee of the Committee on Appropriations, 1950, p. 223.

57. *New York Times*, March 29, 1951, p. 29.
58. U.S. Congress. Senate Subcommittee on Immigration and Naturalization of the Committee on the Judiciary, 1954, p. 4.
59. Interview with Carter, quoted in García, 1980, p. 178.
60. *New York Times*, September 16, 1953, p. 31.
61. *New York Times*, September 7, 1953, p. 1.
62. *Ibid.*
63. *Ibid.*, p. 10.
64. Letter to the President of the National Agricultural Workers Union, quoted in *Congressional Record*, 1954, p. 15175.
65. García, 1980, p. 164; letter from the Chairman of the CIO, quoted in *Congressional Record*, 1954, p. 15175.
66. *New York Times*, June 27, 1954, p. 36.
67. Hayes, *et al.*, 1955, pp. 17, 21.
68. U.S. Congress. Senate Subcommittee of the Committee on Appropriations, 1954, p. 215; emphasis added.
69. *New York Times*, June 10, 1954, p. 25.
70. García, 1980, p. 183.
71. U.S. Immigration and Naturalization Service, *Annual Report*, 1955, pp. 9–12; U.S. Immigration and Naturalization Service, *I and N Reporter*, 1956, p. 8; García, 1980, p. 183.
72. *New York Times*, June 28, 1954, p. 3.
73. U.S. Immigration and Naturalization Service, *I and N Reporter*, 1974, p. 15; *New York Times*, June 20, 1954, p. 75.
74. U.S. Immigration and Naturalization Service, *Annual Report*, 1955, pp. 9–12. This figure is probably somewhat exaggerated. The INS estimated elsewhere that by July 27—that is, after the peak of Operation Wetback—only 52,374 Mexicans had been deported (cited in García, 1980, p. 193). It may be that the inflated figure for fiscal year apprehensions either included INS estimates of the number of aliens who departed on their own, and/or was a political creation generated to demonstrate the "success" of the drive. In any case, even the lower figure represents an unprecedented apprehension rate.
75. Copp, 1963, pp. 96–97.
76. U.S. Immigration and Naturalization Service, *I and N Reporter*, 1974, p. 15.
77. U.S. Immigration and Naturalization Service, *I and N Reporter*, 1956, p. 7.
78. Morgan, 1954, pp. 49–50.
79. INS records, cited in García, 1980, p. 195.
80. *New York Times*, June 23, 1954, p. 35.
81. U.S. Immigration and Naturalization Service, *Annual Report*, 1955, p. 15.
82. U.S. Congress. House Subcommittee on Equipment, Supplies, and Manpower of the Committee on Agriculture, 1960, p. 417; see Appendix B.
83. U.S. Immigration and Naturalization Service, "Report to the American Section of Joint Commission on Mexican Migrant Labor," 1954, p. 34. Unpublished Report. Accession 67A3254, Box 8. This and all subsequent references to an "Accession" number refer to internal INS files housed at the Suitland, Maryland facility.

84. Department of Labor, "Report on Mexican Labor Situation as Result of Immigration Service Wetback Cleanout," 1954, pp. 1–2. National Archives. Record Group 174, Box 54.
85. U.S. Immigration and Naturalization Service, "Report to the American Section of Joint Commission on Mexican Migrant Labor," 1954, p. 9. Accession 67A3254, Box 8.
86. Pfeffer, 1980, p. 25; emphasis added.
87. President's Commission, 1951, p. 20.
88. *Congressional Record*, 1958, pp. 17654; 17658.
89. Oral History Interview with Senator Arthur Watkins, p. 60. Eisenhower Administration Project, Columbia University Library, 1968; hereafter, Interview with Watkins.
90. Quoted in Anderson, 1963, p. 1.
91. Quoted in Lyon, 1954, p. 229.
92. U.S. Congress. House Committee on Agriculture, 1961, pp. 11–13.
93. U.S. Immigration and Naturalization Service. Border Patrol. Monthly Sector Activity Report. Yuma, Arizona. February, 1961. Accession 64A1851, Box 161; emphasis added.
94. Moore, 1965, p. 83.
95. Anderson, 1963, p. 12.
96. Interview with Watkins, 1968, pp. 57–59.
97. U.S. Immigration and Naturalization Service. Border Patrol. Monthly Sector Activity Report. Brownsville, Texas. August 1957. Accession 63 A1359, Box 3.
98. Not surprisingly, some migrants *preferred* the risks of an illegal status to the controls imposed on braceros. According to a report from INS officials at Livermore, Texas, "Illegal entrants have told officers that they would rather enter illegally than as a contract laborer because they can select the better paying jobs and locations" (U.S. Immigration and Naturalization Service. Border Patrol. Intelligence Report. Livermore, Texas. October 1957. CO 660.4–P. This and all subsequent references to a "CO" number refer to INS "Central Office" files).
99. U.S. Immigration and Naturalization Service, "Report to the American Section of Joint Commission on Mexican Migrant Labor," 1954, p. 35. Accession 67A3254, Box 8.
100. Hayes, *et al.*, 1955, p. 17.
101. Galarza, 1977, p. 265.
102. U.S. Immigration and Naturalization Service, "Report to the American Section of Joint Commission on Mexican Migrant Labor," 1954, page 41. Accession 67A3254, Box 8.
103. *Ibid.*, page 41.
104. U.S. Department of Labor, "Report on Mexican Labor Situation as Result of Immigration Service Wetback Cleanout," 1954, p. 4. National Archives, Record Group 174, Box 54.
105. *New York Times*, August 2, 1954, p. 8; see also Myers, 1971, pp. 90–91.
106. Hayes, *et al.*, 1955, pp. 17–21.
107. U.S. Immigration and Naturalization Service, *I and N Reporter*, 1955, p. 15.
108. U.S. Immigration and Naturalization Service, Border Patrol.

Monthly Sector Activity Report, El Centro, California, August 1957. CO 660.4–P.

109. U.S. Department of Labor, March 19, 1954. National Archives, Record Group 174, Box 54.

110. Hayes, *et al.*, 1955, p. 17.

111. U.S. Department of Labor. "Report on Mexican Labor Situation as Result of Immigration Service Wetback Cleanout," 1954, p. 2. National Archives. Record Group 174, Box 54.

112. U.S. Immigration and Naturalization Service, *Public Opinion Survey*. Brownsville, Texas. July 29, 1957, pp. 4–5. Accession 67A233, Box 6.

113. U.S. Immigration and Naturalization Service, *Public Opinion Survey*. McAllen, Texas. July 30, 1957, p. 3. Accession 67A233, Box 6.

114. *Ibid.*, p. 10.

115. U.S. Immigration and Naturalization Service, *Public Opinion Survey*. Yuma, Arizona, July 31, 1957, p. 1. Accession 67A233, Box 6.

116. Galarza, 1964, pp. 70, 111–114; Hayes *et al.*, 1955, pp. 17, 21.

117. U.S. Department of Labor, 1954, p. 1. National Archives. Record Group 174, Box 54.

118. "Report to American Section of Joint Commission on Mexican Migrant Labor," 1954, p. 106. Accession 67A3254, Box 8.

119. U.S. Immigration and Naturalization Service, *Public Opinion Survey*. Yuma, Arizona, July 31, 1957, pp. 4, 1. Accession 67A233, Box 6.

120. California State Senate. Senate Fact Finding Committee on Labor and Welfare, 1961, p. 110.

121. U.S. Immigration and Naturalization Service, *Public Opinion Survey*. Southwest Region, August 23, 1957, p. 4. Accession 67A233, Box 6.

122. Pfeiffer, 1979, p. 80.

123. *Hispanic American Report*, 1957, p. 520; Pfeiffer, 1979, p. 80; Lessard, 1984, pp. 83–84. The total amount of the bribes varied, but at the peak of the program it was estimated at approximately $50 per bracero (Pfeiffer, 1979, p. 81; Lessard, 1984, p. 84). The bracero often had to go into debt to pay these bribes, and was thus rendered a more docile worker since repayment of his debt depended on his continued stay in the United States regardless of the abuses to which he might be subjected (Pfeiffer, 1979, p. 81).

124. Memo to Marcus Neelly, District Director, El Paso, Texas, from Ernest Hover. Chief, Examinations Branch, El Paso, Texas, May 31, 1956. Accession 58A733, Box 195.

125. *Congressional Record*, 1951, pp. 4420–4421.

126. Some regions and crops were notoriously undesirable. Imperial Valley in California, and Yuma, Arizona, offered among the lowest wages and presented the most arduous working conditions, with desert temperatures of 110 degrees not uncommon (Anderson, 1963, p. 28).

127. *Ibid.*, pp. 28–29; Galarza, 1964, p. 83.

128. U.S. Immigration and Naturalization Service, Border Patrol. Monthly Sector Activity Report, Yuma, Arizona, October 1958. Accession 63A1359, Box 3.

129. U.S. Immigration and Naturalization Service, Border Patrol. Monthly Sector Activity Report, El Paso, Texas, November 1960. Accession 64A1851, Box 161.

130. U.S. Congress. Senate Subcommittee on Labor and Labor-Manage-

ment Relations of the Committee on Labor and Public Welfare, 1952, pp. 250–251.

131. *69 Stat.* 615.

132. U.S. Congress. House. Subcommittee on Equipment, Supplies, and Manpower of the Committee on Agriculture, 1961, p. 354.

133. *Ibid.*, pp. 361–362.

134. *New York Times*, March 28, 1951, p. 34; Galarza, 1977, p. 158.

135. U.S. Immigration and Naturalization Service, Border Patrol. Monthly Sector Activity Report, Marfa, Texas, June 1957. CO 660.4–P.

136. PL 78 had authorized the INS not only to report users of illegal aliens so that they would be denied access to braceros in the future, but to remove braceros from farms and ranches where illegal aliens were employed (Section 504).

137. *Ibid.*

138. U.S. Immigration and Naturalization Service, *INS Information Bulletin*, June 2, 1955, pp. 1–2.

139. *Ibid.*, p. 2.

140. *Ibid.*, p. 1.

141. *Ibid.*, p. 1. With no apparent irony intended, the *Bulletin* added, "Workers who have been required to accept sub-standard wages are not being penalized" (*Ibid.*, p. 2).

142. *New York Times*, October 8, 1953, p. 27.

143. *New York Times*, January 16, 1954, p. 15.

144. *New York Times*, February 2, 1954, p. 3.

145. *Hispanic American Report*, 1954, p. 1.

146. Letter from the Comptroller General of the United States to the Secretary of Labor, February 2, 1954. National Archives, Record Group 174, Box 54.

147. *Congressional Record*, 1951, p. 7540; see also *Ibid.*, pp. 7256, 7259, 7264.

148. Scruggs, 1988, p. 447.

149. State Department Files, quoted in Scruggs, 1988, p. 452.

150. *New York Times*, July 14, 1951, p. 11.

151. *Congressional Record*, 1952, p. 792.

152. *Ibid.*, pp. 792, 795.

153. *Ibid.*, pp. 792–793.

154. *Ibid.*, p. 795.

155. *Ibid.*, p. 792.

156. *Ibid.*, p. 393.

157. *Ibid.*, p. 393.

158. *Ibid.*, p. 394.

159. *Ibid.*, p. 795.

160. *Ibid.*, p. 794.

161. *Ibid.*, p. 797.

162. *Ibid.*, p. 797.

163. *Ibid.*, p. 798–811.

164. *Ibid.*, p. 808.

165. *Ibid.*, p. 806. In fact, the Douglas Amendment applied to employment in general and made no specific reference to farmers.

166. *Ibid.*, p. 808. Ironically, Mexican pressure to pass an employer sanctions law was the rationale for introducing S.1851 in the first place, and was now used to sabotage a more effective version of the bill.

167. PL 283. Two years later, in the spring of 1954, legislation (S.3660) was considered that would have authorized an injunction against employers who knowingly employed illegal aliens. This less punitive version of Douglas' proposal, specifying no criminal penalties, was never acted on (see *Congressional Record*, 1954, p. 15174). It was not until the Immigration Reform and Control Act of 1986 that the knowing employment of unauthorized aliens was explicitly prohibited.

168. Lyon, 1954, pp. 378–383.

169. *Ibid.*, p. 378.

170. 60 *Stat.* 238; 5 U.S.C., p. 1003.

171. U.S. Immigration and Naturalization Service, "Notice of Amendments to Part 60 of Chapter I, Title 8 of the Code of Federal Regulations." March 21, 1952. Unpublished INS document, 56192/582–A.

172. *Congressional Record*, 1952, pp. 795, 800. A member of the House described the emasculation of S.1851 metaphorically: "As originally introduced in the Senate in S.1851 . . . the legislation contained the teeth necessary to really bite into the problem. But, as passed by the Senate, so much dental surgery has been applied that the measure cannot begin to do the job it should do" (*Ibid.*, p. 1413).

173. Mexican officials were well aware that S.1851 was not in fact an employment prohibition measure and thus did not technically meet their demands (*New York Times*, February 9, 1952, p. 7). However, according to some observers (Craig, 1971, p. 97; Scruggs, 1988, p. 463), they too were eager to renew the contract agreement and used Senate passage of the bill to justify an extension.

174. U.S. Congress. Senate Committee on Agriculture and Forestry, 1951, pp. 56–72 and 93–123.

175. Halsell, 1978, pp. 8–9.

176. Cited in *Congressional Record*, 1961, pp. 20757–74. Despite the overall increase in farm wages, they lost ground relative to manufacturing wages. Whereas in 1946, agricultural wage rates were 47.9% of manufacturing rates, by 1955 they had declined to just over 36% (Hadley, 1956, p. 356).

177. California State Senate. Senate Fact Finding Committee on Labor and Welfare, 1961, pp. 115–117.

178. Telegram from Joe T. Gore, Texas Producers Cooperative, to James C. Mitchell, Secretary of Labor, May 25, 1954. National Archives, Record Group 174, Box 54; emphasis added.

179. California Legislature. Assembly. Legislative Reference Service, 1965, p. 7.

180. Cited in *Ibid.*, p. 13.

181. Craig, 1971, p. 10; U.S. Congress. House Subcommittee on Equipment, Supplies, and Manpower of the Committee on Agriculture, 1961, p. 354.

182. *New York Times*, April 5, 1959.

183. Galarza, 1977, p. xii.

184. For a detailed, first-hand account of union activity in response to the Bracero Program in this period, see Galarza, 1977.

185. California Legislature. Assembly. Legislative Reference Service, 1965, pp. 5–6.
186. U.S. Immigration and Naturalization Service, *INS Information Bulletin*, March 3, 1956, p. 1.
187. U.S. Immigration and Naturalization Service, *I and N Reporter*, 1955, p. 16.

Notes to Chapter 4

1. Galarza, 1977, p. 83.
2. U.S. Congress. House Committee on Government Operations. Subcommittee on Legal and Monetary Affairs, 1955, pp. 1–2; Congressional Research Service, 1980a, p. 70.
3. U.S. Immigration and Naturalization Service, Border Patrol. Monthly Sector Activity Reports (MSARs), Tucson, Arizona, September 1957; El Centro, California, August 1958. CO 660.4–P; hereafter cited as MSAR, with appropriate dates and locations.
4. Semi-Annual Report from L.W. Gilman, Associate Deputy Regional Commissioner, Southwest Region, July 13, 1962. Accession 67A233, Box 6.
5. MSAR, Livermore, Texas, June 1958. Accession 63A1359, Box 4.
6. *Ibid.*
7. MSAR, Yuma, Arizona, June 1958. Accession 63A1359, Box 4.
8. U.S. Immigration and Naturalization Service, *Annual Report*, 1964, p. 60.
9. MSAR, Del Rio, Texas, June 1958. Accession 63A1359, Box 4. This increase in wages as the number of braceros was reduced, and at a time of severe recession, seriously strains the argument of Bracero Program advocates that the contract labor system had no adverse effect on farm wages.
10. *Ibid.*
11. MSAR, Yuma, Arizona, May 1958; Del Rio, Texas, June 1958; Livermore, Texas, June 1958. Accession 63A1359, Box 4.
12. When Commissioner Swing reorganized INS regions and Border Patrol sectors in 1955, Arkansas fell through the cracks. Swing had apparently intended for the state to be included in the Southeast region of the INS, but for Border Patrol enforcement to stay in the Southwest region, for reasons that remain unclear. The confusion resulted in an absence of full-time Border Patrol officers in Arkansas for several years (Memorandum for the File, from Donald R. Coppock, Deputy Assistant Commissioner, Border Patrol, October 14, 1960. Accession 67A3254, Box 8).
13. Memorandum for the File, from Donald R. Coppock, Deputy Assistant Commissioner, Border Patrol, October 14, 1960. Accession 67A3254, Box 8.
14. U.S. Immigration and Naturalization Service, *Annual Report*, 1955, p. 15.
15. Memo from David H. Carnahan, Regional Commissioner, Southwest Region, to District Directors, Southwest Region, May 24, 1956. Accession 58A733, Box 195; emphasis in the original.
16. *Ibid.*
17. Memo from Robin J. Clack, Acting Chief Patrol Inspector, McAllen,

Texas, to Regional Commissioner, Southwest Region, August 29, 1956. Accession 58A733, Box 195.

18. Memo from A. C. Ohswaldt, Regional Chief of Investigations, to M.R. Toole, Acting Regional Commissioner, Southwest Region, June 15, 1956. Accession 58A733, Box 195.

19. *Ibid.*

20. Undated memo. Accession 58A733, Box 195.

21. *Notes*, from Irvin Shrode, June 15, 1956. Accession 58A733, Box 195.

22. Memo from Commissioner Swing to David Carnahan, Southwest Regional Commissioner, June 29, 1956. Accession 58A733, Box 195.

23. *Ibid.*; emphasis in the original.

24. Anderson, 1963, p. 45. With union representation precluded by statute and by the international accord, one of the few avenues for complaint open to braceros was through their local Mexican consuls who on occasion were able to bring pressure to bear on U.S. officials to enforce protections provided in the international accords. However, the degree to which Mexican consuls acted as bracero advocates varied. The Consuls in California rarely acted on behalf of braceros, while the Consul General in Texas set up a "Good Neighbor Commission," the function of which was to press for improved treatment of braceros and other Mexican citizens in the U.S. (Galarza, 1964, p. 232; Gamboa, 1990, p. 77).

25. From 1952 to the end of the Bracero Program in 1964, only 222 aliens of all nationalities were officially deported "due to subversive/anarchistic activities" (Congressional Research Service, 1980a, p. 67). It is difficult to estimate the number of braceros deported for labor activism, since not all of those sent home for such activism were officially labelled, as for example, in the case of the three braceros described here. However, the Monthly Sector Activity Reports and other internal communication suggest that the priority assigned to this mission was disproportionate to the numbers actually involved.

26. 8 U.S.C. 1152. The Immigration and Nationality Act of 1965 provided an overall western hemisphere ceiling of 120,000 effective in 1968, but included no per-country limits.

27. Memo from Acting Officer in Charge, INS Los Angeles Office, to Commissioner Swing, October 1955. Accession 58A733, Box 185.

28. Unpublished notes of El Paso Conference, December 2, 1955. Accession 58A733, Box 186.

29. *Ibid.*

30. *Ibid.*; emphasis added.

31. *Ibid.*; emphasis in original.

32. MSAR, Yuma, Arizona, September 1958. Accession 63A1359, Box 4.

33. MSAR, El Centro, California, February 1958. Accession 63A1359, Box 3.

34. MSAR, Del Rio, Texas, August 1958. Accession 63A1359, Box 4.

35. MSAR, Yuma, Arizona, March 1958. Acceession 63A1359, Box 4.

36. The corporate lawyer/rancher who in his letter complained to Swing about the attitude of the Attorney General toward the "proletariat such as myself" (*sic*), understood the *de facto* power of the immigration bureaucracy to make policy. He urged Swing, "I know that your duties are largely 'enforcement', but certainly enforcement includes at times the matter of policy" (letter to Commissioner Swing, June 11, 1956. Accession 58A733, Box 195).

37. Letter from the President of the Texas Sheep and Goat Raisers' Association to Commissioner Joseph Swing, July 2, 1958. Accession 67A233, Box 6.

38. MSAR, Brownsville, Texas, April 1958. Accession 63A1359, Box 4.

39. *Ibid.*

40. See, for example, U.S. Congress. House Committee on Agriculture, 1951, pp. 88–92.

41. U.S. Congress. House Committee on Agriculture. Subcommittee on Equipment, Supplies, and Manpower, 1958, p. 450.

42. *Ibid.*, p. 450.

43. *Ibid.*, pp. 453, 454, 456.

44. MSAR, Brownsville, Texas, June 1958. Accession 63A1359, Box 4; see also MSAR, McAllen, Texas, July 1958. Accession 63A1359, Box 4.

45. MSAR, Yuma, Arizona, April 1957. CO 660.4–P.

46. U.S. Immigration and Naturalization Service, "Report to the American Section of the Joint Commission on Mexican Migrant Labor," September 3, 1954, p. 102. Accession 67A3254, Box 8; hereafter cited Joint Commission on Mexican Migrant Labor; emphasis added.

47. Untitled document, November 1955. Accession 58A733, Box 185.

48. The Immigration and Nationality Act of 1952 allowed for the importation of foreign workers for non-agricultural employment for specified periods of time upon certification of employer need [Section 101(a)(15)(H)(ii)]. The INS was recommending that something comparable to this "H-2" program be opened up to growers, despite the plentiful supply of farm labor available under the Bracero Program. A 1954 memorandum from the INS General Counsel to Commissioner Swing suggests that the Service had also explored the possibility of using the H-2 program as an alternative to the Bracero Program to import Mexican farm workers should negotiations with Mexico fail or Congress terminate funding (December 6, 1954. Accession 67A233, Box 6).

49. The 1951 agreement, as a compromise measure, had provided for border reception centers to which Mexican braceros were transported after their initial recruitment in the interior. In 1954, after Mexico's bargaining position had been eroded by the unilateral recruitment episode, border recruitment stations were opened in Mexicali, Monterrey, and Chihuahua (Craig, 1971, p. 121–123).

50. Memo from Commissioner Swing, to INS District Directors, August 25, 1954. Accession 67A3254, Box 8.

51. Letter from Commissioner Swing to Rep. Bolton, October 5, 1955. Accession 58A733, Box 185.

52. Joint Commission on Mexican Migrant Labor.

53. *Ibid.*

54. Letter from A. C. Devaney, Assistant Commissioner, to Walter S. Alexander, July 28, 1955. Accession 58A733, Box 185.

55. Letter from Commissioner Swing to Senator Fulbright, July 12, 1955. Accession 58A733, Box 185; emphasis added.

56. Memo from Acting Assistant Commissioner to the Regional Commissioner of the Southwest Region, December 15, 1955. Accession 58A733, Box 185.

57. Memo of telephone conversation from Mr. Sneed to Irvin Shrode, January 22, 1958. Accession 67A233, Box 6.

58. Memorandum for File from Irvin Shrode, August 19, 1958. Accession 67A233, Box 6. According to an angry letter written by the Assistant Secretary of Labor to the State Department in 1955, the INS had originally planned to treat the I-100 card as both necessary and sufficient for entry, thereby effectively nullifying the role of the Department of Labor in certifying the unavailability of qualified domestic workers prior to the importation of braceros (letter from Rocco C. Siciliano, Assistant Secretary of Labor, to Hon. Robert Murphy, Deputy Under Secretary of State, June 27, 1955. Accession 58A733, Box 185). The I-100 card had been a source of jurisdictional contention between the INS and the Department of Labor since its inception (See Chapter 5).

59. Memo from Southwest Regional Commissioner, to the Assistant Commissioner, Central Office, July 23, 1958. Accession 67A233, Box 6.

60. U.S. Immigration and Naturalization Service, *INS Information Bulletin*, August 10, 1955, p. 3.

61. Joint Commission on Mexican Migrant Labor, pp. 97, 95, 81–82; emphasis in original.

62. *Ibid.*, pp. 90, 104.

63. U.S. Congress. Senate Subcommittee on Appropriations, 1956, p. 142.

64. U.S. Immigration and Naturalization Service, "Notice to Mexican Nationals Contracted as Braceros," September 1955. Accession 58A733, Box 185.

65. Quoted in Anderson, 1963, p. 26.

66. *Ibid.*, p. 44–45.

67. Memo to Rocco Siciliano, September 21, 1954. National Archives. Record Group 174, Box 54.

68. Memo to Commissioner Swing, July 23, 1955. Accession 58A733, Box 185.

69. Memo from Acting Regional Commissioner of the Southwest Region to Assistant Commissioner, Central Office, July 22, 1955. Accession 58A733, Box 185.

70. Memo of meeting with Mexican officials, from Irvin Shrode, Chief, Examinations Division, to Commissioner Swing, May 2, 1956. Accession 58A733, Box 185.

71. Memo from Ernest Hover, Chief of INS Examinations Branch in El Paso, Texas, to Marcus Neelly, District Director, El Paso, Texas, May 31, 1956. Accession 58A733, Box 195.

72. Agricultural Producers Labor Committee, *Newsletter*, August 27, 1954. Accession 67A3254, Box 8.

73. Letter from Trailback Plantation to the District Director, San Antonio, Texas, August 12, 1955. Accession 58A733, Box 185.

74. Letter from Commissioner Swing to Senator Fulbright, July 12, 1955. Accession 58A733, Box 185.

75. Letter from the President of the Webb County Farm Bureau to Senator Lyndon B. Johnson, July 26, 1954. National Archives. Record Group 174, Box 54.

76. Letter from Assistant Secretary of Labor, Rocco C. Siciliano, to Hon. Robert Murphy, Deputy Under Secretary of State, June 27, 1955. Accession 58A733, Box 185.

77. Memo from the Southwest Regional Commissioner, David H. Carna -
han, to the Assistant Commissioner, Central Office, March 20, 1956. Accession
58A733, Box 185.

78. U.S. Immigration and Naturalization Service, *I and N Reporter*, November, 1955, p. 16.

79. Memo from Southwest Regional Commissioner, David Carnahan, to
the Assistant Commissioner, Central Office, March 20, 1956. Accession
58A733, Box 185.

80. *Ibid.*

81. Memo of telephone conversation from Irvin Shrode, Examinations
Division, to Mr. Beechie, Mexico City, February 19, 1958. Accession 67A233,
Box 6; letter from Walter A. Sahli, District Director, San Antonio, Texas, to
Commissioner Swing, June 14, 1956. Accession 58A733, Box 195.

82. Memo of telephone conversation, from Mr. Beechie, INS Mexico City
representative, to Irvin Shrode, Chief, Examinations Division, February 19,
1958. Accession 67A233, Box 6.

83. Memo from Department of State to Department of Labor, May 15,
1956. National Archives. Record Group 174, Box 140.

84. See Chapter 5 for details of this suspension.

85. Memorandum for file from Irvin Shrode, Chief, Examinations Division, July 30, 1958. Accession 67A233, Box 6.

86. U.S. Congress. Senate Committee on Appropriations, 1954a, p. 13.

87. Letter from Commissioner Swing to Honorable Henry F. Holland,
Assistant Secretary of State, August 18, 1955. Accession 58A733, Box 185.

88. Letter from William Rogers, Deputy Attorney General, to Senator Carl
Hayden, July 2, 1956. Accession 58A733, Box 195.

89. Memo from Walter Sahli, District Director, San Antonio, Texas, to
Commissioner Swing, June 4, 1956. Accession 58A733, Box 195.

90. MSAR, Tucson, Arizona, January 1958. CO660.4–P. A margin note
by Commissioner Swing observed, "Good public relations."

91. MSAR, Del Rio, Texas, March 1958. Accession 63A1359, Box 4.

92. Memo from Edward Rudnick, Executive Assistant to the Commissioner, to Albert Del Guercio, Assistant Commissioner, November 17, 1955.
Accession 58A733, Box 185. Braceros who already had I-100 cards deposited
their laminated cards at their port of entry upon arrival and carried paper
facsimiles while in the U.S.

93. Memo from Ernest Hover, Chief, Examinations Branch, El Paso,
Texas, to Marcus Neelly, District Director, El Paso, Texas, March 28, 1956.
Accession 58A733, Box 185.

94. Memo from Ernest Hover, Chief, Examinations Branch, El Paso,
Texas, to Marcus Neelly, District Director, El Paso, Texas, May 31, 1956.
Accession 58A733, Box 195.

95. *Ibid.*

96. U.S. Congress. House Committee on Appropriations, 1957, p. 163;
emphasis added.

97. *Ibid.*, p. 163.

98. Memo from Commissioner Swing to District Directors in San Antonio,
El Paso, Los Angeles, San Francisco, August 25, 1954. Accession 67A3254,
Box 8; emphasis added.

99. "Important Notice to Employers of Mexican Agricultural Workers," September, 1955. Accession 58A733, Box 185.

100. Memo from Edward Rudnick, Executive Assistant to Commissioner Swing, to Albert Del Guercio, Assistant Commissioner, November 17, 1955. Accession 58A733, Box 185; see also memo from Masil Mason, Inspector, Examinations Division, to Albert Del Guercio, Assistant Commissioner, January 18, 1956. Accession 58A733, Box 185.

101. Memo from N. Thomas Sherfy, Officer in Charge, Hidalgo, Texas, to David Carnahan, Southwest Regional Commissioner, May 15, 1956. Accession 58A733, Box 185.

102. *Ibid.*; see also Memorandum for file, from Walter Sahli, San Antonio District Director, May 14, 1956. Accession 58A733, Box 195.

103. See MSAR's, Southwest Region, 1958. Accession 63A1359, Box 4.

104. Memo from Irvin Shrode, Chief Inspector, Examinations Division, to Commissioner Swing, May 2, 1956. Accession 58A733, Box 185.

105. *Ibid.*

106. Undated Memorandum for file, from Irvin Shrode, Chief Inspector, Examinations Division. Accession 58A733, Box 185.

107. *Ibid.* All negotiations involving the possible termination of the I-100 card system in exchange for an agreement on the Special Program took place informally in the hotel lobby, where growers and their representatives—who were not admitted to the official meetings—were active participants. The INS used the fact that "[n]othing had been said during the official conference about the dependence of the predesignated workers program on the elimination of the form I-100," to avoid having to take action on the proposed exchange.

108. Undated Memorandum for file, from E. DeWitt Marshall. Accession 58A733, Box 185.

109. After a temporary suspension of the Special system by Mexican officials at various migratory centers, this favorite program of employers continued to operate by fits and starts until its demise in the early 1960s.

110. Memorandum for file from Irvin Shrode, Chief, Examinations Division, February 19, 1958. Accession 67A233, Box 6.

111. Undated memo for file. Accession 67A233, Box 6.

112. Memorandum for file from Irvin Shrode, Chief, Examinations Division, February 19, 1958. Accession 67A233, Box 6. This vague reference to the "welfare of the growers" is never clarified, but may allude to the possibility of a Mexican backlash or reprisals for the unilateral action that the ranchers requested.

113. *Ibid.*

114. *Ibid.*

115. U.S. Congress. House Committee on Appropriations, 1955b, pp. 230–231.

116. U.S. Congress. House Committee on Government Operations. Subcommittee on Legal and Monetary Affairs, 1955, pp. 15–18.

117. *Ibid.*, p. 37.

118. U.S. Congress. Senate Committee on Appropriations, 1956, p. 134.

119. The *New York Times*, May 12, 1956, p. 40.

120. U.S. Congress. House Committee on Goverment Operations. Subcommittee on Legal and Monetary Affairs, 1956; see also the *New York Times*,

July 7, 1956, p. 14; July 26, 1956, p. 9; October 1, 1956, p. 24; October 12, 1956, p. 42.

121. *Ibid.*, Appendix, p. 62.

122. U.S. Congress. House Committee on Government Operations. Subcommittee on Legal and Monetary Affairs, 1955, pp. 14, 18, 26–37; *Congressional Record*, 1956, pp. 5174–5176, 5279–5294, 6995–6998; see also the *New York Times*, May 11, 1955, p. 32; June 6, 1955, p. 49.

123. *Congressional Record*, 1956, pp. 5174–5176, 5281–5286.

124. *Ibid.*, p. 5284.

125. *Ibid.*, pp. 5175, 5284, 5289.

126. Personal correspondence with the author, January 18, 1988. This official maintains that some members of Congress tried to have Commissioner Swing ousted from office. Another former senior INS official confirms the report, adding that it was Swing's personal connection to President Eisenhower and the President's lobbying on his behalf that "saved" Swing (Personal interview, November 18, 1988).

127. Oral History Interview with INS Commissioner Joseph Swing, 1971. Columbia University Library.

128. U.S. Congress. House Committee on Appropriations, 1955b, pp. 230–231; INS, "Administrative Reforms in the Immigration and Naturalization Service," 1955, Accession 67A3254, Box 8.

129. Oral History Interview with INS Commissioner Joseph Swing, 1971, pp. 27–28. Columbia University Library.

130. *Ibid.*, p. 28.

131. *Ibid.*, p. 75.

132. See Fiorina, 1977, pp. 43–46.

133. Oral History Interview with INS Commissioner Joseph Swing, 1971, p. 20. Columbia University Library.

134. *Ibid.*, pp. 75–76.

135. U.S. Congress. Senate Committee on Appropriations, 1957, pp. 226–227; *Congressional Record*, 1958, pp. 7952–7953; see also the *New York Times*, June 26, 1958, p. 18.

136. The *New York Times*, January 28, 1961, p. 8. Commissioner Swing was eventually replaced by INS career official Raymond Farrell, reportedly "to get a man who would be more responsive to the Attorney General [Robert Kennedy] than General Swing had been" (the *New York Times*, November 23, 1961, p. 27).

137. U.S. Congress. House Committee on Agriculture, 1951, p. 3.

138. *Ibid.*, p. 4; emphasis added.

139. *Ibid.*, pp. 89–90; emphasis added.

140. As enacted, PL 78 contained no such provision to legalize those already in the United States, and later bilateral agreements with Mexico explicitly forebade the practice.

141. MSAR, Laredo, Texas, March 1958. Accession 63A1359, Box 4.

142. MSAR, Yuma, Arizona, June 1958. Accession 63A1359, Box 4.

143. MSAR, El Paso, Texas, September 1958. Accession 63A1359, Box 4.

144. Letter from Deputy Attorney General William P. Rogers, to Senator Carl Hayden of Arizona, July 2, 1956. Accession 58A733, Box 195.

145. U.S. Congress. House Committee on Appropriations, 1953c, p. 9.

Notes to Chapter 5

1. Memo from E. L. Keenan, Department of Labor, to Rocco Siciliano, Assistant Secretary of Labor, September 21, 1954. National Archives. Record Group 174, Box 54.
2. Letter from Rocco Siciliano to Honorable Henry F. Holland, October 5, 1955. Accession 58A733, Box 185.
3. Handwritten note from James L. Hennessy, Executive Assistant to the Commissioner, to A. C. Devaney, Assistant Commissioner, Examinations Division, attached to letter from Rocco Siciliano, Assistant Secretary of Labor, to Undersecretary of State, June 27, 1955. Accession 58A733, Box 185.
4. Memo from Walter A. Sahli, District Director, San Antonio, Texas, to M. R. Toole, Deputy Regional Commissioner, San Pedro, California, September 28, 1955. Accession 58A733, Box 185.
5. Memo from Irvin Shrode, Chief Inspector, Examinations Division, to Commissioner Swing, May 2, 1956. Accession 58A733, Box 185.
6. Undated Memorandum for File from Irvin Shrode, Chief Inspector, Examinations Division. Accession 58A733, Box 185.
7. Letter from L. W. Williams, INS Assistant Commissioner, to Don Larin, Chief, Farm Placement Service, Bureau of Employment Security, Department of Labor, December 17, 1957. Accession 67A233, Box 6.
8. Letter from Commissioner Swing to Newell Brown, July 24, 1958. Accession 67A233, Box 6.
9. Letter from Commissioner Swing to Hon. Henry Holland, August 8, 1956. Accession 58A733, Box 195.
10. Letter from Commissioner Swing to Rocco C. Siciliano, Assistant Secretary of Labor, March 26, 1956. Accession 58A733, Box 185.
11. Memo from Newell Brown, Assistant Secretary of Labor, to Secretary Mitchell, August 5, 1958. National Archives. Record Group 174, Box 234.
12. The Labor Department's own interpretation of what they had accomplished was much more optimistic—an interpretation that seems to be supported by the reaction of growers (see text below).
13. Memoranda for File from Irvin Shrode, Chief Inspector, Examinations Division, July 30 and 31, 1958. Accession 67A233, Box 6.
14. Memo from E. DeWitt Marshall, District Director, San Antonio, Texas, to L.W. Gilman, Associate Deputy Regional Commissioner, San Pedro, California, June 9, 1960. Accession 67A233, Box 6.
15. Memo from Irvin Shrode to the Deputy Associate Commissioner, July 30, 1963. Accession 67A233, Box 6.
16. Hawley, 1966, p. 165.
17. Anderson, 1963, p. 48.
18. Letter from Ernesto Galarza to W. Willard Wirtz, Secretary of Labor, June 3, 1963. National Archives. Record Group 174, Box 75. Galarza was a member of the National Agricultural Workers Union and its precursor the

National Farm Labor Union, and was an active participant in the struggle against the Bracero Program.

19. Galarza, 1956.

20. Galarza, 1977, pp. 250–256.

21. Letter from Jesse W. Tapp, President of the San Francisco Chamber of Commerce, to James P. Mitchell, Secretary of Labor, January 19, 1954. National Archives. Record Group 174, Box 54.

22. Letter from the Secretary of Labor to Senator Estes Kefauver, July 7, 1953. National Archives. Record Group 174, Box 6.

23. Letter from Rep. O.C. Fisher to James Mitchell, Secretary of Labor, July 7, 1958. National Archives. Record Group 174, Box 234.

24. Letter from Secretary of Labor James Mitchell to Rep. O.C. Fisher, July 23, 1958. National Archives. Record Group 174, Box 234.

25. Memorandum for File from Irvin Shrode, INS Examinations Division, July 30, 1958. Accession 67A233, Box 6.

26. *Ibid.*

27. Memo from Newell Brown, Assistant Secretary of Labor, to James Mitchell, Secretary of Labor, August 5, 1958. National Archives. Record Group 174, Box 234.

28. Memo from Newell Brown, Assistant Secretary of Labor, to James Mitchell, Secretary of Labor, April 10, 1958. National Archives. Record Group 174, Box 235.

29. Memo from Newell Brown, Assistant Secretary of Labor, to James Mitchell, Secretary of Labor, April 29, 1958. National Archives. Record Group 174, Box 235.

30. Plumb, 1958, p. 10.

31. Quoted in MSAR, Yuma, Arizona, July, 1958. Accession 63A1359, Box 4.

32. Quoted in MSAR, Brownsville, Texas, July, 1958. Accession 63A1359, Box 4.

33. MSAR, Yuma, Arizona, June, 1958. Accession 63A1359, Box 4.

34. Letter from Texas businessman to Secretary of Labor Mitchell, June 25, 1958. National Archives. Record Group 174, Box 235.

35. U.S. Congress. House Committee on Agriculture. Subcommittee on Equipment, Supplies, and Manpower, 1958, p. 4.

36. MSAR, Brownsville, Texas, July 1958. Accession 63A1359, Box 4.

37. U.S. Congress. House Committee on Agriculture. Subcommittee on Equipment, Supplies, and Manpower, 1958, pp. 302–316, 460–469, 493–598.

38. Moore, 1965, p. 110.

39. Telegram from the president of the San Joaquin Farm Produce Association to Glenn Brockway, Regional Director of the BES, October 30, 1963. National Archives. Record Group 174, Box 76.

40. Letter from Millard Cass, Deputy Under Secretary of Labor, to the president of the San Joaquin Farm Produce Association, November 15, 1963. National Archives. Record Group 174, Box 76.

41. *Brownsville Herald*, June 12, 1960, p. 1.

42. Letter from Rep. O.C. Fisher, to Arthur J. Goldberg, Secretary of Labor, November 10, 1961. National Archives. Record Group 174, Box 54.

43. Letter from a California grower, to John Henning, Under Secretary of Labor, July 30, 1963. National Archives. Record Group 174, Box 76.
44. Quoted in Mayer, 1961, p. 35.
45. U.S. Congress. House Committee on Agriculture. Subcommittee on Equipment, Supplies, and Manpower, 1960, pp. 2–14, 61–69, 352–354.
46. U.S. Congress. House Committee on Agriculture. Subcommittee on Equipment, Supplies, and Manpower, 1961, pp. 10–14.
47. Brooks, 1971, p. 369.
48. Hawley, 1966, p. 166.
49. Jacobs, 1963, p. 193; Brooks, 1971, p. 369.
50. Jenkins, 1985, p. 114.
51. In 1965, the Agricultural Workers Organizing Committee (AWOC) merged with the National Farm Workers Association led by Cesar Chavez, forming the United Farm Workers Organizing Committee (UFWOC). UFWOC became the United Farm Workers union (UFW) in 1972.
52. Galarza, 1977.
53. *Ibid.*, p. 205.
54. *Ibid.*, p. 216.
55. Moore, 1965, pp. 156–157.
56. Letter from C. Al Green, Director, AWOC, to John F. Henning, Under Secretary of Labor, August 9, 1963. See also letters, June 27, 1963 and August 13, 1963. National Archives. Record Group 174, Box 76.
57. *Ibid.*
58. Letter from C. Al Green to John F. Henning, August 9, 1963. National Archives. Record Group 174, Box 76.
59. Memo from Millard Cass to John Henning, July 29, 1963. National Archives. Record Group 174, Box 76.
60. Memo from Newell Brown, Assistant Secretary of Labor, to James Mitchell, Secretary of Labor, May 28, 1958. National Archives. Record Group 174, Box 235.
61. Unsigned memo to John Henning, Under Secretary of Labor, February 7, 1964. National Archives. Record Group 174, Box 165.
62. Letter from Carl N. Carr, President, Central Labor Council of Salinas, California, AFL-CIO, to John F. Henning, Under Secretary of Labor, August 7, 1963. National Archives. Record Group 174, Box 76.
63. See for example, *Farm Labor Newsletter*, February, 1953, p. 3; and *The Reporter*, January 22, 1959, p. 20.
64. Memo from W. Willard Wirtz, Secretary of Labor, to Millard Cass, Deputy Under Secretary of Labor, September 11, 1963. National Archives. Record Group 174, Box 76.
65. *Ibid.*, pp. 50–51.
66. Craig, 1971, p. 199.
67. Anderson, 1963, p. 47.
68. Quoted in Rourke, 1969, p. 20.
69. Ferejohn, 1987, p. 448. The concept of agency "clienteles" is similar to Rourke's (1969, pp. 13, 85) "attentive publics" or "constituencies."
70. *Ibid.*, p. 13.
71. Mitchell, 1959, p. 20.
72. *Hispanic American Report*, March 1957, p. 63.

73. The *New York Times*, August, 18, 1957, p. 50.

74. Bailey and Vernoff, 1959, pp. 12–14.

75. U.S. Department of Labor. Bureau of Employment Security, 1959.

76. *Congressional Record*, 1961, p. 20642.

77. Williams, 1962, p. 31.

78. Craig, 1971, pp. 178–179.

79. "Semi-Annual Report," from the Regional Commissioner, Southwest Region, to the Assistant Commissioner, Examinations Division, July 23, 1958. Accession 67A233, Box 6.

80. MSAR, Marfa, Texas, November 1961. Accession 64A1851, Box 161.

81. MSAR, Port Isabel, Texas, April 1962. Accession 64A1851, Box 162.

82. MSAR, Marfa, Texas, December 1961. Accession 64A1851, Box 161.

83. MSAR, Yuma, Arizona, May 1960. Accession 63A1359, Box 5.

84. Memo from Irvin Shrode, Assistant Commissioner, Examinations, to Mr. Hardin, Assistant Commissioner, Special Projects, March 30, 1960. Accession 67A233, Box 6.

85. MSAR, Del Rio, Texas, June 1958. Accession 63A1359, Box 4.

86. MSAR, Marfa, Texas, May 1960. Accession 63A1359, Box 5.

87. Memo from J.G. Frye, Acting Assistant Regional Commissioner, Special Projects, Southwest Region, to I.F. Shrode, Assistant Commissioner, Examinations, May 5, 1960. Accession 67A233, Box 6; emphasis added.

88. Memo from E. DeWitt Marshall, District Director, San Antonio, Texas, to L. W. Gilman, Assistant Deputy Regional Commissioner, June 9, 1960. Accession 67A233, Box 6; emphasis added.

89. Memo from E. L. Keenan, Department of Labor, to Rocco Siciliano, Assistant Secretary of Labor, September 21, 1954. National Archives. Record Group 174, Box 54.

90. The draft legislation was eventually shelved, apparently as a result of active opposition from Secretary of Agriculture Benson and White House Administrative Assistant Jack Anderson, who himself used braceros on his California farm (Mayer, 1961, p. 35).

91. Memo from Irvin Shrode, Assistant Commissioner, Examinations, to J. M. Wehler, Assistant Executive Assistant [*sic*], March 18, 1960; see also memo from Frank H. Partridge, Deputy Associate Commissioner, to J. M. Wehler, March 18, 1960; memo from Commissioner Swing to the Deputy Attorney General, March 18, 1960; all Accession 63A1359, Box 10.

92. Handwritten note for file, from J. M. Wehler, March 21, 1960. Accession 63A1359, Box 10.

93. Letter from Rocco Siciliano, Assistant Secretary of Labor, to Robert Murphy, Deputy Under Secretary of State, June 27, 1955. Accession 58A733, Box 185.

94. Memo from Irvin Shrode, Assistant Commissioner, Examinations, to J. M. Wehler, Assistant Executive Assistant, March 18, 1960. Accession 63A1359, Box 10.

95. Memo from Frank H. Partridge, Deputy Associate Commissioner, to J. M. Wehler, March 18, 1960. Accession 63A1359, Box 10; emphasis added.

96. Letter from Rocco Siciliano, Assistant Secretary of Labor, to Robert Murphy, Deputy Under Secretary of State, June 27, 1955. Accession 58A733, Box 185.

97. INS, *Public Opinion Survey*, McAllen, Texas, pp. 7, 10. Accession 67A233, Box 6.

98. Memo from A.D. Sneed, Acting Special Projects Officer, Southwest Region, to M.R. Toole, Acting Regional Commissioner, Southwest Region, June 21, 1956. Accession 58A733, Box 195.

99. *Ibid.*

100. Letter from Glenn E. Brockway, Regional Director, BES, to Manager of the Yuma Producers Cooperative Association, August 7, 1957. Accession 67A233, Box 6.

101. Letter from the Manager of the Yuma Producers Cooperative Association, to Alfred J. Norton, BES, August 20, 1957. Accession 67A233, Box 6.

102. Letter from M. R. Toole, Acting Regional Commissioner, Southwest Region, to Glenn E. Brockway, Regional Director, BES, September 16, 1957. Accession 67A233, Box 6.

103. Memo from M. R. Toole, Acting Regional Commissioner, Southwest Region, to J. M. Swing, Commissioner, December 30, 1955. Accession 58A733, Box 185.

104. Memo from Edward Bruder, District Director, Phoenix, Arizona, to Regional Commissioner, Southwest Region, September 6, 1957. Accession 67A233, Box 6.

105. Letter from M. R. Toole, to Glenn E. Brockway, September 16, 1957. Accession 67A233, Box 6.

106. Unsigned INS memo for file, June 14, 1956. Accession 58A733, Box 195.

107. Quoted in U.S. Congress. House Committee on Agriculture. Subcommittee on Equipment, Supplies, and Manpower, 1958, p. 615.

108. *Ibid.*, pp. 608–610.

109. MSAR, Marfa, Texas, April 1960. Accession 63A1359, Box 5.

110. U.S. Congress. House Committee on Agriculture. Subcommittee on Equipment, Supplies, and Manpower, 1960, p. 423.

111. U.S. Congress. House Committee on Agriculture. Subcommittee on Equipment, Supplies, and Manpower, 1958, p. 457.

112. Letter from the president of the California Growers Association, Inc., to Commissioner Swing, April 7, 1958; see also letter from the manager of the Agricultural Producers Labor Committee, to Commissioner Swing, April 2, 1958. Accession 67A233, Box 6.

113. Quoted in U.S. Congress. House Committee on Agriculture. Subcommittee on Equipment, Supplies and Manpower, 1958, p. 471.

114. *Brownsville Herald*, June 12, 1960, pp. 1, 11.

115. INS memo for file, April 13, 1956. Accession 58A733, Box 185.

116. Handwritten note attached to *Ibid*.

117. Letter from Commissioner Swing to Rocco C. Siciliano, August 15, 1955. Accession 58A733, Box 185; emphasis added.

118. Memo from Irvin Shrode to Commissioner Swing, May 2, 1956. Accession 58A733, Box 185.

119. Letter from Commissioner Swing to Robert Murphy, July 18, 1955. Accession 58A733, Box 185.

120. Letter from Rocco C. Siciliano to Henry F. Holland, Assistant Secretary of State, March 29, 1956. Accession 58A733, Box 185.

121. Memo from the Secretary of State to the Secretary of Labor and the

Commissioner of the INS, May 15, 1956. National Archives. Record Group 174, Box 140.

122. Cited in memo from the Assistant Commissioner of the INS to the Deputy Associate Commissioner, July 30, 1963. Accession 67A233, Box 6.

123. Anderson, 1963, p. 47.

124. Congressional Research Service, 1980b, p. 58.

Notes to Chapter 6

1. U.S. Department of Labor, 1963, pp. 42–44.

2. Moore, 1965, p. 88.

3. U.S. Department of Labor. Bureau of Employment Security, 1959, p. 273.

4. Moore, 1965, p. 95.

5. This amendment was a reaction to the DOL regulation in 1959 that established minimum wages and working conditions for domestic farm workers recruited by the Farm Placement Service. Referred to as the "New Wagner-Peyser Regulations," the policy was hotly contested by growers who feared an increasing DOL role in setting not just bracero wages, but domestic wages as well (U.S. Congress. House Committee on Agriculture. Subcommittee on Equipment, Supplies, and Manpower, 1960, p. 5). The amendment sought to void the regulation by specifying that nothing in PL 78 authorized the Secretary of Labor to establish wages and working conditions for domestic farm workers (*Ibid.*, pp. 2–3).

6. *Ibid.*, pp. 3–4. For an excellent discussion of these proceedings, see Craig, 1971, pp. 155–163.

7. See generally, U.S. Congress. House Committee on Agriculture. Subcommittee on Equipment, Supplies, and Manpower, 1961, pp. 37–38; Senate Committee on Agriculture and Forestry, 1961, pp. 5–18, 159–166.

8. U.S. Congress. House Committee on Agriculture. Subcommittee on Equipment, Supplies, and Manpower, 1963, pp. 29–38, 92–96, 102–105; U.S. Congress. House, 1963. *House Report #274*; *Congressional Record*, 1963, pp. 23155, 23174, 23223. It has been widely argued that even this extension would not have been possible without persistent pressure from Mexico and related State Department recommendations not to terminate the program abruptly (Congressional Research Service, 1980b, pp. 53–56; Craig, 1971, p. 185).

9. Congressional Research Service, 1980b, p. 51.

10. Craig, 1971, p. 164; Hawley, 1966, p. 172.

11. *Ibid.*, pp. 172, 176.

12. Keisker, 1961, p. 202. For the effect of "Harvest of Shame" on the Bracero Program, see Hawley, 1966, p. 172.

13. Craig, 1971, p. 204.

14. Cover letter to *Semi-Annual Report*, INS Southwest Region. July 13, 1962. Accession 67A233, Box 6. While many growers and ranchers stopped importing braceros as a result of the stricter regulations, others simply ignored the regulatory formalities. According to a Labor Department report to Congress, in the second half of 1963, the DOL found violations in 33% of its 1425

investigations of bracero working conditions, and housing standards violations were uncovered in 30% of its 3621 inspections (Department of Labor, "Report on Operations of Mexican Farm Labor Program," 1963. National Archives. Record Group 174, Box 76).

15. Runsten and Leveen, 1981, pp. 53–55.

16. *Ibid.*, p. 53.

17. *Ibid.*, p. 56.

18. California Legislative Assembly. Legislative Reference Service, 1965, pp. 5–6.

19. Block, 1987, pp. 84, 16. See Chapter 7 for further discussion of Block's contributions to state theory.

20. Personal interviews with former INS and Border Patrol officials (6/8/87; 11/17/88; 11/18/88; 12/9/88).

21. Letter from Lawrence W. Walsh, Deputy Attorney General, to Senator Eugene McCarthy, November 18, 1960. CO 659.4P; memo from M. F. Fargione, Deputy Regional Commissioner, Southwest Region, to Commissioner Raymond F. Farrell, July 24, 1963. Accession 67A233, Box 6.

22. Personal interview, 11/18/88.

23. Memo from J. G. Frye, Special Projects Officer, Southwest Region, to Irvin Shrode, February 3, 1961. Accession 67A233, Box 6; MSAR, Livermore, California, June 1960. Accession 63A1359, Box 5.

24. Telegram from Clive Knowles, International Representative of the United Packing House Workers of America, and Norman Smith, Director of the Agricultural Workers Organizing Committee, AFL-CIO, to Arthur Goldberg, Secretary of Labor, February 7, 1961. Accession 67A233, Box 6.

25. Memo from DeWitt Marshall to General Partridge, October 12, 1956. C0845-P.

26. Memorandum for File from James F. Greene, Assistant Commissioner for Enforcement, January 3, 1961. Accession 67A233, Box 6.

27. *Ibid.*

28. Letter from Robert C. Goodwin to Edmund Dores, Deputy Administrator, Bureau of Security and Consular Affairs, Department of State, November 2, 1960. Accession 67A233, Box 6.

29. MSAR, Yuma, Arizona, November 1960. Accession 64A1851, Box 161; MSAR, Yuma, Arizona, June 1960. Accession 63A1359, Box 5.

30. U.S. Congress. House Committee on the Judiciary. Subcommittee Number 1, 1963, p. 50.

31. The interest that immigration officials showed with regard to strike activity derived in part from their concern with the potential for labor activism among braceros. At least as important, they worried that growers would turn to illegal labor if precluded from hiring domestic workers or braceros during a strike.

32. Memorandum of telephone call from T. H. Armstrong, Special Projects Officer, San Pedro, California, to J. W. Bowser, Deputy Assistant Commissioner, October 25, 1960. Accession 67A233, Box 6. According to one observer who interviewed immigrants, domestic migrants, growers, crew leaders, union leaders, and social workers, some growers collected the visas of their immigrant workers and held them until the end of the season, thereby rendering them as captive as braceros (Moore, 1965, p. 89).

NOTES TO CHAPTER 6

33. *Ibid.*, p. 89.
34. California Legislative Assembly. Legislative Reference Service, 1965, p. 8.
35. North, 1970, p. 83.
36. U.S. Congress. House Committee on Agriculture. Subcommittee on Equipment, Supplies, and Manpower, 1958, pp. 457–459; and, 1963, p. 53.
37. Section 101 (a)(15)(H)(ii).
38. California Legislative Assembly. Legislative Reference Service, 1965, pp. 16, 20.
39. The *New York Times*, December 1, 1964, p. 25; Hawley, 1966, p. 175.
40. Quoted in Congressional Research Service, 1980b, p. 65.
41. Letter from Charles Donahue, Solicitor of Labor, U.S. Department of Labor, to Alberto Becerra-Sierra, Minister Counsellor, Embassy of Mexico, Washington, D.C., August 17, 1965. CO 214h.10-P.
42. Memo from Donald R. Coppock to Deputy Associate Commissioner, Domestic Control, January 25, 1965. CO 659-P; emphasis added.
43. *Ibid.*
44. INS Enforcement Division. "Field Operations," November 1962. Accession 67A3254, Box 8; emphasis added.
45. *Ibid.*
46. President's Commission on Migratory Labor, 1951, pp. 73–74.
47. Personal interview with senior INS official from the Swing and Farrell Administrations, 6/8/87. This central office civil servant explained simply, "Illegals are good for the economy."
48. Memorandum for File, from James F. Greene, Deputy Associate Commissioner, Domestic Control, December 22, 1964. CO 214h.10-P; emphasis added. Commissioner Farrell's name is conspicuously absent from INS correspondence in this period, suggesting that he took a far less active role in the formation of policies relating to foreign labor and border control than had his assertive and seemingly ever-present predecessor.
49. Internal INS Report, "A Plan to Bolster the Border Patrol Force on the Mexican Border," May 14, 1965. CO 659-P.
50. Memo from James F. Greene, to Southwest Regional Commissioner, January 22, 1965. CO 659-P. It is interesting to note that after termination of the Bracero Program, INS officials consistently blamed their problems on immigrants who sought employment in the United States, and all reference to the role of employers hiring illegal workers as a trigger for illegal migration—a constant theme in INS communication during the Bracero Program—was dropped. Perhaps the shift was due to an ideological reluctance to place the blame for the growing problem on employers, or perhaps it was simply an unstated assumption that growers would hire illegal workers in the absence of a legal source.
51. Greene, 1969a, p. 405.
52. Unpublished INS report, October 21, 1971. CO 214h.
53. Congressional Research Service, 1980b, p. 43.
54. Personal interview, 9/24/86.
55. PL 89–236; 79 *Stat.* 911.
56. Gordon, 1969, p. 181.
57. *Ibid.*, p. 182.

58. *Karnuth v. Albro*, 279 U.S. 231.

59. For more detailed description of this regulation and subsequent INS decisions, see Gordon, 1969.

60. I & N Decision 716. Board of Immigration Appeals, 1954.

61. Hearings before the Select Commission on Western Hemisphere Immigration, 1968 (Part 2), pp. 101–102.

62. *Ibid.*, Part 3, p. 49. It is revealing that this grower put the date of the enactment of PL 78 (passed in 1951) in 1954—the year of Operation Wetback, and the exchange of illegal workers for braceros. See also statement of Morris Atlas, on behalf of the Rio Grande Valley Farm Bureau, *Ibid.*, Part 3, pp. 61–62.

63. These surveys and their deficiencies are discussed in North, 1970, pp. 22–31.

64. *Ibid.*, pp. 22–31; Gordon, 1969, pp. 183–184; U.S. Congress. Senate, 1968. *Senate Report* No. 1006, pp. 10–11.

65. North, 1970, p. 24.

66. Report prepared by the Bureau of Employment Security, Department of Labor, for the Select Commission on Western Hemisphere Immigration, reprinted in U.S. Congress. Senate Committee on Labor and Public Welfare. Subcommittee on Migratory Labor, 1969, p. 2645.

67. *Amalgamated Meatcutters v. Rogers*, 186 F.Supp. 114 (D.D.C. 1960).

68. *Texas AFL-CIO v. Kennedy*, 330 F.2d 217 (D.C. Cir. 1964), cert. denied, 379 U.S. 826 (1964).

69. 8 C.F.R. Section 211.1(b)(1).

70. U.S. Congress. Senate Committee on the Judiciary. Subcommittee on Immigration and Naturalization, 1967. Unpublished transcript, p. 27; hereafter, Senate Immigration Subcommittee, 1967. For additional criticisms of this aspect of the regulation, see comments of Rep. James O'Hara of Michigan, U.S. Congress. House Committee on Education and Labor. Subcommittee on Labor, 1969, p. 88; North, 1970, p. 55.

71. Senate Immigration Subcommittee, 1967, pp. 82–83.

72. Comments of James L. Hennessy. U.S. Congress. House Committee on Education and Labor. Subcommittee on Labor, 1969, p. 87.

73. *Ibid.*, p. 29.

74. *Ibid.*, p. 52.

75. North, 1970, p. 56.

76. Senate Immigration Subcommitee, 1967, p. 28.

77. *Ibid.*, pp. 76–77; Select Commission on Western Hemisphere Immigration, 1968, pp. 107–109; Greene, 1969b, p. 491.

78. Select Commission on Western Hemisphere Immigration, 1968, pp. 112–114; Senate Immigration Subcommittee, 1967, pp. 76–77.

79. Greene, 1972, p. 443.

80. U.S. Congress. House Committee on the Judiciary. Subcommittee Number 1, 1972, p. 1351.

81. U.S. Congress. Senate Committee on Labor and Public Welfare. Subcommittee on Migratory Labor, 1969, p. 2591.

82. *Ibid.*, p. 2582; emphasis added.

83. *Ibid.*, pp. 1, 2584; Greene, 1972, p. 442.

84. Senate Immigration Subcommittee, 1967, p. 1.

85. *Ibid.*, p. 33.

86. *Ibid.*, p. 61.

87. *Ibid.*, p. 33.

88. *Gooch v. Clark*, Civil No. 49,5000 (N.D. Cal., June 24, 1969).

89. Greene, 1972, p. 448.

90. Select Commission on Western Hemisphere Immigration, Part 1, 1968, pp. vi–vii.

91. Senate Immigration Subcommittee, 1967, pp. 37–38; 66–67. See also, U.S. Congress. Senate Committee on Labor and Public Welfare. Subcommittee on Migratory Labor, 1969, p. 2591.

92. Select Commission on Western Hemisphere Immigration, 1968a, Part 2, p. 160.

93. *Ibid.*, pp. 82, 87; 1968a, Part 3, pp. 8–9; U.S. Congress. House Committee on the Judiciary. Subcommittee on Immigration, Citizenship, and International Law, 1972, p. 1351.

94. Senate Immigration Subcommittee, 1967, pp. 77, 53.

95. Select Commission on Western Hemisphere Immigration, 1968a, Part 2, pp. 82–83; Part 3, pp. 42–43, 49, 61–73.

96. Personal interview, 12/9/88.

97. North, 1970, p. 72.

98. Personal interview, 12/9/88.

99. Clinard and Yeager, 1980; Clinard *et al.*, 1979; Braithwaite, 1979, 1982, 1984; Coleman, 1985; Barnett, 1982; Snider, 1987, 1990, 1991; Levi, 1981; Stone, 1978.

100. Donnelly, 1982; Calavita, 1983b; Snider, 1991.

101. Schrecker, 1989; Molotch, 1973; Coleman, 1985.

102. The *New York Times*, November 23, 1961, p. 26.

103. Personal interviews, 9/24/86; 6/8/87; 11/17/88; 12/9/88.

104. Personal interview, 6/8/87.

105. Personal interview, 9/24/86.

106. Schuck, 1975, p. xii.

107. *Ibid.*, p. 18. One of the many bills that was allowed to die in Eastland's committee was a 1974 "employer sanctions" measure that would have made it illegal to hire undocumented immigrants. One cynical Justice Department official sent his colleague a news clipping reporting that Eastland's committee was "sitting on" the bill. He attached a handwritten note: "And the Hill blames the *Department* for not being able to control the 'alien problem.' Who's kidding whom???" (Department of Justice File #51–537, Item 127; emphasis in the original).

108. Crewdson, 1983, p. 126.

109. Personal interviews, 9/24/86; 6/8/87; 1/17/88; 12/9/88; personal letter, 1/18/88.

110. Personal interview, 9/24/86.

111. Letter to the Select Commission on Immigration and Refugee Policy, July 1, 1980, Select Commission Notes, reel 11.

112. Personal interview, 9/24/86.

113. *Ibid.*

114. Personal interview, 11/17/88.

115. Personal interviews, 9/24/86; 11/17/88

116. Personal interview, 11/17/88.

117. Personal interview, 11/17/88.

118. *Ibid.*
119. Congressional Research Service, 1980a, pp. 65, 76, 90.
120. Unpublished INS report, "A Plan to Bolster the Border Patrol Force on the Mexican Border," March 14, 1965. CO 659-P.
121. Weinraub, 1980, p. B9.
122. Personal interview, 9/24/86.
123. *Ibid.*
124. U.S. Congress. House Committee on the Judiciary. Subcommittee on Immigration, Citizenship, and International Law, 1971, p. 479.
125. *Ibid.*, p. 85.
126. Personal interview, 9/24/86.
127. *Ibid.*
128. Personal interview, 11/17/88.
129. Personal interview, 9/24/86.
130. U.S. Congress. House Committee on the Judiciary. Subcommittee on Immigration, Citizenship, and International Law, 1972, pp. 1263–1264.
131. U.S. Congress. House Committee on the Judiciary. Subcommittee on Immigration, Refugees, and International Law, 1979, p. 1.
132. *Ibid.*, p. 70.
133. U.S. Congress. Senate Committee on the Judiciary, 1980, p. 551.
134. U.S. Congress. House Committee on Appropriations. Subcommittee on State, Justice, and Commerce, and the Judiciary, 1977, p. 444.
135. U.S. General Accounting Office, 1980.
136. Quoted in U.S. Congress. House Committee on the Judiciary. Subcommittee on Immigration, Refugees, and International Law, 1982, p. 6.
137. Maxwell, 1980, p. 6.
138. *U.S. News and World Report*, June 22, 1981, p. 27.
139. Crewdson, 1983, p. 114.
140. Personal interview, 9/24/86.
141. Comments of Michael Harpold, President, National INS Council, quoted in U.S. Congress. Senate Committee on the Judiciary, 1980, pp. 558–559; emphasis added.
142. Personal interview, 11/17/88.
143. Bach, 1978; Burawoy, 1976.
144. U.S. Congress. Senate Committee on the Judiciary, 1980, p. 174.

Notes to Chapter 7

1. See the Select Commission on Immigration and Refugee Policy, 1981.
2. U.S. Immigration and Naturalization Service, *Statistical Yearbook*, 1986, p. 95.
3. Bach, 1978; Burawoy, 1976; Bustamante, 1978; Lopez, 1981.
4. Marshall, 1978, p. 169.
5. Maram, 1980, pp. 31–32.
6. San Francisco Human Rights Commission, cited in Dygert and Shibata, 1975, p. 66.
7. Bustamante, 1978, p. 187.
8. Recent studies draw a distinction between "sojourners" who cross the border for a temporary period of work in the United States and "settlers" who

stay (Chavez, 1988; Cornelius and García y Griego, 1992). While it is true that many sojourners put down extensive roots and remain in the U.S. for long periods of time, most scholars conclude that the public perception of Mexican immigrants as primarily long-term settlers is a myth grounded in, and contributing to, public fears of the immigrant influx (See Lopez, 1981).

9.   American Association of University Women, San Diego monthly meeting. The comment was made subsequent to a presentation by the author on U.S. immigration policy.

10.   *Washington Post*, July 16, 1986.

11.   In addition, the so-called "amnesty" measure provided for the legalization of illegal aliens who could demonstrate that they had lived continuously in the United States since January 1, 1982.

12.   See Gallup, 1980, p. A–22.

13.   U.S. Congress. Senate Committee on the Judiciary. Subcommittee on Immigration and Refugee Policy, 1981, p. 86.

14.   For a discussion of the legislative debates, see Calavita, 1989.

15.   U.S. Congress. House Committee on the Judiciary. Subcommittee on Immigratio, Refugees, and International Law, 1983, p. 265.

16.   Personal interview, 6/8/87.

17.   Personal interview, 11/19/87.

18.   U.S. General Accounting Office, 1982a.

19.   This employer was interviewed as part of a study of the effects of employer sanctions on immigrant-dependent employers and on migration patterns. The study was conducted at the Center for U.S.-Mexican Studies at the University of California, San Diego. For a discussion of the methodology and findings of the study, see Calavita, 1990.

20.   U.S.-Mexico border apprehensions went from 1,615,854 to 854,939 from fiscal year 1986 to fiscal year 1989. However, apprehensions increased by more than 32% in the last two quarters of 1989, and by over 50% in 1990. The most comprehensive study to date of the effect of employer sanctions on the volume of illegal border crossings (Crane *et al.*, 1990) concludes that the early reductions were less a product of employer sanctions than they were a consequence of IRCA's legalization provisions, which legalized close to three million immigrants, many of whom periodically crossed the border illegally prior to legalization.

21.   Mills, 1959.

22.   See Skocpol, 1985, pp. 4–9, for a discussion of this distinction.

23.   C. Wright Mills' *The Power Elite* (1956) was one of the only systematic critiques of the pluralist model in the early period, and was never a serious contender for pluralists' paradigmatic dominance, sparking only a brief flurry of angry rebuttals (see Domhoff and Ballard, 1968).

24.   The most extensive scholarly study to date on the politics of the Bracero Program (Craig, 1971) provides an excellent example of the ostensible merits of the pluralist perspective, as well as its limitations. Focusing on the "group processes" and special interests affecting bracero policies, Craig underplays both the broader structural context within which negotiations were embedded, and consistent patterns of U.S. agricultural dominance.

25.   See Domhoff, 1967, 1970, 1978, 1979; Miliband, 1969.

26.   1966, p. 165. See Chapter 5 for the details of Hawley's allegations.

27.   1963, p. 48. See Chapter 5.

28. See Calavita, 1984, pp. 138–161.
29. See Offe, 1974, p. 35; Poulantzas, 1969, pp. 67–71. For further critique of the instrumentalist model, see Block, 1987, pp. 9–16.
30. Althusser, 1971.
31. Poulantzas, 1969; 1973.
32. Poulantzas, 1969.
33. Central to this objective relation, the state must promote capital accumulation since its own survival depends on tax revenues derived from successful profit-making activity, as well as on the political stability that is contingent on economic growth. In addition to this accumulation function, the state must actively pursue "political integration" (Friedland *et al.*, 1977), "social harmony" (O'Connor, 1973), or "the cohesion of the social formation" (Poulantzas, 1969) in the interests of political survival and the economic growth upon which it depends. This ideological cohesion is accomplished through extensive "state ideological apparatuses," such as schools, the mass media, and churches.
34. Poulantzas, 1969; 1973.
35. Pfeffer, 1980.
36. *Ibid.*, p. 39.
37. Bach, 1978, p. 63.
38. This neglect of human agency is a potential danger in all theories that emphasize the causal primacy of social structure, with structural-functionalism providing another notable example. However, the neglect of the human subject seems not to be motivated entirely by intellectual considerations. In Poulantzas' 1969 critique of Miliband's instrumentalist view, he accuses Miliband of sharing the same "epistemological terrain" with pluralists. Poulantzas claims that Miliband, with his focus on human beings rather than structures as causal agents, commits the "problematic of the subject" (Poulantzas, 1969, p. 70). That is, "men" are the subjects of action, rather than being simply the "bearers" of structure. Given the political context within which the split from pluralism occurred, and the ideological commitments of these state theorists, the accusation carried the implication that Miliband's perspective was not just intellectually inaccurate, but politically undesirable. As Block says, ". . . if focusing on the role of capitalists in staffing the government and influencing politicans put one on the epistemological terrain of pluralists, who would want to do it?" (Block, 1987, p. 7).
39. Chambliss, 1979.
40. Whitt, 1979. See also, Whitt, 1982.
41. See, for example, Calavita, 1984.
42. Skocpol, 1985, pp. 4–7.
43. Skocpol's pathbreaking work on the French, Russian, and Chinese Revolutions concludes that both the revolutions themselves and the nature of the New Regimes depended less on conflicts and tensions in civil society, than on the organization of the pre-revolutionary states, revenue pressures, and subsequent conflicts between the state and the landed classes.
44. Alfred Stepan (1978) documents the role of state elites in Peru in the 1960s in promoting economic reforms and staving off threats to the political order. Similarly, Trimberger (1978) examines *Revolutions from Above*, describing the role of state elites in Japan, Turkey, Egypt, and Peru in redefining the economic order and effectively eroding the power of the existing aristocracy.

45. Skocpol and Finegold, 1982.
46. *Ibid.*, p. 271.
47. Hooks, 1990, p. 32; emphasis in the original. See also Evans, *et. al*, 1985, pp. 347–366.
48. Skocpol, 1980, p. 201.
49. See in particular, Block, 1987, pp. 3–35; 81–96.
50. *Ibid.*, p. 21.
51. *Ibid.*, p. 84.
52. *Ibid.*, p. 84. Block points out that the result is asymmetrical: "In social formations dominated by the capitalist mode of production, the dominant historical pattern has been the development of a *modus vivendi* that is highly favorable to the owners of capital" (p. 84). The arrangement hammered out between the Immigration Service and growers was consistent with this pattern.
53. *Ibid.*, pp. 85–87.
54. It is in the interest of state managers, Block points out, to improve their relative standing within both the world economy and the state political competition. This is so because a high standing on each of these dimensions increases the resources available to the state, and because a low standing—in the worst-case scenario, military defeat—depletes resources and jeopardizes state managers' political control.
55. Rosenbloom, 1983, p. 23. Rosenbloom points out further that "members of Congress have developed an inclination to delegate not just authority, but also controversial political issues to public administrators. By doing so, they . . . avoid making enemies of those who would oppose their policy stands" (p. 24; see also Fiorina, 1977, pp. 43–46).
56. Davis, 1970, pp. 133–134.
57. Scher, 1971.
58. Aberbach, 1979.
59. Ripley and Franklin, 1984, p. 252.
60. Redford, 1969, pp. 40–41; see also Davis, 1969; Davidson, 1977; and Lowi, 1969.
61. Wildavsky, 1971, p. 390.
62. *Ibid.*, p. 390; see also Rourke, 1969, pp. 15–16.
63. Rourke, 1969, pp. 19, 22–23, 85; Lowi, 1969; Ripley and Franklin, 1984, p. 69. This literature on administrative agencies and the internal and external forces that affect decision-making has some fundamental weaknesses. Although it is almost without exception general, it is seldom explicitly theoretical. Instead, it is based loosely on pluralist notions about the nature of political and social power in the United States—notions that remain implicit and thus serve less as a theoretical guide than as untested background assumptions. This lack of a coherent theoretical framework may explain the *ad hoc* pasting together of disparate levels of analysis in many of these studies.
64. U.S. Congress. Senate Immigration Commission, 1911, pp. 690–691.
65. Evans *et al.*, 1985, p. 360.
66. *Ibid.*, p. 350.
67. Galarza, 1964, p. 255.
68. Skocpol, 1985, p. 16.
69. Hooks, 1990, p. 30.

APPENDIX

Appendix A.   Illegal Aliens Apprehended by the INS, 1940–1976

Year	No. Apprehended	Year	No. Apprehended
1940	10,492	1959	45,336
1941	11,294	1960	70,684
1942	11,784	1961	88,823
1943	11,715	1962	92,758
1944	31,174	1963	88,712
1945	69,164	1964	86,597
1946	99,591	1965	110,371
1947	193,657	1966	138,520
1948	192,779	1967	161,608
1949	288,253	1968	212,057
1950	468,339	1969	283,557
1951	509,040	1970	345,353
1952	528,815	1971	420,126
1953	885,587	1972	505,949
1954	1,089,583	1973	655,968
1955	254,096	1974	788,145
1956	87,696	1975	766,600
1957	59,918	1976	875,915
1958	53,474		

Source: U.S. Immigration and Naturalization Service, *Annual Report*, 1959, p. 54; Congressional Research Service, 1980a, pp. 65 and 76.

Appendix B.   Mexican Foreign Workers Admitted Under the Bracero
              Program, 1942–1964

Year	No. Admitted	Year	No. Admitted
1942	4,203	1954	309,033
1943	52,098	1955	398,650
1944	62,170	1956	445,197
1945	49,454	1957	436,049
1946	32,043	1958	432,857
1947	19,632*	1959	437,643
1948	35,345*	1960	315,846
1949	107,000*	1961	291,420
1950	67,500*	1962	194,978
1951	192,000	1963	186,865
1952	197,100	1964	177,736
1953	201,380		

Source: Congressional Research Service, 1980a, p. 65.

* The 1947–1950 figures do not accurately reflect the number of braceros
actually employed, since illegal workers legalized as braceros were not consistently included in the tabulations. For example, the 1947 figure does
not include approximately 55,000 illegal Mexican farm workers who were
contracted as braceros in the United States.

Appendix C.   Mexicans Admitted on Permanent Visas, 1940–1971

Year	No. Admitted	Year	No. Admitted
1940	1914	1956	65,047
1941	2068	1957	49,154
1942	2182	1958	26,712
1943	3985	1959	23,061
1944	6399	1960	32,684
1945	6455	1961	41,632
1946	6805	1962	55,291
1947	7775	1963	55,253
1948	8730	1964	32,967
1949	7977	1965	37,969
1950	6841	1966	45,163
1951	6372	1967	42,371
1952	9600	1968	43,563
1953	18,454	1969	44,623
1954	37,456	1970	44,469
1955	50,772	1971	50,103

Source: Cardenas, 1975, p. 90.

BIBLIOGRAPHY

Aberbach, Joel D. 1979. "Changes in Congressional Oversight." *American Behavioral Scientist,* Vol. 22: 493–515.

Aleinikoff, Thomas Alexander and David A. Martin. 1985. *Immigration Process and Policy.* St. Paul, Minnesota: West Publishing Co.

Althusser, Louis. 1971. *Lenin and Philosophy and Other Essays.* New York: Monthly Review Press.

American Farm Bureau Federation. 1942. *AFBF Official Newsletter,* March 27.

American G.I. Forum and Texas State Federation of Labor. 1976. "What Price Wetbacks?" In *Mexican Migration to the United States.* The Chicano Heritage. New York: Arno Press.

American Library Association. 1984. *Less Access to Less Information By and About The U.S. Government.* Chicago: American Library Association.

Anderson, Henry. 1963. *Fields of Bondage: The Mexican Contract Labor System in Industrialized Agriculture.* Mimeograph. Berkeley, California.

Bach, Robert L. 1978. "Mexican Immigration and U.S. Immigration Reforms in the 1960s." *Kapitalistate,* Vol. 7: 73–80.

Bailey, Linwood K. and Samuel Vernoff. 1959. "Agricultural Wage Policy Developments during 1958." *Employment Security Review,* Vol. 20 (Fall): 12–14.

Barnett, Harold. 1982. "The Production of Corporate Crime in Corporate Capitalism." In P. Wickham and T. Dailey (eds.) *White Collar and Economic Crime.* Toronto: Lexington Books.

Braithwaite, John. 1979. "Transnational Corporations and Corruption: Towards Some International Solutions." *International Journal of Sociology of Law.* Vol. 7: 125–142.

———. 1982. "Enforced Self-Regulation: A New Strategy for Corporate Crime Control." *Michigan Law Review,* Vol. 80: 1466–1507.

———. 1984. *Corporate Crime in the Pharmaceutical Industry.* London: Routledge and Kegan Paul.

Brownsville Herald. 1960. "Valley Farmers Bombard Secretary Mitchell with Petitions." June 12.

Block, Fred. 1987. *Revising State Theory: Essays in Politics and Post-Industrialism.* Philadelphia: Temple University Press.

Brooks, Thomas R. 1971. *Toil and Trouble: A History of American Labor.* New York: Delacorte Press.

Burawoy, Michael. 1976. "The Functions and Reproduction of Migrant Labor: Comparative Material from Southern Africa and the United States." *American Journal of Sociology,* Vol. 81, No. 5 (March): 1050–1087.

Business Week. 1953. "Wetbacks in Middle of Border War." October 24: 64–66.

Bustamante, Jorge. 1978. "Commodity-Migrants: Structural Analysis of Mexican Immigration to the U.S." In Stanley Ross (ed.) *Views Across the Border.* Albuquerque, New Mexico: University of New Mexico Press.

Calavita, Kitty. 1983a. "California's 'Employer Sanctions' Legislation: Now You See it, Now You Don't." *Politics and Society,* Vol. 12, No. 2: 205–230.

———. 1983b. "The Demise of the Occupational Safety and Health Administration: A Case Study in Symbolic Action." *Social Problems,* Vol. 30, No. 4 (April): 437–448.

———. 1984. *U.S. Immigration Law and the Control of Labor: 1820–1924.* London: Academic Press.

———. 1986. "Worker Safety, Law, and Social Change: The Italian Case." *Law and Society Review,* Vol. 20, No. 2: 189–227.

———. 1989. "The Contradictions of Immigration Lawmaking: The Immigration Reform and Control Act of 1986." *Law and Policy,* Vol. 11, No. 1 (January): 17–47.

———. 1990. "Employer Sanctions Violations: Toward a Dialectical Model of White-Collar Crime." *Law and Society Review,* Vol. 24, No. 4: 1041–1069.

California Legislative Assembly, Legislative Reference Service. 1965. *The Bracero Program and Its Aftermath: An Historical Summary.* Prepared for the Use of the Assembly Committee on Agriculture, John C. Williamson, Chairman, April 1.

California State Senate, Senate Fact Finding Committee. 1961. "California's Farm Labor Problems." Part I. *Report of the Senate Fact Finding Committee on Labor and Welfare.*

Cardenas, Gilberto. 1975. "United States Immigration Policy Toward Mexico: An Historical Perspective." *Chicano Law Review,* Vol. 2: 66–91.

Carnegie, Andrew. 1886. *Triumphant Democracy, or Fifty Years' March of the Republic.* New York: Charles Scribner's Sons.

Castles, Stephen and Godula Kozack. 1973. *Immigrant Workers and Class Structure in Western Europe.* London: Oxford University Press.

Chambliss, William J. 1979. "Contradictions and Conflicts in Law Creation." In Steven Spitzer, (ed.) *Annual Review of the Sociology of Law.* Greenwich, Connecticut: JAI-In Press.

Chavez, Leo R. 1988. "Settlers and Sojourners: The Case of Mexicans in the United States." *Human Organization,* Vol. 47: 95–108.

Clinard, Marshall B. and Peter C. Yeager. 1980. *Corporate Crime.* New York: The Free Press.

Clinard, Marshall B., Peter C. Yeager, Jeanne Brissette, David Petrashek, and Elizabeth Harries. 1979. *Illegal Corporate Behavior.* Washington DC: U.S. Government Printing Office.

Coleman, James W. 1985. *The Criminal Elite.* New York: St. Martin's Press.

Congressional Record. 1882. 47th Congress. 1st Session.

———. 1884. 48th Congress. 1st Session.
———. 1885. 48th Congress. 2nd Session.
———. 1947. 80th Congress. 1st Session.
———. 1949. 81st Congress. 1st Session.
———. 1951. 82nd Congress. 1st Session.
———. 1952. 82nd Congress. 2nd Session.
———. 1954. 83rd Congress. 2nd Session.
———. 1956. 84th Congress. 2nd Session.
———. 1958. 85th Congress. 2nd Session.
———. 1960. 86th Congress. 2nd Session.
———. 1961. 87th Congress. 1st Session.
———. 1963. 88th Congress. 1st Session.

Congressional Research Service. 1980a. *History of the Immigration and Naturalization Service*. A Report prepared for the use of The Select Commission on Immigration and Refugee Policy. Washington, D.C.: U.S. Government Printing Office.

———. 1980b. *Temporary Worker Programs: Background and Issues*. A Report Prepared at the Request of Sen. Edward M. Kennedy, Chairman of the Senate Committee on the Judiciary, for the Use of the SCIRP. Washington, D.C.: U.S. Government Printing Office.

Copp, Nelson G. 1963. "Wetbacks' and Braceros: Mexican Migrant Laborers and American Immigration Policy, 1930–1960." PhD Dissertation. Boston University.

Cornelius, Wayne A. and Manuel García y Griego. 1992. *Mexican Migration to the United States: Dependent Communities, Dependent Industries, and the Limits of Government Intervention*. Stanford, California: Stanford University Press (forthcoming).

Craig, Richard B. 1971. *The Bracero Program: Interest Groups and Foreign Policy*. Austin, Texas: University of Texas Press.

Crane, Keith, Beth Asch, Joanna Zorn Heilbrunn, and Danielle C. Cullinane. 1990. *The Effect of Employer Sanctions on the Flow of Undocumented Immigrants to the United States*. Lanham, MD: University Press of America.

Crewdson, John. 1983. *The Tarnished Door: The New Immigrants and the Transformation of America*. New York: Times Books.

Dahl, Robert. 1961. *Who Governs?* New Haven: Yale University Press.

Davidson, Roger H. 1977. "Breaking Up Those Cozy Triangles; An Impossible Dream?" In Susan Welch and John G. Peters (eds.) *Legislative Reform and Public Policy*. New York: Praeger Publishers.

Davis, James W. 1970. *The National Executive Branch*. New York: Free Press.

Davis, Kenneth Culp. 1969. *Discretionary Justice*. Baton Rouge: Louisiana State University Press.

Domhoff, G. William. 1967. *Who Rules America?* Englewood Cliffs, New Jersey: Prentice Hall.

———. 1970. *The Higher Circles*. New York: Random House.

———. 1978. *Who Really Rules?* Santa Monica, California: Goodyear Publishing.

———. 1979. *The Powers That Be*. New York: Random House.

Domhoff, G. William and Hoyt B. Ballard (eds.). 1968. *C. Wright Mills and the Power Elite*. Boston: Beacon Press.

Donnelly, Patrick. 1982. "The Origins of the Occupational Safety and Health Act of 1970." *Social Problems,* Vol. 30: 13–25.

Dygert, Harold Paul III and David Shibata. 1975. "Chinatown Sweatshops: Wage Law Violations in the Garment Industry." University of California, *Davis Law Review,* Volume 8: 63–83.

Eckels, Richard P. 1954. "Hungry Workers, Ripe Crops, and the Non-Existent Mexican Border." *The Reporter,* April 13: 28.

Ericson, Anna-Stina. 1970. "The Impact of Commuters on the Mexican-American Border Area." *Monthly Labor Review,* August: 18–27.

Evans, Peter B., Dietrich Rueschemeyer, and Theda Skocpol. 1985. "On the Road Toward a More Adequate Understanding of the State." In Evans, Rueschemeyer, and Skocpol (eds.) *Bringing the State Back In.* Cambridge: Cambridge University Press.

Farm Labor Developments. 1968. "Long-Term Trends in Foreign Worker Employment." February: 11–14.

Farm Labor Newsletter. 1953. *A Monthly Report on Farm Labor Conditions in California.* February.

Federal Register. 1943. May 11: 6013.

Ferejohn, John A. 1987. "The Structure of Agency Decision Processes." In Matthew D. McCubbins and Terry Sullivan (eds.) *Congress: Structure and Policy.* Cambridge: Cambridge University Press.

Fiorina, Morris P. 1977. *Congress: Keystone of the Washington Establishment.* New Haven, Connecticut: Yale University Press.

Fisher, Lloyd H. 1953. *The Harvest Labor Market in California.* Cambridge, Mass.: Harvard University Press.

Fragomen, Austin T., Jr. and Lydio F. Tomasi (eds.) 1980. *In Defense of the Alien,* Vol. 2. *Immigration Law and Legal Representation.* Proceedings of the 1979 Annual Legal Conference on Aliens' Rights: Options for the 1980s. March 29–30, 1979. New York: Center for Migration Studies.

Friedland, Roger, Frances Fox Piven, and Robert Alford. 1977. "Political Conflict, Urban Structure, and the Fiscal Crisis." In D. Ashford (ed.) *Comparative Public Policy: New Approaches and Methods.* Sage Yearbook in Politics and Public Policy. Beverly Hills, California: Sage Publications.

Fuller, Varden. 1955. *Labor Relations in Agriculture.* Institute of Industrial Relations, University of California, Berkeley.

Galarza, Ernesto. 1956. *Strangers in Our Fields.* Washington, D.C.; Joint U.S.-Mexico Trade Union Committee.

———. 1964. *Merchants of Labor: The Mexican Bracero Story.* Sage Yearbook in Politics and Public Policy. Santa Barbara, California: McNally & Loftin, Publishers.

———. 1977. *Farm Workers and Agri-business in California, 1947–1960.* Notre Dame: University of Notre Dame Press.

Gallup, George. 1980. "Most U.S. Citizens Favor a Hard Line Toward Illegal Aliens." *San Diego Union,* November 30: A22.

Gamboa, Erasmo. 1990. *Mexican Labor and World War II: Braceros in the Pacific Northwest, 1942–1947.* Austin, Texas: University of Texas Press.

García, Juan Ramon. 1980. *Operation Wetback: The Mass Deportation of*

Mexican Undocumented Workers in 1954. Westport, Connecticut: Greenwood Press.

Garth, Bryant. 1986. "Migrant Workers and Rights of Mobility in the European Community and the United States: A Study of Law, Community, and Citizenship in the Welfare State." Series A: Law. Vol. 1, Book 3. Edited by Mauro Cappelletti, Monica Seccombe, Joseph Weiler. Florence, Italy: European University.

Gordon, Charles. 1969. "The Amiable Fiction—Alien Commuters Under Our Immigration Laws." *Case Western Journal of International Law.* Vol. 1, No. 2 (Spring): 181–187.

Greene, Sheldon L. 1969a. "Wetbacks, Growers and Poverty." *The Nation,* Vol. 209, No. 13: 403–405.

———. 1969b. "Immigration Law and Rural Poverty: The Problem of the Illegal Entrant." *Duke Law Journal,* No. 3 (June): 475–494.

———. 1972. "Public Agency Distortion of Congressional Will: Federal Policy Toward Non-Resident Alien Labor." *George Washington Law Review,* Vol. 40. No. 3 (March): 440–463.

Hadley, Eleanor. 1956. "A Critical Analysis of the Wetback Problem." *Law and Contemporary Problems.* Vol. 21: 334–57.

Halsell, Grace. 1978. *The Illegals.* New York: Stein and Day.

Hamilton, Alexander. 1791. *Report on Manufacturing.* American State Papers, Finance I.

Hawley, Ellis W. 1966. "The Politics of the Mexican Labor Issue, 1950–1965." *Agricultural History,* Vol. 40, No. 3 (July): 157–176.

Hayes, Edward F., Richard H. Salter, Roy Plumlee, Robert B. Lindsey. 1955. "Operation 'Wetback'—Impact on the Border States." *Employment Security Review,* Vol. 22 (March): 16–21.

Heclo, Hugh. 1977. *A Government of Strangers: Executive Politics in Washington.* Washington, D.C.: The Brookings Institute.

Hispanic American Report. 1954. February: 1.

———. 1957. November: 520; March: 63

Hoffman, Abraham. 1974. *Unwanted Mexican Americans: The Great Depression Repatriation Pressures, 1929–1939.* Tucson: University of Arizona Press.

Hooks, Gregory. 1990. "From an Autonomous to a Captured State Agency: The Decline of the New Deal in Agriculture." *American Sociological Review,* Vol. 55 (February): 29–43.

Iowa Law Review. 1970. "The Secret Law of the Immigration and Naturalization Service," Vol. 56, No. 1 (October): 140–151.

Jacobs, Paul. 1963. *The State of the Unions.* New York: Atheneum.

Jenkins, J. Craig. 1985. *The Politics of Insurgency: The Farm Worker Movement in the 1960s.* New York: Columbia University Press.

Jones, Robert C. 1945. *Mexican War Workers in the United States: The Mexico-United States Manpower Recruiting Program and Its Operation.* Washington D.C.: Pan American Union.

Keisker, Sue. 1961. "Harvest of Shame." *The Commonwealth.* May 19: 202–205.

Kibbe, Pauline R. 1953. "The Economic Plight of Mexicans." In Edward C. McDonagh and Eugene S. Richards (eds.) *Ethnic Relations in the United States.* New York: Appleton-Century-Crofts, Inc.

Kirstein, Peter Neil. 1973. *Anglo Over Bracero: A History of the Mexican Workers in the United States from Roosevelt to Nixon.* Ph.D. Dissertation, Saint Louis University.

Kiser George C. and Martha Woody Kiser (eds.) 1979. *Mexican Workers in the United States: Historical and Political Perspectives.* Albuquerque, New Mexico: University of New Mexico Press.

Landau, Jack. 1981. "A Pattern of Censorship." *The Washington Post,* November 28: A23.

Lessard, David Richard. 1984. "Agrarianism and Nationalism: Mexico and the Bracero Program, 1942–1947." Ph.D. Dissertation. Tulane University.

Levi, Michael. 1981. *The Phantom Capitalists: The Organization and Control of Long Term Fraud.* London: Heinemann.

———. 1984. "Giving Creditors the Business: The Criminal Law in Inaction." *International Journal of the Sociology of Law,* Vol. 12: 321–333.

Life Magazine. 1951. "Wetbacks Swarm In." May 21: 30–37.

Lopez, Gerald P. 1981. "Undocumented Mexican Migration: In Search of a Just Immigration Law and Policy." *UCLA Law Review,* 28 (April): 615–714.

Lorch, Robert S. 1969. *Democratic Process and Administrative Law.* Detroit: Wayne State University Press.

Lowi, Theodore J. 1969. *The End of Liberalism.* New York: W. W. Norton.

Lyon, Richard Martin. 1954. "The Legal Status of American and Mexican Migratory Farm Labor: An Analysis of U.S. Farm-Labor Legislation, Policy and Administration." Ph.D. Thesis. Cornell University.

Maram, Sheldon L. 1980. "Hispanic Workers in the Garment and Restaurant Industries in Los Angeles County." *Working Papers in U.S.-Mexican Studies,* No. 12. La Jolla, Calif.: Center for U.S.-Mexican Studies, University of Calif., San Diego.

Markovits, Andraei S. and Samantha Kazarinov. 1978. "Class Conflict, Capitalism, and Social Democracy: The Case of Migrant Workers in the Federal Republic of Germany." *Comparative Politics,* Vol. 10, No. 2: 373–391.

Marshall, Ray. 1978. "Economic Factors Influencing the International Migration of Workers." In Stanley Ross (ed.) *Views Across the Border.* Albuquerque, New Mexico: University of New Mexico Press.

Maxwell, Evan. 1980. "INS Swamped: For 'Huddled Masses,' L.A. is Ellis Island." *Los Angeles Times,* October 19.

Mayer, Arnold. 1961. "The Grapes of Wrath, Vintage 1961." *The Reporter,* Feb. 2: 34–37.

McWilliams, Carey. 1968. *North From Mexico.* New York: Greenwood Press.

Miliband, Ralph. 1969. *The State in Capitalist Society.* London: Winfield and Nicholson.

Miller, Mark J. 1981. *Foreign Workers in Western Europe: An Emerging Political Force.* New York: Praeger Publishers.

Miller, Mark J. and Philip L. Martin. 1982. *Administering Foreign-Worker Programs: Lessons from Europe.* Lexington, Mass.: Lexington Books.

Mills, C. Wright. 1956. *The Power Elite.* London and New York: Oxford University Press.

———. 1959. *The Sociological Imagination.* New York: Oxford University Press.

Mitchell, James. 1959. "An Interview with Secretary Mitchell." *The Reporter,* January 22.

Mollenkopf, John. 1975. "Theories of the State and Power Structure Research." *Insurgent Sociologist,* Vol. 5, No. 3: 245–264.

Molotch, Harvey. 1973. "Oil in Santa Barbara and Power in America." In William J. Chambliss (ed.) *Sociological Readings in the Conflict Perspective.* Reading, MA: Addison-Wesley.

Montgomery, David. 1972. "The Shuttle and the Cross: Weavers and Artisans in the Kensington Riots of 1847." *Journal of Social History,* Vol. 5, No. 4: 411–446.

Moore, Truman. 1965. *The Slaves We Rent.* New York: Random House.

Morgan, Patricia. 1954. *Shame of a Nation: A Documented Story of Police-State Furor Against Mexican-Americans in the U.S.A.* Los Angeles: Los Angeles Committee for the Protection of the Foreign Born.

Morris, Milton D. 1985. *Immigration: The Beleaguered Bureaucracy.* Washington, DC: The Brookings Institution.

Mosher, Frederick C. 1968. *Democracy and the Public Service.* New York: Oxford University Press.

Myers, John Myers. 1971. *The Border Wardens.* Englewood Cliffs, NJ: Prentice-Hall, Inc.

New York Journal of Commerce. 1892. December 13.

New York Times. 1950. "Big Farmers Blamed for Migrant Woes." August 13: 63.

——. 1951. "Mexican Labor Discussed." January 27: 3; "Million a Year Flee Mexico Only to Find Peonage Here." March 25: 41; "Peons Net Farmer A Fabulous Profit." March 26: 25; "Peons In the West Lowering Culture." March 27: 31; "Southwest Winks at 'Wetback' Jobs." March 28: 34; "Interests Conflict on 'Wetback' Cure." March 29: 29–30; "Truman Approves the 'Wetback' Bill." July 13: 24; "Text of Truman's Message on 'Wetbacks.' " July 14: 11; "McCarran Charges Alien Infiltering." August 21: 11.

——. 1952. "Mexican Workers Here Face Loss of Jobs With Agreement Ending." February 9: 7; "Union Coup Stops Alien-Labor Trek." March 3: 6.

——. 1953. "Brownell Tours 'Wetback' Border." August 16: 1; " 'Wetbacks' Called a Major Problem." August 17: 11; "Eisenhower Backs 'Wetbacks' Drive." August 18: 16; "California Seeks More 'Wetbacks'." September 7: 1; "Wetback' Traffic Again Sets Record." September 16: 31; "U.S. Weighs Change in Pact." October 8: 27.

——. 1954. "U.S. Sets Program on Mexican Labor." January 16: 15; "Mexico Resents U.S. Hiring Policy." January 24: 10; "Mexican Border Mix-Up." January 27: 14; "Mexicans Seeking U.S. Farm Jobs." January 29: 7; "Thousands of Mexican Farm Workers Battle to Cross U.S. Boundary." February 2: 3; "Brownell Scouts Spy Ring Reports." May 3: 12; "Senators Study Maid Recruiting." May 12: 40; " 'Wetbacks' Patrol to be Stepped Up." June 10: 25; "700 on Coast Open 'Wetback' Drive." June 18: 14; " 'Wetback' Stream Stemmed in Part." June 20: 75; "Border Patrol Fund Asked." June 23: 35; "Plan Gains to End Use of 'Wetbacks'." June 27: 36; " 'Wetback' Drive Irks the Valley." August 2: 8.

———. 1955. "Generals Approved As Aides of Swing." May 11: 32; "Two Ruled Overpaid as U.S. Consultants." June 6: 49.

———. 1956. "Senators Study Maid Recruitings." May 12: 14; "U.S. Aide Scored on Hunting Trips." July 7: 14; "House Unit Assails Swing Hunting Trips." July 12: 9; "Brownell Scored on Swing Inquiry." October 1: 24; "Curb on Report Denied." October 12: 42.

———. 1957. "Mexicans in Jobs on Farms at Issue." August 18: 50.

———. 1958. "Fund Bill is Passed." June 26: 18.

———. 1961. "New Immigration Chief." November 23: 26; "Swing Keeps Immigration Post Until June as Walter Backs Him." January 28: 8.

———. 1964. "Foes Resist Plan for Bracero Use." December 1: 25.

Newsweek. 1946. "Wetbacks." March 11: 70–71.

North, David S. 1970. *The Border Crossers: People Who Live in Mexico and Work in the United States.* Washington, DC: Trans Century Corporation.

O'Connor, James. 1973. *The Fiscal Crisis of the State.* New York: St. Martin's Press.

Offe, Claus. 1974. "Structural Problems of the Capitalist State: Class Rule and the Political System. On the Selectiveness of Political Institutions." In K. Von Beyme (ed.) *German Political Studies.* London: Sage Publications.

Pfeffer, Max J. 1980. "The Labor Process and Corporate Agriculture: Mexican Workers in California." *The Insurgent Sociologist,* Vol. 10, No. 2 (Fall): 25–44.

Pfeiffer, David G. 1979. "The Bracero Program in Mexico." In George C. Kiser and Martha Woody Kiser (eds.) *Mexican Workers in the United States: Historical and Political Perspectives.* Albuquerque, New Mexico: University of New Mexico Press.

Plumb, Milton. 1958. "Growers Fight Labor Department's Try to Enforce Mexican Labor Law." *AFL-CIO News,* May 10: 10.

Portes, Alejandro. 1983. "Of Borders and States: A Skeptical Note on the Legislative Control of Immigration." In Wayne A. Cornelius and Ricardo A. Montoya (eds.) *America's New Immigration Law: Origins, Rationales, and Potential Consequences.* La Jolla, California: Center for U.S.-Mexican Studies, University of California, San Diego.

Poulantzas, Nicos. 1969. "The Problem of the Capitalist State." *New Left Review,* Vol. 58 (Nov–Dec): 67–87.

———. 1973. *Political Power and Social Classes.* London: New Left Books.

President's Commission on Migratory Labor. 1951. *Migratory Labor in American Agriculture.* Report of the President's Commission on Migratory Labor. Washington, D.C.: U.S.-Government Printing Office.

Preston, William. 1963. *Aliens and Dissenters: Federal Suppression of Radicals, 1903–1933.* Cambridge, Massachusetts: Harvard University Press.

Rasmussen, Wayne D. 1951. *A History of the Emergency Farm Labor Supply Program, 1943–1947.* Agricultural Monograph, No. 13. U.S. Department of Agriculture, Bureau of Agricultural Economics, Washington, D.C.

Redford, Emmette S. 1969. *Democracy in the Administrative State.* New York: Oxford University Press.

The Reporter. 1959. "The Forgotten People." January 22: 13–20.

Ripley, Randall B. and Grace A. Franklin. 1984. *Congress, the Bureaucracy, and Public Policy.* Homewood, Illinois: The Dorsey Press.

Rose, Arnold. 1967. *The Power Structure.* New York: Oxford University Press.

Rosenbloom, David H. 1983. *Public Administration and the Law.* New York: Marcel Dekker, Inc.

Rourke, Francis E. 1969. *Bureaucracy, Politics, and Public Policy.* Boston: Little, Brown and Company.

Runsten, David and Phillip Leveen. 1981. "Mechanization and Mexican Labor in California Agriculture." Monographs in U.S.-Mexican Studies, 6. University of California, San Diego, La Jolla, California.

San Francisco Examiner. 1953. "Brownell Urges Action on 'Wetback' Invasion." August 17: 20.

Scher, Seymour. 1971. "Conditions for Legislative Control." In Raymond E. Wolfinger (ed.) *Readings on Congress.* Englewood Cliffs, New Jersey: Prentice-Hall, Inc.

Schmidt, Fred H. 1964. *After the Bracero: An Inquiry into the Problems of Farm Labor Recruitment.* A report submitted by the Institute of Industrial Relations, UCLA, to the Department of Employment of the State of California.

Schrecker, T. 1989. "The Political Context and Content of Environmental Law." In T. Caputo, M. Kennedy, C. Reasons, and A. Brannigan (eds.) *Law and Society: A Critical Perspective.* Toronto: Harcourt Brace Jovanovich.

Schuck, Peter H. 1975. *The Judiciary Committees: A Study of the House and Senate Judiciary Committees.* The Ralph Nader Congress Project. New York: Grossman Publishers.

———. 1984. "The Transformation of Immigration Law." *Columbia Law Review,* Vol. 84, No. 1: 1–90.

Scruggs, Otey M. 1960. "Evolution of the Mexican Farm Labor Agreement of 1942." *Agricultural History.* Vol. 34, No. 3 (July): 140–149.

———. 1988. *Braceros, "Wetbacks," and the Farm Labor Problem: Mexican Agricultural Labor in the United States, 1942–1954.* New York: Garland Publishers.

Select Commission on Immigration and Refugee Policy. 1980a. Letter from Richard Ahern. Select Commission on Immigration and Refugee Policy. "Notes." Microform. Reel 11.

———. 1980b. Letter from Mary Jo Grotenrath, Director of Legal Research to Acting Commissioner of the INS, David Crosland. April 17. Select Commission on Immigration and Refugee Policy. "Notes." Microform. Reel 11.

———. 1981. *U.S. Immigration Policy and the National Interest. Final Report and Recommendations.* March 1. Washington, DC: U.S. Government Printing Office.

Select Commission on Western Hemisphere Immigration. 1968a. "The Impact of Commuter Aliens Along the Mexican and Canadian Borders." Hearings before the Select Commission on Western Hemisphere Immigration. Parts I–IV. Washington, DC: U.S. Government Printing Office.

———. 1968b. *Report of the Select Commission on Western Hemisphere Immigration.* Washington, DC: U.S. Government Printing Office.

Skocpol, Theda. 1979. *States and Social Revolutions: A Comparative Analysis of France, Russia, and China.* Cambridge: Cambridge University Press.

——. 1980. "Political Response to Capitalist Crisis: Neo-Marxist Theories of the State and the Case of the New Deal." *Politics and Society,* Vol. 10, No. 2: 155–201.

——. 1985. "Bringing the State Back In: Strategies of Analysis in Current Research." In Peter B. Evans, Dietrich Rueschemeyer, and Theda Skocpol (eds.) *Bringing the State Back In.* Cambridge: Cambridge University Press.

Skocpol, Theda and Kenneth Finegold. 1982. "State Capacity and Economic Intervention in the Early New Deal." *Political Science Quarterly,* Vol. 97: 255–278.

Snider, Laureen. 1987. "Towards a Political Economy of Reform, Regulation, and Corporate Crime." *Law and Policy,* Vol. 9: 37–68.

——. 1990. "Cooperative Models and Corporate Crime: Panacea or Cop-Out?" *Crime and Delinquency,* Vol. 36: 373–391.

——. 1991. "The Regulatory Dance: Understanding Reform Processes in Corporate Crime." *International Journal of Sociology of Law,* Vol. 19: 209–236.

Stepan, Alfred. 1978. *The State and Society: Peru in Comparative Perspective.* Princeton, New Jersey: Princeton University Press.

Stone, Christopher. 1978. "Social Control of Corporate Behavior." In David M. Ermann and Richard J. Lundman (eds.) *Corporate and Governmental Deviance.* New York: Oxford University Press.

Swing, Joseph M. 1955. "A Workable Labor Program." *I and N Reporter.* Vol. 4 (November): 15–16.

Teitelbaum, Michael S. 1980. "Right Versus Right: Immigration and Refugee Policy—the United States." *Foreign Affairs,* (Fall) Vol. 59, No. 1: 21–59.

Time Magazine. 1951. "Immigration: The Wetbacks." April 9: 24.

Todd, Henry C. 1953. "Labor's Viewpoint on Mexican Nationals and 'Wetbacks'." *The Commonwealth,* April 20: 164.

Tomasi, Silvano M. and Charles B. Keely. 1975. *Whom Have We Welcomed? The Adequacy and Quality of United States Immigration Data for Policy Analysis and Evaluation.* Staten Island, New York: Center for Migration Studies.

Trillin, Calvin. 1984. "Making Adjustments." *The New Yorker,* May 28: 50.

Trimberger, Ellen Kay. 1978. *Revolutions from Above: Military Bureaucrats and Development in Japan, Turkey, Egypt, and Peru.* New Brunswick, New Jersey: Transaction Books.

U.S. Congress House. 1958. "Continuation of Mexican Farm Labor Program." *House Report,* No. 2357. 85th Congress, 2nd Session.

——. 1963. "Continuation of Mexican Farm Labor Program." *House Report,* No. 274. 88th Congress, 1st Session.

——. 1973. "Amending Reorganization Plan No. 2 of 1973." *House Report,* No. 93–303. 93rd Congress, 1st Session.

U.S. Congress. House. Committee on Agriculture. 1947a. "Farm Labor Supply Program." Hearings before the House Committee on Agriculture. 80th Congress, 1st Session.

———. 1947b. "Permanent Farm Labor Program." Hearings before the House Committee on Agriculture. 80th Congress, 1st Session.

———. 1947c. "Foreign Agricultural Labor." Hearings before the House Committee on Agriculture. 80th Congress, 1st Session.

———. 1951. "Farm Labor." Hearings before the House Committee on Agriculture. 82nd Congress, 1st Session.

———. 1954. "Mexican Farm Labor." Hearings before the House Committee on Agriculture. 83rd Congress, 2nd Session.

———. 1955. "Mexican Farm Labor Program." Hearings before the House Committee on Agriculture. 84th Congress, 1st Session.

———. 1958. "Farm Labor and Mexican Labor." Hearings before the Subcommittee on Equipment, Supplies and Manpower of the House Committee on Agriculture. 85th Congress, 2nd Session.

———. 1960. "Extension of Mexican Farm Labor Program." Hearings before the Subcommittee on Equipment, Supplies, and Manpower of the House Committee on Agriculture. 86th Congress, 2nd Session.

———. 1961. "Extension of Mexican Farm Labor Program." Hearings before the Subcommittee on Equipment, Supplies, and Manpower of the House Committee on Agriculture. 87th Congress, 1st Session.

———. 1963. "Mexican Farm Labor Program." Hearings before the Subcommittee on Equipment, Supplies, and Manpower of the House Committee on Agriculture. 88th Congress, 1st Session.

———. 1983. "The Immigration Reform and Control Act of 1983." Hearings before the House Committee on Agriculture. 98th Congress, 1st Session.

U.S. Congress. House. Committee on Appropriations. 1943. "Farm Labor Supply Program." Hearings before the Subcommittee of the Committee on Appropriations. 78th Congress, 1st Session.

———. 1945. "First Deficiency Appropriation." Hearings before the Subcommittee on Deficiency of the House Committee on Appropriations. 79th Congress, 1st Session.

———. 1949. "Department of Justice Appropriation Bill for 1950." Hearings before the Subcommittee of the Committee on Appropriations. 81st Congress, 1st Session.

———. 1952. "Departments of State, Justice, Commerce, and the Judiciary, Appropriations for 1953." Hearings before the Subcommittee of the Committee on Appropriations. 82nd Congress, 2nd Session.

———. 1953a. "Second Supplemental Appropriation Bill, 1953." Hearing before the Subcommittee of the Committee on Appropriations. 83rd Congress, 1st Session.

———. 1953b. "Departments of State, Justice and Commerce Appropriations for 1954." Hearing before the Subcommittee of the Committee on Appropriations. 83rd Congress, 1st Session.

———. 1953c. "Departments of State, Justice and Commerce Appropriations for 1955." Hearing before the Subcommittee of the Committee on Appropriations. 83rd Congress, 2nd Session.

———. 1954. "Departments of State, Justice, and Commerce Appropriations for 1955." Hearing before the Subcommittee of the Committee on Appropriations. 83rd Congress, 2nd Session.

———. 1955a. "The Second Supplemental Appropriations Bill, 1955." Hearing before the Subcommittee of the Committee on Appropriations. 84th Congress, 1st Session.

———. 1955b. "Departments of State and Justice, the Judiciary, and Related Agencies Appropriations for 1956." Hearing before the Subcommittee of the Committee on Appropriations. 84th Congress, 1st Session.

———. 1956. "Departments of State and Justice, the Judiciary, and Related Agencies Appropriations for 1957." Hearing before the Subcommittee of the Committee on Appropriations. 84th Congress, 2nd Session.

———. 1957. "Departments of State, Justice, the Judiciary, and Related Agencies Appropriations for 1958." Hearing before the Subcommittee of the Committee on Appropriations. 85th Congress, 1st Session.

———. 1958. "Departments of State and Justice, the Judiciary, and Related Agencies Appropriations for 1959." Hearing before the Subcommittee of the Committee on Appropriations. 85th Congress, 2nd Session.

———. 1977. "Departments of State, Justice, and Commerce, the Judiciary, and Related Agencies Appropriations for 1978." Hearing before the Subcommittee of the Committee on Appropriations. 95th Congress, 1st Session.

———. 1980. "Departments of State, Justice, and Commerce, the Judiciary, and Related Agencies Appropriations for 1981." Hearing before the Subcommittee of the Committee on Appropriations. 96th Congress, 2nd Session.

U.S. Congress. House. Committee on Education and Labor. 1969. "Employment of 'Green Card' Aliens During Labor Disputes." Hearing before the Special Subcommittee on Labor of the Committee on Education and Labor. 91st Congress, 1st Session.

U.S. Congress. House. Committee on Government Operations. 1955. "Reorganization of the Immigration and Naturalization Service." Hearing before the Subcommittee on Legal and Monetary Affairs of the Committee on Government Operations. 84th Congress, 1st Session.

———. 1956. "Improper Use of Government Equipment and Government Personnel." Hearing before the Subcommittee on Legal and Monetary Affairs of the Committee on Government Operations. 84th Congress, 2nd Session.

U.S. Congress. House. Committee on Immigration and Naturalization. 1919. "Prohibition of Immigration and the Problem of Immigration." Hearing before the Committee on Immigration and Naturalization. 65th Congress, 3rd Session.

U.S. Congress. House. Committee on the Judiciary. 1963. "Study of Population and Immigration Problems." Administrative Presentations. Hearing before Subcommittee No. 1 (Immigration and Nationality) of the Committee on the Judiciary. 88th Congress, 1st Session.

———. 1971. "Illegal Aliens." Part 2. Hearing before the Subcommittee on Immigration, Citizenship, and International Law of the Committee on the Judiciary. 92nd Congress, 1st Session.

———. 1972. "Illegal Aliens." Parts 4–5. Hearing before the Subcommittee on Immigration, Citizenship and International Law of the Committee on the Judiciary. 92nd Congress, 2nd Session.

———. 1973. "Review of the Administration of the Immigration and Nationality Act." Hearing before the Subcommittee on Immigration, Citizenship, and International Law of the Committee on the Judiciary. 93rd Congress, 1st Session.

———. 1979. "Immigration and Naturalization Service." Hearings before the Subcommittee on Immigration, Refugees, and International Law of the Committee on the Judiciary. 96th Congress, 1st Session.

———. 1980. "Immigration and Naturalization Service Oversight." Hearing before the Subcommittee on Immigration, Refugees, and International Law of the Committee on the Judiciary. 96th Congress, 2nd Session.

———. 1982. "Authorization/Oversight on the Immigration and Naturalization Service." Hearing before the Subcommittee on Immigration, Refugees, and International Law of the Committee on the Judiciary. 97th Congress, 2nd Session.

U.S. Congress. Senate. 1951. "Importation of Foreign Agricultural Workers." *Senate Report,* No. 214. 82nd Congress, 1st Session.

———. 1963. "Extension of Mexican Farm Labor Program." *Senate Report,* No. 391. 88th Congress, 1st Session.

———. 1968. "The Migratory Farm Labor Problem in the United States." *Senate Report,* No. 1006. 90th Congress, 2nd Session.

U.S. Congress. Senate. Committee on Agriculture and Forestry. 1947. "Farm Labor Supply Program." Hearing before the Committee on Agriculture and Forestry. 80th Congress, 1st Session.

———. 1951. "Farm Labor Program." Hearing before the Committee on Agriculture and Forestry. 82nd Congress, 1st Session.

———. 1953. "Extension of the Mexican Farm Labor Program." Hearing before the Committee on Agriculture and Forestry. 83rd Congress, 1st Session.

———. 1961. "Extension of Mexican Farm Labor Program." Hearing before the Committee on Agriculture and Forestry. 97th Congress, 1st Session.

U.S. Congress. Senate. Committee on Appropriations. 1950. "Departments of State, Justice, Commerce, and the Judiciary, Appropriations for 1951." Hearing before the Subcommittee of the Committee on Appropriations. 81st Congress, 2nd Session.

———. 1952. "Departments of State, Justice, Commerce, and the Judiciary, Appropriations for 1953." Hearing before the Subcommittee of the Committee on Appropriations. 82nd Congress, 2nd Session.

———. 1953. "Departments of State, Justice, Commerce, and the Judiciary, Appropriations for 1954." Hearing before the Subcommittee of the Committee on Appropriations. 83rd Congress, 1st Session.

———. 1954a. "Departments of State, Justice, and Commerce, and the United States Information Agency Appropriations, 1955." Hearing before the Subcommittee of the Committee on Appropriations. 83rd Congress, 2nd Session.

———. 1954b. "The Supplemental Appropriation Bill, 1955." Hearing before the Subcommittee of the Committee on Appropriations. 83rd Congress, 2nd Session.

———. 1955. "Departments of State and Justice, the Judiciary and Related Agencies Appropriations, 1956." Hearing before the Subcommittee of the Committee on Appropriations. 84th Congress, 1st Session.

———. 1956. "Departments of State and Justice, the Judiciary, and Related

Agencies Appropriations, 1957." Hearing before the Subcommittee of the Committee on Appropriations. 84th Congress, 2nd Session.

———. 1957. "Departments of State and Justice, the Judiciary, and Related Agencies Appropriations, 1958." Hearing before the Subcommittee of the Committee on Appropriations. 85th Congress, 1st Session.

U.S. Congress. Senate. Committee on the Judiciary. 1949. "Admission of Foreign Agricultural Workers." Hearing before a Subcommittee of the Committee on the Judiciary. 81st Congress, 1st Session.

———. 1954. "To Control Illegal Migration." Hearing before the Subcommittee on Immigration and Naturalization of the Committee on the Judiciary. 83rd Congress, 2nd Session.

———. 1967. "Alien Commuter 'Green Card' System." Unpublished transcript of hearing before the Subcommittee on Immigration and Naturalization of the Committee on the Judiciary. 90th Congress, 1st Session.

———. 1980. "Department of Justice Authorization and Oversight for Fiscal Year 1981." Hearing before the Committee on the Judiciary. 96th Congress, 2nd Session.

———. 1981. "The Knowing Employment of Illegal Immigrants." Hearing before the Subcommittee on Immigration and Refugee Policy of the Committee on the Judiciary. 97th Congress, 1st Session.

U.S. Congress. Senate. Committee on Labor and Public Welfare. 1952. "Migratory Labor." Hearing before the Subcommittee on Labor and Labor-Management Relations of the Committee on Labor and Public Welfare. 82nd Congress, 2nd Session.

———. 1969. "Migrant and Seasonal Farmworker Powerlessness." Hearings before the Subcommittee on Migratory Labor of the Committee on Labor and Public Welfare. 91st Congress, 1st Session.

U.S. Congress. Senate. Immigration Commission. 1911. *Immigration Commission Report.* Senate Document, No. 747. 61st Congress, 3rd Session.

U.S. Department of Labor. 1963. "The Admission of Aliens into the United States for Temporary Employment." In *Study of Population and Immigration Problems.* Special Series No. 11. House Judiciary Committee, Subcommittee No. 1. Washington, DC: U.S. Government Printing Office.

U.S. Department of Labor. Bureau of Employment Security. 1959. "Mexican Farm Labor Program, Consultants' Report." Washington, DC: U.S. Government Printing Office.

———. 1962. "Cotton Harvest Mechanization: Effect on Seasonal Hired Labor." Report No. 209. June 1962. Washington, DC: U.S. Government Printing Office.

U.S. Department of State. 1943. "Temporary Migration of Mexican Agricultural Workers." Executive Agreement Series No. 278. Washington, DC: U.S. Government Printing Office.

U.S. General Accounting Office. 1980. "Prospects Dim for Effectively Enforcing Immigration Laws." Report to the Congress of the United States. Nov. 5. GGD–81–4. Washington, DC: U.S. Government Printing Office.

———. 1982a. "Information on the Enforcement of Laws Regarding Employment of Aliens in Selected Countries." GAO/GGD–82–86. Washington, DC: U.S. Government Printing Office.

———. 1982b. "Problems and Options in Estimating the Size of the Illegal Alien Population." Report to the Chairman of the Subcommittee on Immigration and Refugee Policy of the Senate Committee on the Judiciary. September 24. GAO/IPE–82–9. Washington, DC: U.S. Government Printing Office.

U.S. Immigration and Naturalization Service. *Annual Reports of the Immigration and Naturalization Service, 1951–1959.* Washington, DC: U.S. Government Printing Office.

———. 1955. *Information Bulletin.* Volume V, Number 21. June 2.

———. 1955. Volume V, Number 26, August 10.

———. 1956. Volume VI, Number 5. March 3.

———. 1955. *Reporter.* "The Wetback Issue." Vol. 2, No. 3 (January): 37–39.

———. 1955. "A Workable Labor Program." Vol. 4, No. 2 (November): 15–16.

———. 1956. "Importation of Alien Laborers." Vol. 5, No. 1 (July): 4–8.

———. 1958. "Supplemental Labor Program in California." Vol. 7, No. 1 (July): 5–7.

———. 1974. "The First Fifty Years." Vol. 23, No. 1 (Summer): 2–20.

———. 1986. *Statistical Yearbook.* Washington, DC: U.S. Government Printing Office.

U.S. *News and World Report.* 1981. "The Great American Immigration Nightmare." June 22: 27–31.

Ware, Caroline. 1931. *Early New England Cotton Manufacture: A Study in Industrial Beginning.* New York: Houghton Mifflin.

Washington Post. 1952. April 14: 6.

———. 1986. "The Immigration 'Compromise.' " July 16: A14.

Wasserman, Jack. 1976. "Freedom of Information and the Right to Privacy." *Interpreter Releases,* Vol. 53, No. 39 (October 7): 325.

Weinraub, Bernard. 1980. "Immigration Bureaucracy is Overwhelmed by its Work." *New York Times.* January 17: A1, B9.

Whitt, Allen. 1979. "Toward a Class-Dialectical Model of Power." *American Sociological Review,* Vol. 44 (February): 81–99.

———. 1982. *Urban Elites and Mass Transportation: The Dialectics of Power.* Princeton, New Jersey: Princeton University Press.

Wildavsky, Aaron. 1971. "Budgetary Strategies of Administrative Agencies." In Raymond E. Wolfinger (ed.) *Readings on Congress.* Englewood Cliffs, New Jersey: Prentice-Hall, Inc.

Williams, Lee G. 1962. "Recent Legislation Affecting the Mexican Labor Program." *Employment Security Review,* February 1962: 29–31.

Statutes and Laws Cited

PL 45
PL 78
PL 89–487

PL 93–502
22 *Stat.* 214
39 *Stat.* 875

57 *Stat.* 70–73; 643
58 *Stat.* 11; 853
59 *Stat.* 361; 645
60 *Stat.* 238
61 *Stat.* 55
65 *Stat.* 119

69 *Stat.* 615
79 *Stat.* 911
80 *Stat.* 250
88 *Stat.* 1562
5 U.S.C. 552
8 U.S.C. 1152

INDEX

Aberbach, Joel, 178, 216
Administrative Procedure Act; access to INS records and, 12; Texas Proviso and, 70
Administrative discretion, 178; administrative creation of Bracero Program, 1–3, 18, 23, 73, 113; extension of contract labor system, 2, 25–27, 73; INS power to admit the inadmissible, 23, 28; border recruitment, 23–24, 29–30, 73, 87, 186; INS legalization of undocumented workers, 24, 28–29, 41; lax enforcement of contracts, 29, 64–65; tolerance of illegal immigration, 35–36, 40; Congress and, 9, 25–27, 39–40, 107, 113, 181, 216; unilateral admission of braceros, 29, 65–66, 73, 186, 198; Texas Proviso, 66–70; El Paso conference and, 80–82; 1-100 card system and, 87–95, 199; Special Program and, 87, 92–95; "green-card commuters" and, 152–159
"Adverse effect," 44, 63–64, 113, 121, 127, 130, 141, 154
AFL-CIO, 120, 122, 142–143, 145, 155
Agricultural wages and working conditions, 2–3, 19, 22, 24, 26, 30–31, 38–39, 47, 55–57, 64, 70–71, 74–77, 128, 139, 141–142, 148, 180, 195–196, 208
Agricultural Workers Organizing Committee (AWOC), 122–123, 143, 205, 209
Aleinikoff, Thomas Alexander and Martin, David A., 188
Althusser, Louis, 3, 173, 184, 215
Amalgamated Meatcutters v. Rogers, 211

American Farm Bureau, 22, 44, 186
American Federation of Labor, 44, 64
American G.I. Forum of Texas, 48
American Library Association; FOIA and, 12
An Act to Encourage Immigration, 4
Anderson, Henry, 57, 64, 79, 90, 117, 125, 139, 172, 184–185, 187, 189, 192–193, 197, 199, 203, 205, 208
Anti-Alien Contract Labor Law, 5–6, 23, 179
Apprehensions of illegal aliens, 8, 32–41, 49, 52, 54–55, 64–65, 77, 101, 146, 149–151, 167, 170, 214, 217
Armstrong, T. H., INS Special Projects Officer, 209
Autonomy of the state, 175–176, 179, 182; bureaucratic interests and, 9–10, 73–74, 82, 95–102, 111–112, 172

Bach, Robert, 3, 173, 184, 213, 215
Bailey, Linwood K. and Vernoff, Samuel, 206
Barnett, Harold, 212
Bentson, Representative Lloyd, 35
Blacklisting, 63, 90, 114
Block Fred, 144, 166, 176–177, 179, 209, 215–216
Board of Immigration Appeals, 153
Border Patrol; pressures not to apprehend illegal aliens, 32–41, 52, 99; budget reductions, 36–37, 52; "Operation Wetback" and, 52, 54–61, 99; Sector Activity Reports, 75, 82–83; opposition to Department of Labor regulations, 128–129; "green-card commuters" and, 155; demoralization, 164–165

235

Border recruitment, 23–24, 28–30, 86–89, 93, 95–96
Bowser, J. W., Deputy Assistant INS Commissioner, 209
Bracero captivity, 21–22, 56–58, 74–77
Bracero contracts, 20–22, 24, 29, 62–63
Bracero, definition of, 1
Bracero desertions, 42–43, 58, 75–77, 87
Bracero employers; requests for Mexican contract labor, 19–20, 25, 43; political power of, 19, 22, 24–26, 44–45, 117–121, 133–134, 142; obligations of, 20, 22, 27, 43, 46; benefits of Bracero Program for, 3, 21–22, 30–31, 42, 55–61, 70–74; violations of contracts, 2, 24, 29, 65, 128, 208–209; direct grower-bracero contracts, 27–31; threats to use illegal immigrant labor, 74, 83–84, 127–130; INS lobbying on behalf of, 84–86, 88–89, 101, 133; pressures on Department of Labor, 117–122, 124–125, 136; alliance with INS, 131–136, 181, 216; opposition to Department of Labor regulations, 131–136, 197, 208–209 (see also growers)
Bracero processing, 62–63
Bracero unemployment and underemployment, 19, 42–43, 46, 57, 66, 76
Bracero vulnerability, 10, 74–82, 90, 95, 111
Bracero wages and working conditions, 2, 19–24, 29, 38, 42, 46, 56–58, 63, 123, 182, 193, 208
Braithwaite, John, 212
Bribes, 62, 91, 94, 187, 193
Brockway, Glenn, Regional Director, Bureau of Employment Security (BES), 204, 207
Brooks, Thomas, 205
Brown, Governor Edmund G., 50, 148
Brown, Newell, Assistant Secretary of Labor, 115, 203–205
Brownell, Attorney General Herbert, 11, 48–53, 96, 111
Bruder, Edward, Phoenix District Director, INS, 207
Budget, INS, 34, 36–37, 52, 54, 162–163, 167
Burawoy, Michael, 184, 213

Bureau of Employment Security (BES), 63, 117–118, 121, 132, 146
Bureau of Immigration, 4
Bustamante, Jorge, 213

Calavita, Kitty, 184, 212, 214–215
California Rural Legal Assistance, 151, 156
Carnahan, David, INS Commissioner, Southwest Region, 78, 196–197, 200–201
Carnegie, Andrew, 4–5, 184
Carter, Harlan, Field Director of "Operation Wetback," 52
Carter, President Jimmy, 13, 166
Cass, Millard, Deputy Under Secretary of Labor, 138, 204–205
Castillo, Leonel, INS Commissioner, 166
Castles, Stephen and Kozack, Godula, 184
Certification of labor shortage, 20, 29, 44, 62–63, 83, 116, 123–124, 128–129, 131, 146–149, 152, 199
Chambliss, William J., 184, 215
Chapman, Leonard, INS Commissioner, 166
Chavez, Cesar, United Farm Workers Union, 155, 205
Chavez, Leo R., 214
Chavez, Senator Dennis, 68
Clientele groups, 40, 126, 179, 205
Clinard, Marshall B. and Yeager, Peter C., 212
Clinard, Marshall B.; Yeager, Peter C.; Brissette, Jeanne; Petrashek, David; and Harries, Elizabeth, 212
Cold War; fears of illegal immigration and, 49–51; deportations of "subversive" braceros and, 77–80
Coleman, James W., 212
Congress of Industrial Organizations (CIO), 44
Congressional Reorganization Act, 45
Control of agricultural labor, 55–59, 74; bracero captivity and, 56–58, 61, 74–77, 180, 209; deportation of "subversives" and troublemakers, 77–80, 87, 145, 197; denying braceros visas and, 80–82; 1-100 card system and, 87–95, 97–98
Copp, Nelson, 187, 191

Coppock, Donald, Deputy Assistant INS Commissioner, 149–150, 196, 210
Cornelius, Wayne A. and Garcia y Griego, Manuel, 214
Craig, Richard, 24, 125, 142–143, 186, 189, 195, 198, 205–206, 208, 214
Crane, Keith; Asch, Beth; Heilbrunn, Joanna Zorn; and Cullinane, Danielle C., 214
Crewdson, John, 161, 164, 188, 212–213
Crosland, David, INS Commissioner, 13, 185

Davidson, Roger H., 216
Davis, James W., 178, 216
Davis, Kenneth Culp, 216
Dahl, Robert, 170
DeConcini, Senator Dennis, 164
Del Guercio, Albert, Assistant INS Commissioner, 81, 200–201
Deportations; "Operation Wetback" and, 53–61, 191; of braceros for "subversive" activity, 77–80, 87, 145, 197
Devaney, A. C., Assistant INS Commissioner, 198, 203
Dialectical-structuralism, 8–9, 174–175, 179
Dillingham Immigration Commission, 180
Domhoff, G. William, 171–172, 214
Domhoff, G. William and Ballard, Hoyt B., 214
Donnelly, Patrick, 212
Douglas, Senator Paul, 67, 69, 168
Douglas Amendment, 67, 69
Dygert, Harold Paul III and Shibata, David, 213

Eastland, Senator James, 107, 160–163, 212
Eckels, Richard, 190
Eilberg, Representative Joshua, 164
Eisenhower Administration Project, 11, 190, 192
Eisenhower, President Dwight D., 33, 48, 51, 104, 108, 142, 202
"El Paso Incident," 29–30, 198
Ellender, Senator Allen, 37, 43–45, 67–68

Employer sanctions, 7–8, 53, 67–69, 168–169, 179, 195, 212, 214
Enforcement of bracero contracts; lax enforcement of wages and working conditions protections, 29, 42, 64–65, 70
European guest workers, 6
Evans, Peter B.; Rueschemeyer, Dietrich; and Skocpol, Theda, 182, 185, 216
Extensions of Bracero Program, 24–27, 45, 142

Fargione, M. F., Deputy INS Commissioner, Southwest Region, 209
Farm Placement Service, 56, 117–118, 172, 208
Farm Security Administration (FSA), 20, 22, 47, 186
Farrell, Raymond, INS Commissioner, 144, 155, 158–163, 166, 178, 182, 202, 209–210
Ferejohn, John, 205
Fiorina, Morris, 188, 202, 216
Fisher, Lloyd, 186
Fisher, Representative O. C., 36, 101, 119, 134, 204
Freedom of Information Act (FOIA), 12–15
Friedland, Roger; Piven, Frances Fox; and Alford, Robert, 215
Frisch, Max, 6
Frye, J. G., INS Special Projects Officer, 129, 206, 209
Furloughs, 132–133

Galarza, Ernesto, 71, 73, 118, 122–123, 182, 184, 187, 189, 192–193, 195–197, 203–205, 216
Gamboa, Erasmo, 20, 185, 189, 197
Garcia, Juan Ramon, 184, 188, 190
Garth, Bryant, 184
Gathings, Representative E. C., 84–85, 121
Gilman, L. W., Associate Deputy INS Commissioner, Southwest Region, 196, 203, 206
Goldberg, Arthur J., Secretary of Labor, 204, 209
Gompers, Samuel, President, American Federation of Labor, 126

Gonzalez, Representative, Henry, 8
Gooch v. Clark, 157, 212
Goodwin, Robert, Director, Bureau of Employment Security, 209
Gordon, Charles, INS General Counsel, 152–153, 156–157, 210–212
Gossett, Representative Edward, 49
Green, C. Al, Director of Agricultural Workers Organizing Committee, 123–124, 205
"Green-card commuters," 152–159, 211
Greene, James, Deputy Associate INS Commissioner, 150–151, 209–211
Growers; requests for Mexican contract labor, 19–20, 25, 43, 189; political power of, 8, 19, 22, 24–26, 35–38, 44–45, 114, 117–121, 124, 133–134, 142, 168, 214; benefits of Bracero Program for, 18, 21–22, 30–31, 42, 55–61, 70–74; violations of contracts, 24, 29, 128, 208–209; direct grower-bracero contracts, 27–31; pressures on INS, 34–35, 83–84, 100, 136, 145, 158, 172; cooperation with INS on "Operation Wetback," 9, 53, 59–60, 74, 96; advantages of "Operation Wetback" for, 55–61; increases in growers' associations, 61, 99; Texas Proviso and, 66–70; pressures on Department of Labor, 117–122, 124–125, 136; alliance with INS, 131–136, 162, 181, 216; opposition to Department of Labor regulations, 131–136, 208–209; "green-card commuters" and, 153–154, 158; employment of illegal aliens following Bracero Program, 167–170, 210 (*see also* bracero employers)

H-2 Program, 10, 99, 116, 134, 148–152, 158, 184–185, 198
Hadley, Eleanor, 32, 36, 187–188, 195
Halsell, Grace, 184, 195
Hamilton, Alexander, 4, 184
Harpold, Michael, President of National INS Council, 164–165, 213
"Harvest of Shame," 143, 208
Hawley, Ellis, 117–118, 122, 171, 190, 203, 205, 208, 214
Hayden, Senator Carl, 200, 203
Hayes, Edward; Salter, Richard;

Plumlee, Roy; and Lindsey, Robert, 191–193
Hays, Representative Wayne, 104
Hennessy, James, Executive Assistant to INS Commissioner, 84, 203, 211
Henning, John, Under Secretary of Labor, 116, 123–124, 205
Hickenlooper, Senator Bourke, 38
Hill, Gladwyn, 71
Holland, Henry, Assistant Secretary of State, 114, 200, 203, 207
Holtzman, Representative Elizabeth, 164
Hooks, Gregory, 176, 179, 182, 216
Hover, Ernest, Chief, INS Examinations Branch, El Paso, Texas, 193, 199–200
Howard, Brig. Gen. Edwin, 103
Humphrey, Senator Hubert, 36–37, 50, 67–68

I-100 card system, 87–100, 110, 114–115, 130, 132–133, 137–138, 172, 199, 200–201
Illegal immigration, 2, 7–8, 18, 28–41, 46–53, 83; "Operation Wetback" and, 53–61, 75; Texas Proviso and, 67–70; Department of Labor regulations and, 85, 194; expanding pool of potential illegal entrants, 108–112; increases in, following Bracero Program, 152, 159, 161, 167–170
Immigration and Nationality Act, 23, 28, 134, 148, 152–153, 156–157, 164, 184, 197–198
Immigration policies, history of, 4–8; contradictions surrounding, 4–10, 38–41, 52–53, 102, 107–108, 110–112, 120–127, 135–137, 139, 158, 161, 163, 166–168, 170, 179–181; literacy test requirement, 7; repatriation of Mexicans in the 1930s, 7 (*see also individual acts*)
Immigration Reform and Control Act of 1986 (IRCA), 7–8, 168–170, 214
Instrumentalism, 3, 9, 73, 95, 111, 118, 171–173, 215
Industrial Workers of the World (IWW), 122

Jacobs, Paul, 205
Japanese contract labor, 134–135

Jenkins, J. Craig, 205
Johnson, Senator Lyndon, 103, 105, 199
Joint Commission on Mexican Migrant Labor, 85, 88–89, 198–199
Jones, Robert, 186

Karnuth v. Albro, 211
Kefauver, Senator Estes, 119, 204
Keisker, Sue, 208
Kelly, Willard, Chief of Border Patrol, 33, 35, 37, 49, 109
Kem, Senator James, 25
Kennedy, Senator Edward, 155–158
Kennedy, President John, 108, 128, 142, 160
Kennedy, Attorney General Robert, 202
Kilgore, Senator Harley, 67–69
Kincaid, T. A., President of Texas Sheep and Goat Raisers Association, 101, 198
Kirstein, Peter Neil, 23, 25, 30, 185–187
Knowles, Clive, United Packing House Workers of America, 209
Korean War, 3, 43–44, 65
Kuchel, Senator Thomas, 80

Labor turnover, 56–58, 74, 76–77
Larin, Don, Chief, Farm Placement Service, 203
League of United Latin American Citizens (LULAC), 158
Legalization, 2, 7–8, 24, 28–29, 32, 44, 109, 202, 214
Lessard, David, 193
Levi, Michael, 212
Lopez, Gerald P., 213, 214
Lorch, Robert, 188
Loughran, Edward, Associate INS Commissioner, 160–161
Lowi, Theodore J., 216
Lyon, Richard, 69, 189, 192, 195

Mackey, Argyle, INS Commissioner, 37
Maram, Sheldon L., 213
Marshall, E. DeWitt, San Antonio District Director, INS, 129–130, 201, 203, 206, 209
Marshall, Ray, Secretary of Labor, 167, 213

Martin, Philip, 184
"Marysville Incident," 78
Mason, Masil, Inspector Examinations Division, INS, 201
Mayer, Arnold, 205
McCarran, Senator Patrick, 36, 49–50
McCarran-Walter Act, 77
McCarthy, Senator Eugene, 45, 209
McClellan, Senator John, 69
McClure, Senator, James, 8
McCormack, Representative John, 106, 108
McDonald, Representative Jack, 163–164
McWilliams, Carey, 184–185
Meany, George, President, AFL-CIO, 123
Mechanization of agriculture, 31, 71, 143–144
Mexican workers; during World War I, 6; flexibility of, 6–7, 21, 180; exemptions in immigration laws for, 7; Quota Laws and, 7; repatriation of, 7; Immigration Reform and Control Act and, 7; growers' requests for, 19–20, 25, 43; "El Paso Incident" and, 30; dependence of southwest growers on, 112, 167
"Mexican Maid Incident," 103
Mexico; bilateral agreements with, 2, 19, 20, 25, 28, 30, 43, 45, 62, 65, 132, 198, 202; negotiations with, 19, 28–29, 37–38, 43, 45–46, 65–70, 86–87, 94, 114–115, 137–139, 182, 195, 201; opposition to border recruitment, 28, 65, 86; opposition to illegal immigration, 28, 37–38, 46, 67–70; opposition to I-100 card system, 91; opposition to Special Program, 93–94, 100
Migrant Labor Agreement, 45–46, 68, 70
Miliband, Ralph, 214–215
Miller, Mark, 184
Miller, Watson, INS Commissioner, 26–27, 34
Mills, C. Wright, 170, 182, 185, 214
Mitchell, James P., Secretary of Labor, 119–120, 124, 126–127, 195, 203–205
Mollohan, Representative Robert, 103, 106

Molotch, Harvey, 212
Mondale, Senator Walter, 156
Moore, Truman E., 56–57, 192, 204–205, 208–209
Morgan, Patricia, 191
Morse, Senator Wayne, 67
Mosher, Frederick, 188
Murphy, Robert, Deputy Under Secretary of State, 199, 206–207

National Agricultural Workers Union, 71, 122–123, 191, 203
National Farm Labor Union, 44, 64, 71, 122, 185, 204
National Farm Workers Association, 205
National Farmers Union, 189
Neelly, Marcus, El Paso District Director, INS, 65, 193, 199–200
New York Journal of Commerce, 4, 21, 185
North, David, 158, 210–212
Norton, Alfred, Bureau of Employment Security, 207

Occupational Safety and Health Administration (OSHA), 159
O'Connor, James, 215
O'Dwyer, Frank, 64
Offe, Claus, 215
O'Hara, Representative James, 211
"Operation Cloudburst," 51
Organized labor, 5; opposition to immigration, 5–6; use of immigration to undermine power of, 3; opposition to Bracero Program and, 44, 122–123, 142–144, 203–204; opposition to H-2 Program, 134–135; prohibition against braceros forming unions, 46, 197; concern with illegal immigration, 48, 53; pressures on Department of Labor, 122–126, 143, 174; alliance with Department of Labor, 124; Di Giorgio Fruit Corporation and, 122–123; "green-card commuters" and, 154–156 (*see also individual unions*)
"Operation Wetback," 53–61, 96, 99, 107, 211; abuses by Border Patrol, 54; employers' cooperation with, 53, 59–60, 72, 82; Congress and, 54, 105

Ohswaldt, A. C., Southwestern Regional Chief of Investigations, INS, 197

Partridge, Maj. Gen. Frank H., 103, 130, 206, 209
Permanent resident status, 80, 209; INS opposition to granting visas to potential braceros, 80–82, 146–147; increases in Mexican visas, 81, 147; "green-card commuters" and, 152–159, 218
Pfeffer, Max, 55, 173, 192, 215
Pfeiffer, David, 193
Pickering, George, President of Yuma Producers' Cooperative Association, 153
Piece rate system, 57, 76, 119–121, 127
Plumb, Milton, 120, 124, 204
Pluralism, 40, 171, 173, 214–216
Poage, Representative W. R., 35–36, 43, 45, 109, 133–134
Poulantzas, Nicos, 3, 173, 184, 215
President's Commission on Migratory Labor, 2, 19, 21, 28–31, 41, 43–44, 47–48, 67, 125, 185–190, 192, 210
Preston, William, 185
Prevailing wage, 20, 22–23, 44, 63, 65, 117, 119, 121, 123, 127–128, 148, 171
Public Law No. 40, 25, 27
Public Law No. 45, 22–24
Public Law No. 78, 3, 43–46, 61–64, 66, 71, 85, 113, 116, 119–121, 128, 142, 150, 194, 202, 208, 211
Public Law No. 309, 66
Public Law No. 414, 116, 149
Public Law No. 521, 25
Public Law No. 893, 27, 113
Public opinion survey of INS, 60–61, 131, 207

Quota Laws, 6–7, 172

Rasmussen, Wayne, 185–187
Reception centers, 45, 62–63
Recruitment centers, 20, 27–28, 45, 62
Redford, Emmette, 179, 216
"Relative autonomy," 173
Replenishment Agricultural Workers (RAW), 168–169

Ripley, Randall and Franklin, Grace, 178, 216
Rodino, Representative Peter, 163
Rogers, William, Deputy Attorney General, 96, 200, 203
Rose, Arnold, 170
Rosenbloom, David, 178, 188, 216
Rooney, Representative John, 102, 160–161, 163
Rourke, Francis, 40, 162, 179, 188, 205, 216
Roybal, Representative Edward, 8
Rubottom, Roy, U.S. Department of State, 190
Rudnick, Edward, Executive Assistant to INS Commissioner, 200–201
Runsten, David, and Leveen, Phillip, 46, 189, 209

Sahli, Walter, San Antonio District Director, INS, 65, 99, 200–201, 203
Sasuly, Elizabeth, Representative of the Food, Tobacco, Agriculture, and Allied Workers Union, 26
Scher, Seymour, 178, 216
Schrecker, T., 212
Schuck, Peter H., 212
Scruggs, Otey, 186–189, 194–195
Select Commission on Immigration and Refugee Policy, 13, 161, 185, 212
Select Commission on Western Hemisphere Immigration, 153, 157–158, 211–212
Sherfy, N. Thomas, INS Officer in Charge, Hidalgo, Texas, 201
Shrode, Irvin, Assistant INS Commissioner, 116, 129, 197, 199–201, 203–204, 206–207, 209
Siciliano, Rocco, Assistant Secretary of Labor, 49, 115, 199, 203, 206–207
Simpson, Senator Alan, 8, 169
Skocpol, Theda, 10, 175–176, 179, 182, 185, 214–216
Skocpol, Theda and Finegold, Kenneth, 175–176, 179, 216
Smith, Norman, Director, Agricultural Workers Organizing Committee, 209
Sneed, Abner, INS Special Projects Officer, 101, 199, 207
Snider, Laureen, 212
"Sociological imagination," 170

Southern Farmers Tenant Union, 122
Special Agricultural Worker (SAW), 168–169
Special Committee on Importation of Mexican Labor, 2, 19
Special Program, 87, 92–97, 100–101, 114–116, 119, 129, 133–134, 137–147, 172, 201
State-centered theory, 170, 175–176, 179
State Extension Services, 22
Stepan, Alfred, 215
Stone, Christopher, 212
Strikes, 64, 122–123, 145, 147, 154, 189, 209; prohibition against using braceros to break strikes, 46, 123, 145–147; "green-card commuters" and, 154–156, 211
Structuralism, 3, 9–10, 40, 111, 165–166, 173–175, 177, 215
"Subject Index," INS, 14
Swing, Joseph, INS Commissioner, 11, 33, 49, 51, 53–55, 58–59, 61, 65, 72, 75, 78–79, 83–84, 86–88, 90–92, 96–98, 101–108, 115, 130–131, 137–138, 141, 144, 159, 190, 196–203, 206–207

Teitelbaum, Michael, 188
Termination of Bracero Program, 142–146, 148–160, 165, 167, 210
Texas; exclusion from bracero eligibility, 20, 23–24, 29, 34, 46; legalization of undocumented workers in, 24; "El Paso Incident", 29–30; "Operation Wetback" and, 53–54, 59–60
Texas AFL-CIO v. Kennedy, 211
Texas Proviso, 66–70, 195
Theories of the state, 3, 8–10, 73, 111, 118, 139, 144, 165–166, 170–183, 214–216
Todd, Henry, 190
Toole, M. R., Acting INS Commissioner, Southwest Region, 197, 203, 207
Trimberger, Ellen Kay, 215
Truman, President Harry S., 2, 19, 45, 67, 185

United Farm Workers Organizing Committee (UFWOC), 205

United Farm Workers Union (UFW), 122, 156, 205

U.S. Congress; wartime Bracero Program and, 2, 18; Anti-Alien Contract Labor Law and, 5; Quota Laws and, 6, 7, 172; Immigration Reform and Control Act and, 8; endorse the Bracero Program, 18, 22; pressures on INS, 24, 35–37; abdication of policymaking power, 9, 25–27, 39–40, 178, 181, 216; Cold War hysteria and, 49; "Operation Wetback" and, 53–54; Texas Proviso and, 66–70; hostility to Commissioner Swing, 102–108, 159; pressures on Department of Labor, 119–121, 124, 133–134; extension of Bracero Program, 24–25, 45, 142; opposition to Bracero Program, 142, 156; "green-card commuters" and, 156–158; alliance with INS under Commissioner Farrell, 160–163; criticisms of INS, 163–164; exercise of oversight, 27, 178

U.S. Congress. House Committee on Agriculture, 26–27, 35, 45, 84–85, 133, 149, 186–188, 191–192, 197, 204, 207–208

U.S. Congress. House Subcommittee on Appropriations, 102

U.S. Congress. House Subcommittee on Immigration and Naturalization, 6, 107

U.S. Congress. House Subcommittee on Legal and Monetary Affairs, 102–103

U.S. Congress. Senate Subcommittee on Appropriations, 51

U.S. Congress. Senate Subcommittee on Immigration and Naturalization, 49, 51

U.S. Department of Agriculture, 2, 19–20, 26, 68, 70–71, 109, 113, 117, 122, 126, 175–176, 182

U.S. Department of Justice, 19, 66, 96–97, 114, 125, 145–146, 151, 164–165

U.S. Department of Labor (DOL), 2, 4, 10, 15–17, 19, 29–30, 55–56, 58–64, 66, 71, 73, 77, 79, 84, 88–90, 94, 100–101, 112–140, 144–150, 152, 154–155, 158–159, 174, 181–182, 185, 199, 203

U.S. Department of Labor Consultants' Report, 127, 141–142

U.S. Department of State, 2, 19–20, 23, 25, 30, 45, 66–67, 70, 80–81, 86–89, 125, 137–138, 146–147, 181–182, 185

U.S. Employment Service (USES), 6, 20, 27, 29, 30, 113, 117, 185

U.S. Immigration and Naturalization Service (INS); authority over Bracero Program, 1, 9, 21, 23, 26; launching of Bracero Program, 2, 19; legalization of undocumented workers, 2, 24, 28–29, 32, 41, 73, 109; reluctance to apprehend illegal aliens, 2, 32–41, 52, 99, 167; secrecy of, 12–15, 185; disorganization of files, 15; FOIA and, 12–15; Public Law 45 and, 23–24, 113–114, 186; use of authority to satisfy bracero employers, 3, 18, 23–24, 30, 61, 73, 85, 180–181; agency interests, 4, 9, 73–74, 95–102; enforcement of bracero contracts, 29, 64–65; "El Paso Incident" and, 29–30; budget of, 34, 36–37, 52, 54, 162–163, 167; Cold War fears and, 49–50, 79; criticisms of, 51–52, 163–164, 166; "Operation Wetback" and, 53–55; interpretation of Texas Proviso, 70; autonomy of, 73–74, 95–102; reorganization of, 74, 102, 105–106, 196; control of bracero "skips", 75–77; "subversives" and, 77–80; opposition to permanent visas for braceros, 81–82, 146–147; conflicts with Department of Labor, 4, 9–10, 16, 113–140, 181; dilemmas of, 9, 18, 31–41, 52–53, 74, 107–112; "united front" with Department of Labor, 10, 136–140; bracero vulnerability and, 10, 74–82, 90, 95–111; maximization of bracero supply, 9–10, 82–85; Department of Labor regulations and, 85, 128–132; termination of Bracero Program and, 145–166; organized labor and, 145, 147; "green-card commuters" and, 152–159; connections to members of Congress, 160–163; demoralization in, 164–165

Utt, Representative James, 80

Walsh, Lawrence W., Deputy Attorney General, 209

Walter, Representative Francis, 107–108
War Food Administration, 20, 22, 34
War Manpower Commission, 2, 19
Warren, Governor Earl, 48
Wartime Emergency Program, 18–25; termination of, 25
Wasserman, Jack, 185
Watkins, Senator Arthur, 56–57, 192
Weber, Max, 176
Wehler, J. M., Executive Assistant to INS Commissioner, 206
Weinraub, Bernard, 212

Welker, Senator Herman, 69
Whitt, Allen, 174, 215
Wildavsky, Aaron, 179, 216
Williams, Lee G., 206
Williams, L. W., Assistant INS Commissioner, 203
Williams, Senator Harrison, 156
Wirtz, Willard, Secretary of Labor, 118, 148–149, 151, 155, 203, 205

Yarborough, Senator Ralph, 157–158